ADVANCE PRAISE FOR

WIDENING CIRCLES

Let this voice enter your life at a deeper level,
and your own future story may not be the same.
This memoir is a masterpiece — as is the life it describes.
— Daniel Ellsberg, who released the Pentagon Papers

This account of a spiritual life will undoubtably become a classic.
This is no airbrushed memoir but a deep exploration
of how a soul is formed.
— Susan Griffin, author of *What Her Body Thought*

Tracing her journey into an engaged spirituality that spans both
meditative practice and political activism, Joanna Macy's book reads like
a novel, full of suspense, humor, and rich relationships.
— Starhawk, author of *The Spiral Dance* and *The Fifth Sacred Thing*

A gem for all young people seeking to create a life of meaning,
passion and purpose. Joanna Macy is a woman who will help
to light our path for generations to come.
— Michele and Ocean Robbins, Executive Director and Founder,
Youth for Environmental Sanity

Beautifully written and endearing.
I take Joanna as my teacher.
— Robert Aitken, author of *Taking the Path of Zen* and
Original Dwelling Place

A woman of fiery passion, rigorous intellect, profound tenderness for all life,
and commitment to the delight, the love and pleasure awaking in each
moment: this is Joanna Macy revealed in *Widening Circles*.
— Sandy Boucher, author of *Hidden Spring* and *Opening the Lotus*

Wonderful! I am deeply inspired to read about a woman's life that breaks all the rules in just the ways they should be broken.
— Polly Young-Eisendrath, author of *The Resilient Spirit* and *Women and Desire*

Intimate, poetic and wise. I am uplifted, inspired and humbled by this encounter with a truly great being.
— Vicki Robin, co-author with Joe Dominguez of *Your Money or Your Life*

A rich and inspiring tale, a journey of great breadth and integrity.
— Jack Kornfield, author of *After the Ecstasy, the Laundry* and *A Path with Heart*

Every chapter provides a riveting tale of the eros of connection, of opening to the flow of life through her experiences around the globe. We need stories like Joanna's to know ourselves as part of the whole, to experience the universe moving through our individual lives.
— Sarah A. Conn, Ecopsychology Institute, Center for Psychology and Social Change Cambridge, MA

Over and over again, this country has witnessed the emergence of extraordinary women who, in the face of our human blindness, give voice to the cry of life... From her earliest years, Joanna Macy instinctively and then fiercely guarded a space for that cry in her own soul. And she has widened the circles of that space to allow the terror and desperation to be not denied, but carried by a stronger voice for sanity, imagination, and hope. Her story leaves us grateful for the possibilities we also carry.
— Sister Miriam Therese MacGillis, Genesis Farm

WIDENING
CIRCLES

WIDENING
CIRCLES

A MEMOIR

Joanna Macy

NEW SOCIETY PUBLISHERS

Cataloguing in Publication Data:
A catalog record for this publication is available from the National Library of
Canada.

Cover design by Val Speidel from a photo by Don Bonsey, Stone Images.

Printed in Canada on acid-free, partially recycled (20 percent post-consumer) paper
using soy-based inks by Transcontinental/Best Book Manufacturers.

New Society Publishers acknowledges the support of the Government of Canada
through the Book Publishing Industry Development Program (BPIDP) for our
publishing activities, and the assistance of the
Province of British Columbia through the British
Columbia Arts Council.

BRITISH
COLUMBIA
ARTS COUNCIL
Supported by the Province of British Columbia

Paperback ISBN: 0-86571-420-7

Inquiries regarding requests to reprint all or part of *Widening Circles* should be
addressed to New Society Publishers at the address below.

To order directly from the publishers, please add $4.00 shipping to the price of the
first copy, and $1.00 for each additional copy (plus GST in Canada). Send check or
money order to:

New Society Publishers
P.O. Box 189, Gabriola Island, BC V0R 1X0, Canada

New Society Publishers aims to publish books for fundamental social change
through nonviolent action. We focus especially on sustainable living, progressive
leadership, and educational and parenting resources. Our full list of books can be
browsed on the worldwide web — see below.

NEW SOCIETY PUBLISHERS
Gabriola Island BC, Canada   www.newsociety.com

DEDICATION

In gratitude

to all my companions and teachers
who opened my eyes to the beauty of this world,
and walked with me into challenge and change,

to Dugu Choegyal Rinpoche
for the treasure of his friendship and wisdom,

to Anita Barrows
for her unflagging and essential support of this book,

and especially to my beloved Fran,
Chris, Jack, and Peggy,
who have so wondrously graced my life.

CONTENTS

I live my life in widening circles
that reach out across the world.
I may not ever complete the last one,
But I give myself to it.

I circle around God, that primordial tower.
I have been circling for thousands of years,
and I still don't know:
am I a falcon, a storm,
or a great song?

Rainer Maria Rilke, *The Book of Hours*
— translated by Anita Barrows and Joanna Macy

THE GIFTS AT THE START

The Farm

APPROACHING THE MAIN HOUSE on my grandfather's farm, you would see a maple tree, standing alone beside the road, tall and graceful. She did not live in a cluster of her own kind, as the fruit trees did; she seemed more self-reliant and self-contained. I knew her for seven summers — from the time I was nine until I was sixteen.

She opened out a good distance from the ground, so I had to leap and scramble to hoist myself up. Straddling the lowest, waist-thick branch and slowly pulling upright, I entered a solitude that was more than my own. It was a protected solitude, like the woods near the north pasture, but different because here one single, living being was holding me. My hands still remember the feel of her: the texture of the gray bark, the way it rippled in folds near the joints, its dusting of powder. As I climbed up into her murmuring canopy, my heart quickened — from fear of falling, and from awe. Caution felt like reverence.

Here in the maple I didn't play games, the way I did in the wide old apple tree near the south barn that my older brother Harty had rigged with platforms. There I played practically every day, not with Harty, who returned to his own pursuits, but with my little brother John. The scarred, angular old apple became a schooner, a submarine, a space ship, cliffs and ledges for our assaults on Everest, jungle encampments in the heart of Africa, bombers and fighter planes dodging Hitler's anti-aircraft batteries. From a high branch hung a swing whose ropes could be drawn up and grabbed from within the tree. And each adventure required, at some point, that heart-stopping leap from the heights: a timeless second of free fall before the ropes caught and the board swung you out over the speeding ground.

The maple tree did not invite pretending games. I only went there alone. It was a place to be quiet, a place to disappear into a kind of shared presence: the being that was tree and me, with the light coming through. The light is what I remember most of all; high and wide around me, it shaped a luminous, breathing bowl. It danced through the leaves, glowing them green and gold. It stroked the limbs with flickering shadows. When I sat very quiet, the play of light seemed to go right through my body, and my own breath was part of the maple's murmuring.

Being there was sufficient. I didn't think about my life. I didn't talk to the maple about the cares and fears I had begun to carry. The maple took me into a vast, lit stillness beyond all that. She let me glimpse a wild serenity at the heart of my world.

The maple, my cloister, was not remote; she stood diagonally in front of the house, beside the road that linked us to town. She held her stillness and mystery right in the midst of things. Traffic on our farm road passed almost under her branches, although, with gas rationing, the cars and wagons and tractors were few those years, even after the road was paved in 1943. After the war, when the traffic got heavier and faster, the road was widened and the maple disappeared. I had gone by then.

Along the north side of the house ran my grandfather's half-acre vegetable garden. That's where I first saw Spotty, the summer I came to the farm. I was nine that year, and he probably had a dozen years on me, because even then he was known to be old. He still had good strong teeth, though, which makes all the difference if you're a horse.

Ouie, as we called my grandfather because his name was Lewis, had brought him down the road from the big barn, the realm of the tenant farmer, and harnessed him up to the little single-pronged plow he liked to use for cultivating between the rows. I never saw him actually plow with it in the spring, for the same reason I never saw the apple trees bloom: my school in New York City never let out soon enough.

That particular day I looked on with great interest. I could not keep my eyes off the big, raw-boned, piebald horse. He had red-brown markings splotched on a coat of white, a white mane, a black forelock, and a long black tail. He would have looked comical except for his great dignity.

I asked Ouie if I could help out and he suggested that I lead Spotty and make sure he stayed right in the middle between the rows and not reach for bites of the fresh green leaves of corn. Ouie explained that Spotty was not well-trained to farm work and did not much like it either, having been more of a saddle horse in his younger days. So I reached up to grab hold of the halter, and skipped along in front of him to keep my feet clear of his hooves. That big soft mouth just bobbed along right over my shoulder. I felt his breath blowing on me. When we finished, Ouie gave me a hand up as he unbuckled the harness, and I climbed astride. As my grandfather led the horse up the road to the big barn, I was riding on Spotty's back. I rode him all the way. It was as big a happiness as I had yet experienced in my whole life.

I don't remember asking, but after that Spotty was mine each summer, given over to my care. My grandmother Daidee probably had a hand in that decision, because she'd had her own horse as a girl back in Minnesota — a stallion even. She said how wonderful it was for Spotty at this time of his life to shed his disguise as a draft horse and to rediscover his true nature as a gentle-bred mount. Standing on a box to begin with, I learned how to yank the cinch up around the girth in front of his belly, and to knot it tight. I learned how to handle a pitchfork and clean out the stall every morning; how to be gentle and unafraid with Spotty's mouth, and firm as I fitted the bit behind his teeth; how to brush and curry him out of doors, standing to windward, so as not to start my asthma going.

A year or two later Daidee claimed to have unearthed evidence that in his youth Spotty had performed in the Cole Brothers' Circus. Believing her totally, I undertook a program to help him retrieve his circus skills. From a library book I learned about teaching horse tricks, which he learned quickly and loved almost as much as I. Actually, all he learned to do was to say yes and no — vigorously nodding or shaking his head at a secret signal from me — but that was sufficient to amaze anyone I could get to watch.

The farm lay in the western part of New York state, eight hours by train from Manhattan and fifty miles east of Buffalo, where Ouie had his church. It had been home to five generations of my father's people after they came out from New England in the early eighteen hundreds. I only lived there some three months a year, but still the farm felt like the steadiest part of my life. That's because my parents and brothers and I moved around so much — between rented houses in Los Angeles and then rented apartments in New York City — and also because there was this curious sense of belonging. The solemn, bewhiskered men and the thoughtful, overdressed women posing for the daguerreotypes on the parlor wall were my ancestors. The spidery script in the musty leather-bound books and diaries, the butter-churn, the scythe, the sleigh in the barn, where I played museum on rainy days, were theirs.

Even before the Erie Canal opened western New York to trade in 1820, my great-great-great-grandfather Ebenezer Rogers journeyed out from Connecticut with his wife and grown children to preach religion and make a new life. Like most of his Puritan forebears who had come out from England two centuries earlier, he was a working parson. In the glacier-flattened terrain west of the Finger Lakes and south of Lake Ontario, he took title to 260 acres of woods and arable land — he cleared pastureland and fields for wheat and hay, planted orchards, and built for his family the single-story farmhouse now occupied by Ouie's tenant farmer.

Two miles to the south, beside the canal that linked the Hudson River to Lake Erie, the town of Albion was growing up as a way station for the live-ly traffic of mule-drawn barges. There Ebenezer established a church. It was one of several: there were Methodists and Baptists, circuit-riding preachers and tent revivalists — the religious life in nineteenth-century upstate New York flourished with intensity. The Presbyterians and the Congregationalists, more liberal in theology and less flamboyant in style than the others, made an agree-ment to pool their resources. In consequence Ebenezer, a Congregationalist in Connecticut, founded the First Presbyterian Church in Albion.

His grandson, Lewis B. — a preacher like his father and grandfather — built the present church across from the Albion Town Hall, and on the farm, a proper quarter mile up the road from the barns and barnyards, a more sub-stantial family residence. Like the new church, the new house was made of brick in strong verticals with gables and angular trim, like surprised eyebrows, over tall, narrow windows. There during the Civil War his first son, Lewis Gould Rogers, my grandfather, was born.

Though he kept in close touch with the farm he inherited, Ouie's life took him farther afield — to college back in New England and then to semi-nary, later to a city church in Buffalo, and eventually to sabbatical studies in Europe. The overseas travel was surely encouraged by the woman he married. My grandmother Mary Hartley had already seen a lot of the world.

I loved it when Daidee, as we called her, could be persuaded to tell us about journeying by covered wagon from New Brunswick to Minnesota through Indian territory. She was proud that her family had been "loyalists." At the time of the Revolutionary War, her ancestors stayed true to King George, left their homes in Virginia, and moved to Canada. There, two generations later, Daidee and her two sisters and ten brothers were born. The older brothers ventured west, found land and ore in Minnesota, and brought the rest of the family out to join them when Daidee was ten. Having given her the stallion to ride around the Mesabi Iron Range, these brothers took Daidee's education in hand. Clothing her in furs, they sent her by sail-steamer across the Atlantic before she was twenty. So Daidee, the grandmother who told me about holding her sister as she died of tuberculosis in the covered wagon, the grandmother who taught me Ojibwa words she had learned en route, was also the grandmother who could reminisce about Florence and Paris in the late 1880s and her friendship with the sculptor Auguste Rodin.

Daidee loved languages. At Mount Holyoke College she was teaching classes in Greek, German, and French, when she met Ouie. She didn't let her lot as a minister's wife keep her from returning to the cultural riches of Europe. When their only child, Hartley, was six or seven, she packed off to Paris and put him in a lycée for a year, while Ouie studied theology in Germany. Later she joined her husband for a year in Hannover, and my father found himself in a German school.

I guess Papa got used to being on his own, not only in those foreign schools, but also back in Buffalo where the church took so much of his parents' attention. There Daidee, in addition to organizing church activities, played a leading role in civic and literary societies. With such busy parents, the little boy who would become my father could find himself alone, even at Christmas. Though he never liked people to feel sorry for him, he once told Mama, who then told me, about being left by himself in the house — without a tree or candle or a single present — because his parents were too occupied at church to make Christmas at home.

Papa was the first in his line of Rogers men to choose a life outside the church. After graduating from Yale in the early 1920s, he became a stock broker, and I gather he did quite well for a while, but it was a line of work very hard for me to understand. It preoccupied *him*, though, as if little else mattered.

Mama was the most beautiful and popular girl in Buffalo — I was sure of that from studying her albums filled with news clippings and photographs of her debut in society. Peggy Kinsey was tall and willowy with huge brown eyes that were both fun-loving and trustful; that, I knew, was because she had grown up in such a happy, rollicking family. Her father, Daddy Al, who made a lot of money in real estate, brimmed with affection and laughter and never spoke a cross word, she said. But I didn't know him. After the stock market crash, when I was a baby, he drove to the edge of town and shot himself. No one ever talked about it, so I couldn't figure out why he thought his insurance policy would be more useful to my grandmother Nonnie than his life.

Mama, who had the pick of anyone, chose Papa, even though he came from such a serious family. She admired the seriousness, not having been to college herself, and I always thought she loved Ouie and Daidee more than their own son did. When Papa decided to move to California and open his own investment offices in Los Angeles and Seattle, Mama followed with their first baby, my brother Hartley. On May 2, 1929, I was born in the Good Samaritan Hospital in North Hollywood, and four and a half years later — not long before Papa decided to move back East — came my brother John.

If it felt special to me to be born in southern California, it was because of the light that came from the western sea. Golden-amber, it suffuses the fragmented memories of my first five years — a warm hazy glow surrounding faces, flowers, leaping dogs. Wherever I meet that light again, toward sunset, I stop still and feel it flood my heart. In my first months of life, Mama took me along to the beach where Papa surfed after a day at the office. She had contracted mastitis and to keep her breasts from becoming impacted, she needed me to nurse for hours at a time. She told me later how good it had been for her, as she sat there on the sand, that I just kept sucking away, so strong and willing. Turning this over in my mind, I found it hard to picture Papa doing anything as wide-open and free as surfing, even though I knew he had been an athlete — I'd seen his trophies for tumbling and high-diving at Yale — and that he'd trained as a war pilot. But I could imagine, always, the scene as a whole: the golden orange glow of sea and sky, and the great waves rolling in, out of a bright vastness as safe as my mother's arms.

By 1934 the stock brokerage offices my father had opened in Los Angeles and Seattle in the boom times of the late 1920s had closed. It was time to start over, but not back in Buffalo; Wall Street itself was the place for Papa to begin again. Because his asthma was worsening, he needed to stay right in New York City — in tall buildings far from pollens and growing things. For the next four years, until I was nine, he lived apart from us. First, Mama, my brothers, and I spent a winter with Ouie and Daidee in Buffalo, where I started school. Then we lived in Rye, an hour north of Manhattan, in a rented house which I loved and which still provides the mental floor plan for most novels I read. Papa came out rarely. That was a relief, because when he did there were often arguments and Mama would cry. It didn't bother me — or even occur to me — that I never saw my parents embrace.

I felt lucky to have an older brother, but we hardly ever played together. Mama said how smart Harty was, skipping grades at school, and he always seemed to have more important things to do than notice me. Once, when his friends came over for one of their very complicated war games, he let me make brown sugar sandwiches for them. Through the kitchen window I could see the boys ambushing each other in the yard, as I buttered each slice of bread and spread the crumbly brown sugar very evenly.

One day we were all playing hide and seek together. I ran up to the third floor and crawled under the eaves, closing a little cupboard door behind me. It snapped shut, latching from the outside. The game was long over when I was finally found, weak from screaming and pounding, and still filled with the horror of finding myself trapped, perhaps forever. Harty told me what happened to the bride who played hide and seek on the day of her marriage and hid herself in an old trunk in the attic. The groom and the wedding guests looked for her in vain. Long years later, when the trunk was finally opened, all that remained was a crumbling wedding gown and a grinning skull.

"That's a true story," he said, and I thought about it more than I wanted to. I kept wondering how long the bride had stayed alive, and what it was like for her, confined in that darkness, slowly losing hope of being rescued. I learned how often others meet similar fates. In lurid Sunday supplements I read about doomed coal miners trapped underground by cave-ins; about little children fallen out of sight, out of hearing, in the bottom of wells; about people nailed into coffins before they're really dead and when they come to and open their eyes, they're in the grave. Tom Sawyer was lost a long time in the dark, dripping cavern, and Injun Joe never got out of it. Sometimes people even do it on purpose: they'll bury somebody alive, just wall them up, like the count in the story by de Maupassant. He walled up his wife's lover, brick by brick.

I didn't mind looking after my little brother John. He was adorable and funny, and agreeable to my ideas. He got a little bored, though, with the club I established: the Mister Nobody Club. I was president and he was vice-president and general membership. The club met in interesting places, such as behind the garage or under a spreading bush, but since its main activity consisted in sitting very still and gazing at one or two objects — a leaf, say, or an empty medicine bottle — it never held John's interest for long. When we played church — with me, of course, as minister — there was more for John to do, like getting up and down to sing or pray or pass the plate.

When Papa came out to Rye, it was easy to steer clear of him, because he usually stayed indoors. One day I stopped in my tracks and slowly backed out of the room, when I came upon him and Mama facing each other across the dining table, locked in argument. Over the papers on the table, his face was glowering, hers tearful. The papers were bills, the argument was about how to pay them. Household funds were hard to come by. Papa was the sole disburser of money, but he didn't like it if anyone actually expected him to do it. Even to be asked could anger him, so you had to be careful.

Soon Papa decided that it would be cheaper if we all came to live in the city with him. Mama agreed; she probably figured it would be harder for Papa to ignore our needs if we were living right under his nose in Manhattan. She did not foresee that it would make no difference. So she packed us up and we all squeezed into a thirteenth floor apartment over East 86th Street and started in at city schools.

That meant a private boys school for my brothers and public school for me. After a few months of that, Papa didn't like the street talk I was bringing home. Since I seemed adept at mimicking the speech of others, he decided to send me to a foreign language school, the Lycée Français de New York. He still cherished the memory of his own boyhood year in Paris.

Harty briefed me the night before, teaching me all the French he knew. It consisted of a word and a sentence. The word was *un*, which was useful, he pointed out, since it meant both "a" and "one" — and all you need to do is grunt. The sentence was *"Parlez-vous francais?"* Thus prepared, I embarked on the Lycée schooling that would take me through the rest of my primary and all of my secondary education.

It was during that first year of living in the big city that we began taking the train each June to the farm. The route took us first to the Plymouth Congregational Church in Buffalo. Ouie had been its minister for a long time, ever since his son was a little boy. Daidee helped him, and they lived in a small house three blocks away. Once Sunday service was finally over, you could climb around on Ouie's oaken pulpit and jump from the choir stall. I liked feeling so at home in Ouie's church and considered myself privileged to be allowed to do things like that. I wondered if Papa had been permitted to play in church when he was little, or if back then, as the minister's only child, he was told to behave more like a grown-up.

Ouie's church was a modest, straightforward place, as functional and unpretentious as a ladder or a bus. Clear windows let the light pour in, and the wooden pews helped you sit up straight. "Sit up straight," my brother Harty would hiss at John and me when we started to squirm and peer around at the congregation. Then Daidee would just smile and pull us over against her, so we could lean into her softness, and John could even lie down with his head in her lap. Once in a while, when Ouie's sermon grew long and we grew fidgety, she would rivet our attention with surreptitious entertainment. Knotting the corner of her handkerchief, she would pull the fabric down over her middle three fingers to make the head and arms of a puppet. Sometimes it nodded and gesticulated so emphatically that it was hard not to see the puppet as a pompous little preacher, and hard not to laugh — even for Daidee herself. Consequently, these moments of drollery were usually brief, cut short by Daidee's own efforts to regain her composure.

Our wandering attention was frequently retrieved by Ouie himself, as he preached. Mild-mannered as he was, you could always count on him to get worked up in the course of a sermon. He could really startle you. Once little John let out a loud "Wow!" and the grown-ups laughed. When Ouie shouted and pounded his pulpit, it wasn't to scold people for being sinful so much as to wake people up to being loved. He had strong ideas about what it meant that God had sent Jesus to live with people, just like one of them.

Our arrival in June was the occasion for Ouie and Daidee to move out to the farm for the summer months. From there Ouie would commute back to preach on those Sundays he hadn't arranged for a visiting parson or seminarian to take the pulpit. The Inasmuch Group, Daidee's own Sunday School class for grown-ups, suspended its activities until fall. I thought that was a pretty funny name at first, but Daidee gave me to understand that it had to do with helping the poor and other people in trouble, because Jesus had said, "Inasmuch as ye have done it unto the least of these, ye have done it unto me."

It took all morning to pack Ouie and Daidee's car for the big move. I danced with impatience by the bags and baskets collecting in the driveway, as ever more stuff was remembered and fetched amidst shouts and banging screen doors. Then my brothers and I climbed in back; our heads pushed against the roof and our feet stuck straight out over the piles of bedding. Once under way, the car trip was endless. The fifty miles to Albion and the farm took the rest of the day. Without bypasses or roads wider than two lanes, there was no way to hurry as we drove eastward along the Erie Canal and through the main streets of the canal towns. Harty and I chanted out the names of the towns and never tired of it: "Lockport, Gasport, Middleport, Medina. Lockport Gasport Middleport Medina," over and over. The *mantra* had a meaning: It said the world was a safe place, after all. Albion came next, ten miles after Medina, but the rhythm was better without it.

My father rarely visited us on the farm. I wasn't surprised, for I didn't connect him with open spaces or physical labor, or even with leisure, for that matter.

In the dining room at the farm hung a large, framed etching that dated from his and my grandparents' sojourns in Germany. It pictured, in shadowy detail, another dining room — even plainer than ours — and a peasant family about to sit down. The rough table has only a loaf and pitcher on it, so you can tell they're poor; yet the father, with his arms wide open, is welcoming a stranger. His words are written out to see: *"Komm, Herr Jesu, sei unser Gast."* Clearly, it's Jesus who has just walked in. The mother and children raise their eyes from saying grace, with looks of disbelief and reverence and delight. I could experience these feelings myself, as I gazed at the picture and imagined what it would feel like to be sharing what you had to eat with someone who turned out to be God.

In the flatness from Albion north to Lake Ontario even the smallest rise or dip held drama, like the high bridge over the canal, great for flying down on your bike as fast as the wind, or the lazy, low streambeds, perfect for squatting motionless to hunt tadpoles and crawdads. For all the openness of the land, there were hidden places — derelict barns, abandoned orchards, stands of dark woods — that held their own secrets, and you could find them out if you didn't mind getting a little scared and scratched. And everywhere, in every field and ditch, it was so busy — not with people and cars and machines, but with the aliveness of Earth.

As soon as you stopped for a second and let it in, that simmering, seething vitality barraged your senses. When I hurried to the outhouse after the long car trip, there it was right away, and very strong too, in the chorus of flies zooming up from below as I lifted the lid, and in the higher whine from the wasps' nest overhead. I had to try and not be nervous, as I perched there over the smelly abyss, for I feared the wasps, and also I'd heard from Harty that escaped convicts sometimes hid beneath privies, figuring they'd be undetected in pits of human excrement. I diverted myself by studying the yellowing pages from old catalogues and Sunday supplements that papered the walls.

When I pulled up my pants and went out under the sour cherry trees beside the privy, the din of insect life continued all around me — less menacing now. As I listened, it grew louder and wilder. New parts of the orchestra clicked in with new buzzings and dronings — of gnats, bees, June bugs, of dragonflies and horseflies and hornets — in the grasses around my feet and the cherry branches overhead and in the elderberry bushes behind them. And soon I could hear their chorus coming from farther away, from Ouie's garden and the waist-high grasses on the other side, and from the tomato field and orchard beyond, and the hayfields and woods in the distance. The whole world reverberated with their roar — an ocean of multitudes that could absorb you right into their immeasurable, collective presence. Was this always going on — and we were just too busy to hear it, too self-enclosed to hear the world conspiring with itself?

When the breakfast dishes were done and the beds made, I could head off into the morning on Spotty: down the road on an errand to town, or out along the rutted edges of the cultivated fields toward open pastures and woodland. Having no one to ride with, I wished for human companions, invented them. In a remote field surrounded by woods, I would persuade Spotty to run and, charging about on my loyal steed, his noble heart pounding with the effort, I would become Joan of Arc, leading her troops into battle. Or Scarlett O'Hara galloping to the rescue of Tara, or Queen of the Amazons, shirt unbuttoned, defending her jungle realm.

Often, before supper, we'd be under way again, this time to the north pasture to fetch the cows for milking. The small herd, just nine or ten, included a couple of delicate, pretty-faced Jerseys and two or three hefty Holsteins; the rest were Guernseys. I left the reins on Spotty's neck because he knew better than I how to round them up and keep them moving: out the pasture gate and down the long, grassy lane to the road, and then another quarter mile by road till they reached their stanchions in the big barn. The cows took their time about it, so I would just lounge on Spotty and watch the sky turn colors, the land soften.

Whenever someone came with me to fetch the cows, we would go on foot — and once, at least, that someone was my father. I know that because I learned a poem from him then. Walking up the long lane to the pasture, he spied, across a neighboring field, a tree all overgrown with vines. "See yonder ivy-mantled tower!" he laughed, "that's where the moping owl doth complain."

That was from Gray's "Elegy in a Country Churchyard," he said, and he soon had me repeating the opening lines with him:

> Curfew tolls the knell of parting day,
> the lowing herd winds slowly o'er the lea ...

Papa loved poetry. When he was in a good mood, he would recite whole passages from Tennyson and Coleridge, Matthew Arnold, Rupert Brooke, and "The Rubayyat of Omar Khayyam". He would talk about Professor Billy Phelps and the grand, exciting course he taught at Yale. I began to think that if Papa had become a professor of literature, instead of working in stocks and bonds, he would have found more gladness in himself.

In New York City at the Lycée, too, I began learning poetry by heart — a bunch of it for *récitation* every Friday. The very first poem I committed to memory was by La Fontaine, from Aesop's fable about the crow and the fox. Papa would have me recite it for guests — our first years in New York he still invited people home. I would stand in front of some business friend of his who might not know a word of French, and launch myself into the sonnet:

> Maître Corbeau sur un arbre perché
> tenait en son bec un fromage ...

When the fox saw the crow with a cheese in his beak, he called up to him, "Oh, you have such a beautiful voice, please sing for us!" The stupid crow fell for the flattery, dropped the cheese, and the fox straightaway ran off with it. When Papa asked me to recite before guests, I, too, opened my mouth; but there was nothing for me to lose, no cheese to drop, and for a moment there was his smile. For a moment he would see me and hear me — though I sensed even then that it was not me he was hearing, but the language he loved that he had learned as a child in Paris.

To live in the city, surrounded by sooty concrete, to have to wait to be accompanied to the park each time I wanted to play outside, felt hideously confining, though we found a good hill for sledding, and a real Egyptian tomb to walk around in at the Metropolitan Museum nearby. From my bed in the converted dining room I shared with John, I could see the illumined tower of the Empire State Building glowing in the evening sky. At bedtime, with John and me nestled with her against the pillows, Mama would tell us the latest adventures of the rabbit who lived there. The Empire State Building was this rabbit's home, and so, as you would expect, he was quite sophisticated.

But even relaxed moments like these were overshadowed with tension. The apartment began to feel like a pressure cooker. After a day at the office, Papa shut himself in his separate bedroom with the air filter and we kept our voices down. From the moment we heard his keys in the front door, we tried to do nothing that might set him off. But often, late at night, his shouting would jar us awake. I knew Mama was there with him in his room across the hall, though I couldn't hear her voice. That was when John and I would put our pillows, for saddles, over the foot railings of our beds and ride off together into the night. New adventures awaited us always, and it felt so good to do something, rocking in a canter or crouching forward in a flat-out gallop, hanging on to the reins looped round the bedpost. Except for Manhattan's night glow through the window, we rode in darkness, unable to see each other's faces, calling to each other in whispers as we crossed prairies and forded rivers and raced up rocky gulches with our posses and patrols — just in time, usually, to save people.

After a while those night rides became harder to sustain. I would find myself standing in the hall by that closed door, not wanting to hear but needing to know. My father, I thought, could speak even more forcefully and persuasively than all the preachers he descended from, and once he started, it was hard for him to stop. He could take the mildest mistake and turn it into a terrible offense. And you'd believe him. Or at least I was afraid that Mama would believe him. The way she kept apologizing, it sounded as if she did. Apologies didn't stop Papa anyway. He never seemed to think you were sorry enough.

Sometimes, standing in the hall by his bedroom door, I would start hammering on it with my fists, shouting so he could hear me over his own voice, shouting at him to leave Mama alone. When Papa yanked the door open and advanced on me, Mama would plead with me to run off, looking at me as if I were causing her the most anguish of all.

The few times my father hit me hurt less than the tongue-lashings, but they left me with a fear that was hard to shake. On our first Christmas Eve in New York we were decorating the tree when Papa came home from an office party. He seemed unusually friendly and stayed in the living room, lounging on the sofa to watch us. I pulled at him to join us at the tree and teased him when he refused, saying he was a "stick-in-the-mud" who never wanted to have fun with us. That's when he started after me. What I remember most is how his blows sent me sprawling and spinning, bouncing off the walls of the narrow hallway, and how when I scrambled to lock myself in Mama's room at the far end, he knocked the door down. He did it with his back, by bracing his feet against the opposite wall and pushing. The door, as I watched from inside, bent inwards very slowly, creaking and straining at the hinges more and more, until it couldn't hold out any longer and just gave way. I can't remember what happened next.

No one ever talked about it afterwards. No one ever talked about any suffering in our family — except Mama to me, in the privacy of her room. She had begun confiding in me, pouring out her distress and desperation. And they became my own, became a dense mass inside me, growing heavier as I saw how poorly Mama defended herself. I began to fear that my father would break her spirit in some irreparable way. I tried, as hard as I could, to get her to stand up to him.

"Why don't you stand up for Mama? Don't you see what's going on? Don't you care?" I cried at Harty one afternoon, when we were alone in the apartment. He was home from school with a broken arm, and I seized the chance to speak of my fear for Mama. When Harty said nothing, I shoved him in anger — and he fell off his chair onto the cast around his arm. I was horrified at my own vehemence. Harty was the precious genius of the family, and now I'd damaged him. But as I helped him up, he shook his head at my apologies. "I don't blame you for being worried, and I haven't been much help," he said. That, to my recollection, was the only time he actually acknowledged to me that things were hard.

John, at six, was too young to turn to, except for diversion. Already he was developing his own characteristic response to stress: to ignore it with buoyancy and jokes. Even Mama, except when alone with me, appeared trouble-free. Mostly she followed her own dictum: "If you can't say something nice, don't say anything at all."

Only Berthe, a Swiss woman who came one season to cook and clean, was bold enough to name the suffering. She was brawny and outspoken, with a faint mustache, and it awed me that she was not intimidated by my father. Perched on a kitchen stool, I listened intently as she told of going right down to Wall Street to demand the money he owed her and to admonish him for the way he treated his wife. Then Berthe said to me: "I worry about what he will drive her to do. From this height it would be so easy."

The shaking inside me that began then came not from surprise but confirmation, as if I already had been harboring the fears Berthe brought to the surface. Once Berthe was dismissed, as she soon was, to whom could I speak

those fears? I didn't want to add to Mama's anguish by revealing the extent of
my own or, for that matter, to give her any ideas. But now, each afternoon
when I came home from school, I would run to look in all the rooms and, if I
did not find my mother, peer out the windows to the city pavement thirteen
stories below.

It was 1939. War was gradually engulfing Europe, and Europe was home for
most of my schoolmates. Some had fled across borders with parents who now
took asylum in America. Others were children of diplomats, artists, and mer-
chants whose livelihoods had brought them to New York where they were
stuck now "for the duration." It seemed that all of them, whether seven years
old or seventeen, had lived in places now threatened or occupied by Hitler's
armies. All except me.

From newsreels and magazines, I could imagine the scenes that my
schoolmates and their families had lived through, and that their relatives on
the continent were still experiencing. These ravages were seldom mentioned in
the classroom. Ours was the classical Lycée curriculum, unperturbed by current events. It was more important to learn about Vercingétorix, the club-
wielding chieftain who defended Gaul from Julius Caesar, than about the
ordeal of twentieth-century France. When Madame Brodin, my favorite
teacher, mentioned the fall of Poland one morning and wept for about five seconds, her pupils watched solemnly. Then immediately and for the next two
days, in the lavatories, hallways, and courtyard, they performed exaggerated
imitations.

If the pain of loss and dislocation didn't disappear by itself, there was one
thing you could do with it. You could vent it on the place where you were
forced to be — on stupid, ugly, barbaric America. Since the New World gen-
erously provided much to scoff at, my fellow students never ran out of things
to mock and bemoan. So, as I struggled my way into French culture, I heard
my own culture demeaned. That was worse than the teasing I received for my
beginner's French, but I was not brave enough, let alone fluent enough, to
defend my country — and after a while I lost conviction.

As I made my way at the Lycée, I learned to conceal much: my loneliness, my embarrassment for my country, the extent of my ignorance of French,
the anxiety I carried with me each morning from home. Concealment helped
me survive, but it brought shame in its wake. If feelings have to be hidden, I
concluded, they must be unacceptable.

When the moment came in June to board the Empire State Express at Grand Central Station to return to the farm, I felt as if I had been holding my breath the whole year. Once the train finally started, it seemed to rumble on for ages in the dark. In the dirty window I saw my own face against the blackness of the tunnel walls. They were sootier than the subway walls I'd grown accustomed to, but *these* underground passages seemed almost benign, for they were leading out, into a season in the sun. But not straightaway, for when we emerged at 97th Street, the light was gray, shadowed on both sides by blocks of tenements. For miles, we rattled along close to their windows, so close I could see inside, see the dim clutter, see the faces watching us go by, and sometimes meet their eyes, the impassive eyes of those who know they cannot escape.

Spotty seemed disinterested when I finally located him in a far stretch of the north pasture, but I expected him to be wild and hard to catch after long spring months on the loose. I rattled a pail of oats enticingly. He trotted up close, then shied out of reach, and played the game over and over, until I grew cross and tearful with impatience. Finally he thrust his nose straight into the pail — and let me swing a rope over his head and scratch his neck on his favorite scratching place.

Mud was caked on him from rolling by the stream, and burrs tangled his tail and knotted his mane, but back by the barn I slowly groomed him with currycomb and brush. No impatience then. That June grooming had the effect of ritual: it steadied the mind, eased the heart. How good it was, when we were through, simply to lean against him. My cheek rested higher against his withers than it had the summer before, but it felt the same. In those moments I let myself go still.

That summer on the farm I tried to read the Bible. At night in my cherished, very own room, I sat up in bed with the big heavy book braced on my knees. I had taken it from Ouie's study; it smelled old and musty and earnest, like my Pilgrim ancestors. "In the beginning God created the heavens and the earth." I started on the first page, figuring I would just read straight through. My motivation was strong but vague. I think I wanted to be good, or find some way to become good. But mostly I wanted a vision and a blessing. I figured there *had* to be a meaning to my people's faith more riveting and real than what was conveyed in Sunday School.

Doggedly I persisted through the generations of Noah and Shem and Abraham, but the children of Israel seemed about as relevant to my life as

Vercingétorix, and even less interesting. What interested me was to find out about God, or rather God and me, and whether there was some promise in that mystery, some way of getting at it. I attached little importance to the fact that God did not answer my prayers. When John and I got asthma attacks after playing in the hay loft and I had us kneel together and pray for relief, I was not disheartened, really, that we kept on wheezing. Or when, in Mama's bedroom on that Christmas Eve, I prayed to God that the door would hold against Papa's pushing — and it gave way — I did not take that as a sign that God didn't exist. I hardly expected God to conform to my notions of what God should do. On the contrary, when I didn't surround him with demands and expectations, there was more space — space where we both could breathe and be real.

The God I was reading about in the Bible did not seem very spacious. He wanted you to be good and obedient, period. That felt not very different from the world of the Lycée, which seemed to want you to be smart and cynical, period. Neither allowed much room for fallibility or grief.

From the maple tree I could see Ouie working in his vegetable garden, moving up and down the rows behind the horse and plow. He used Red for the job, now that Spotty was released from farm work, and he proceeded as always without hurry, hour after hour, stopping only to toss a surfaced rock, then lurching forward again, pulled by the plow, the reins slung around his shoulders, his hair ruffling in the air, silver as milkweed. Ouie's attention seemed so steady — he clearly wasn't wondering if he should be doing something else, or if he was tired and should finish another day. Or if this was a suitable activity for a seventy-six-year-old preacher, and he maybe should just ask the tenant farmer to drive the tractor over and do the whole job in forty minutes.

Watching him plod up and down the rows behind the plow, I tried to imagine what it would be like to live that way, with such a calm and doubt-free mind. To live my New York City life like that, without wishing it were different, without hating it so much. To just go to school and not feel stuck inside my loneliness. To ride up the elevator and walk into the apartment and not feel trapped in my own fear. Maybe the secret of being peaceful, like Ouie, was to focus your attention only on what you were doing at that very moment, on what was right under your feet or in your hands — and to close your ears to what you did not want to hear. That would spare you a lot of grief. The problem was that I didn't think I *wanted* to tune things out.

Late one afternoon, when I was ten, my grandfather and I were alone together in the front parlor. He was sitting in the rocker by the window and I perched sideways on his lap, looking out toward the road. I was watching the western sky and the maple tree silhouetted against it. Under me Ouie's knees were bony, and his hand was warm and light on my back. I don't remember what we had been saying, or if we had been talking at all. I rarely, if ever, talked at the farm about life in New York — I didn't want to spoil the summer, and furthermore, Papa was Ouie's son — so I don't know what prompted the words he spoke then. They seemed to just come out of the blue — or out of that apricot-colored sky:

"Come unto me, all ye who labor and are heavy-laden, and I will give you rest."

I had not heard those words before. Instantly I turned on Ouie's lap to face him: "Who said that?"

"Jesus said it," Ouie told me. "God says it through Jesus." And he continued: "'Take my yoke upon you and learn of me, and you shall find rest unto your soul. For my yoke is easy and my burden is light.' Matthew eleven."

"Say it again," I said, and repeated the words after him: "Come unto me all ye who labor and are heavy-laden."

I was stunned. I thought of all the people who lived with heavy burdens. They came now to my mind: the faces in the tenement windows, the outnumbered troops fighting for France, even my father. And when I heard that invitation, I knew I was among them.

That invitation did not alter the circumstances of my life; it removed no hardships. Yet it changed everything.

2

Montaigne's Tower

WHEN I WAS FIFTEEN I MOVED INTO MONTAIGNE'S TOWER. I didn't stay in it for more than a few minutes or hours at a time, but I knew it was there and available. Michel de Montaigne built it in the 1570s on the grounds of his country manor house because he wanted a place to think. When he wasn't in Parliament or on the road through war-torn France, he took refuge in his book-lined sanctuary and composed the essays we read in the *Classe de Seconde* at the Lycée. I could picture it as clearly as if I were entering it myself, climbing the curving stone stairs to the upper story, pushing open the solid wooden door, and closing it behind me.

It was always morning there, with bands of sun on the floor reflecting on leather-bound volumes and quotations carved on the beams. Like Montaigne, I walked back and forth in a leisurely, possessive way — knowing, without counting them, the sixteen paces of the room's diameter. Like him, for a time I let the world outside take care of its own needs. With no interruptions, the mind stilled and filled. Thoughts floated to the surface, turning like dust motes in the shafts of sun.

Religious wars were tearing seventeenth-century Europe apart. Princedoms, duchies, and towns pitted their armies against each other in shifting alliances that I found too boring and stupid to try to understand. But I *could* appreciate Montaigne's desire to hold aloof from the conflict. I wished that I could stay neutral, on the sidelines, in the torment gripping my own family life. *That* suffering was like a toothache through all the studies that increasingly engrossed me.

It was my seventh year at the Lycée, and reading and writing in French was by then as natural to me as in English. The years of struggle to get by in the language without humiliating myself were largely behind me.

The Lycée Français de New York, just off Fifth Avenue, was housed in an elegant mansion built in the style of eighteenth-century France. It was both ornate and light — under tapestry-covered walls a creamy marble staircase curved up to patterned marble floors, and for school assemblies we entered a ballroom of gilt and mirrors. I must have known that Papa had badgered the school's directors into admitting me for free, but the thought did not burden me. During those war years, when my schoolmates included European royalty landing penniless on our shores, available money was no gauge of status. Furthermore, I was making good grades now, especially in literature and math, and this was as gratifying to the directors of the Lycée as it was to me. As an American — some years the only one in my class — I served as living proof of the redeeming power of French culture and the rightness of its *mission civilisatrice*.

Madame Davide was our teacher of French literature in the higher classes. Small and hunched over, in an eternal-looking pastel silk, she was so imperturbably self-contained as to be almost expressionless. Our rambunctious class hushed in her presence. From my front row desk I watched her face, pale as paper under her dyed pink hair, and hung on her every word. When she talked about Montaigne, I didn't listen just so I could feed her ideas back to her in my assignments, though by now I had learned well how to do that. She was suggesting a more challenging use of my wits as she told us how Montaigne shrugged off the opinions of others. He turned to his own experience to find out what was true for him. That's why he invented essays, which he called "the art of being truthful." Finding out what he thought let him find out who he was, said Madame Davide. "Self-portrayal forms a person, delineates his inner self, reveals *le moi profond*." I immediately felt my own desire for precisely that: to find out what I really thought, to know my *moi profond*. That is why Montaigne needed his tower, and why I needed it too.

Attention to his own immediate experience, Montaigne explained, preserved him from the flaming hatreds of his time: *Quand je danse, je danse; quand je dors, je dors.* When I dance, I dance; when I sleep, I sleep. All of nature is present in the simplest of acts, he said, and as we allow ourselves to focus on them without distraction, these actions become calming and even *voluptueuses* — pleasure arises, and understanding. That's how he kept a sense of equilibrium. I wanted that. My own life felt squeezed ever more tightly between conflicting forces.

I had not succeeded in accomplishing the divorce of my parents, the goal I had set myself at nine. I no longer imagined that I could. Despite occasional good moments with Papa, the dread of him was strong in me, compounded now by a sense of failure and the different kind of vulnerability I felt as I moved toward womanhood. I craved his attention — and feared it even more.

The Second World War had resonated in our lives ever since we had moved to New York. Hitler had begun his march across Europe back then, in my first months at the Lycée, and my new schoolmates included boys and girls from Poland, Belgium, and Holland. By the end of my second year they were coming from France itself, as the unthinkable happened. Paris — which the Lycée had caused me to love as if it were my own city — fell to the Third Reich. In flickering newsreels, I saw Nazi troops goose-stepping down the Champs Élysées, and wept. I struggled to understand that terrible things can happen on a huge scale, that inhumanity can triumph, that whole countries with their exquisite civilizations can go under. I prayed for America to enter the war.

Naturally I saw it all in black and white, with none of the ambiguities of the ancient wars I studied. With perils so obvious and doom so near, all who fought for freedom were marvelously heroic figures to me. The young men in uniform who came across my New York horizon — Free French and Royal Air Force (RAF) soldiers in transit to the war zones — moved me thrillingly. Because Mama volunteered at the ANZAC (Australia New Zealand Air Corps) Club and often took me with her to help serve tea, I came to know many young men from "down under" who were on their way to fly for the RAF. With their entrancing accents and gray-blue uniforms, they were very glamorous to me — all except Ron Bellingham, a shy, homesick little guy who'd been raised by his great-aunt in Sydney. He seemed almost as young as I, those weeks he spent in Manhattan when I was fourteen. That's why he wrote to me, I guess; long letters from his base in England, with photographs of his bomber crew standing proud and awkward under the belly of their plane. Blond little Ron, looking like a choirboy, served as forward bombardier.

It was summertime on the farm and I was on Spotty, leaning down from the saddle to take the mail from the box by the road. The letter, from one of his barracks mates, informed me that Ron and his crew had gone down in flames over Germany. I looked around at the maple, the house, the barn. Spotty shook the reins free and began to munch the grass, as I read the letter again. I sat there a long time, my eyes on the far horizon, trying to imagine that Ron's death had some meaning.

Though I sensed the terrible cost of the war, I was marvelously stirred by it too, especially after Pearl Harbor, when my own country engaged full-tilt and I could feel part of a huge and necessary collective effort. I felt it in the Albion summers, when shortage of labor made me useful as a fruit and vegetable picker on nearby farms. Rising at dawn to be ready for the truck, I worked ten hours a day alongside folks of all ages as they joked with each other across the rows or from tree to tree. Filling bushel-baskets with tomatoes or feeling the canvas sling on my waist grow heavy with cherries, I felt as full and simple a satisfaction as I had ever known.

In Manhattan what I loved were the blackouts. The apartment walls dissolved as the whole city went dark. Switching off the lamps, we pulled back the mandatory black curtains and opened the windows wide to starlight and the footsteps of air-raid wardens. I felt such connection then, across the planet, with innumerable others — with sailors on their darkened ships, with Dutch families in the occupied Lowlands, with the hunted French resistance fighters huddling over their short-wave radios — that we seemed to be breathing together in the one vast night.

Papa had a short-wave radio set of his own and, because he loved the German language, he regularly tuned to broadcasts from Berlin. Each night these broadcasts, prepared for the German people in the Third Reich and those scattered in other lands, included a reading of the names of sons and brothers and fathers who had fallen in battle. There was a growing poignancy to those lists of German names, because as the war progressed, it was turning against Germany. And each slowly enunciated litany of names was preceded by a song, the same beautiful, somber song. I knew it by heart. To a slow, muffled drumbeat the great tenor Richard Tauber sang: *"Ich hatt' einen Kameraden."* I had a comrade, a faithful comrade, standing by my side; I turned and saw he had fallen, fallen by my side.

Mama said, please turn the volume lower, neighbors are rumoring we are German sympathizers. Yet I felt strangely comforted, and even proud, that Papa brought these voices into our life. They denationalized my patriotic fervor, and stretched my heart.

The war in my home — or, rather, not war so much as tyranny — was harder to come to terms with. In our series of rented apartments, Papa took the largest bedroom for himself and, when home from the office, spent most of his time sequestered there, safe from the noises and needs of his family. It took a lot of courage to approach him for any money, say for clothing, school books, bus fare. Once Mama was so desperate to pay the grocery bill, she tried to follow him right into his room. Even when he slammed the door on her hand, breaking two fingers, he remained furious, saying it was her own fault for bothering him when he was tired.

Papa's self-isolation did not weaken his determination to rule our lives — especially mine. As I entered my mid-teens and wanted to join occasionally in the social life of my friends, his need to control became ever more extreme. It seemed to stem from a basic distrust of me, as if I couldn't be expected to handle the mildest of pleasures — a ride in the country, a classmate's supper dance — without falling into depravity. I soon found that only deception, fueled by a budding hatred, could save me from feeling buried alive.

The year I was fifteen we moved from the third apartment to a house of our own: a tall, narrow row house, built of brownstone and brick the color of dried blood. Other houses on the street, three blocks from the Lycée and just one from the big 95th Street Armory on Park Avenue, were already being renovated. I watched as façades like ours were freed of their high stoops and repainted smartly in white or gray, fitted with brass knockers and lanterns, decked with flowers. Peering in their enlarged windows, I saw how the interiors had been gutted to fashion spacious rooms brimming with light.

Our house — which Mama and I called Bleak House — had remained untouched since the last century, from the huge old coal-burning furnace in the basement to the topmost floor, where John and I, in closet-sized compartments near the separate bedrooms of our parents, were finally given quarters of our own. A dark staircase climbed from the cellar to the three stories above, its splintering, bare boards clattering under our feet. I learned the exact location of every creak and groan so that, when Papa was home, I could creep up to my room as soundlessly as possible.

Bleak House was purchased with the proceeds from the sale of Ouie and Daidee's home in Buffalo. When Ouie finally retired from the Plymouth Congregational Church, Papa pressured his parents to put it on the market and move out full-time to the farm near Albion. Just one year later, when some shortfall in his business required an immediate infusion of cash, Papa made another demand: that they sell the farm as well. Ouie, still pretty spry, had continued to cultivate his big garden, sit with his ancestors' books of sermons, oversee the farm in his bemused fashion; but he was over eighty now, and never one to be uncooperative. In late 1945, the farm — all two hundred and sixty-seven acres, along with the houses and barns — went for eight thousand dollars. The money disappeared as soon as it was handed over to Papa, nothing to be seen or said of it again. Ouie and Daidee came to live with us in New York — and their needs made it even harder for Mama to break free.

I never knew if the lack of money that made my parents' relations so unbearable was due to genuine penury or Papa's stinginess. Either way, it was virtually impossible for Mama to leave him. New York State laws, she explained, wringing her lovely hands, granted divorce for one cause only: adultery. Without those grounds she could not sue for support. "I'd be out on the street, penniless." Her voice sank to a whisper, though we were alone in her bedroom.

Papa grew more reclusive now, unable to tolerate any guests in the house, and his nighttime furies had a new edge to them. I quivered as I buried my face in my pillow, then tiptoed down the hall to check on John, whose bed stood right against the wall of Papa's room. Harty, who left for Yale at sixteen, had been gone for years. One night, standing in the dark hallway by his door, I could make out that Papa was threatening Mama with some disclosure: "I'm going to tell the children who I found you with and how...." And I heard Mama's fainter voice pleading, "please, please don't do that." I felt sickened with rage and pity. I wanted to pound on Papa's door, as I used to do, and yell at him to stop browbeating her, and I wanted to shout even more loudly to her, "Mama, it doesn't matter, it doesn't matter at all! Don't let him scare you!" But that was precisely what I could not do — conventions were so strong for her, the opinions of others so important.

Soon after that night Mama went to work at Papa's office. I couldn't believe she'd do that: take the subway with him to Wall Street every morning and voluntarily enclose herself with him in those cluttered, sterile cubicles behind the door marked with his name. She indicated, rather tersely, that money was scarcer than ever and that Mildred, Papa's secretary ever since he'd returned from California and his one remaining employee, had to be laid off. Mama had no office skills back then, but she hoped that her willingness to work would help somehow to regularize our finances, get the coal bills and food bills paid. On envelopes and slips of paper she kept writing out budgets, itemizing outstanding debts and recurrent monthly needs, to show to Papa — if she could get him to look. Now and again I found one of those lists; they were tucked into the little book of devotional readings she kept by her bed. I think that was as far as they got.

I was the only one I ever heard talk back to my father, though I did it on Mama's behalf more than on my own. When he cut me off and forbade me to speak, I'd let my anger flame out through my eyes. "Joanna, don't you look at me like that!" he'd command across the dinner table, his furious blue eyes locking my own in cold combat. I almost welcomed my feelings of contempt and rage; they were easier to bear than fear. None of it, strangely, stopped me from treasuring each moment he let us glimpse his whimsy and charm — I turned to them as eagerly as to a drink I thirsted for.

Oh, how he could tell a story. He loved French movies and loved recounting them, even if we had all gone along. Hearing him describe *La Grande Illusion* was even better than seeing for yourself that classic film about war. He relished the turnings in the plot, the suspenseful pauses and moments of recognition; they were more vivid in his descriptions than they had been on the screen. He would choke up sometimes over the humanity of the scenes he evoked, going a little hoarse with emotion, or he'd shake with laughter until he wheezed and had to use his adrenaline inhaler. Always, of course, it was only he who did the talking.

Then there was the poetry. At supper table some Sunday nights, over endless slices of protein toast with muenster cheese, we made a game of quoting poems back and forth. The idea was to come up with a line or stanza that starts with the same letter that ended the last quotation — a game in which I was becoming a good match for Papa because of all the verse I memorized for weekly recitation at the Lycée. So when my father would quote Edgar Allan Poe's

> Helen, thy beauty is to me like those Nycean barcs of yore
> that many a weary traveler bore across the wine-dark sea

I recalled the lines I'd had to learn from Lamartine, and piped up with

> Ainsi, toujours poussés vers de nouveaux rivages,
> dans la nuit éternelle emportés sans retour....

But Mama might beat me to it with "After the ball is over"; she and John were allowed to use songs. As for me, I could cheat a little, changing the French words around to get the letter I wanted, and not be caught. It wouldn't have mattered anyway, because the main and amazing thing was not how we played, but that we played at all. We were not arguing or weeping or smoldering in silence, we were saying beautiful things.

We discovered that mice were eating our Books of Knowledge. Refusing to use spring traps or poison, Papa said we needed a figure-four trap. Very carefully, with a cigar box and safety matches, he and John constructed one. It was the only thing I ever saw him make. The box, when set, tilted atop the delicately angled matches and was armed with cheese on the crossbar of the four. It worked excellently; the barest nibble caused it to fall. Every morning when we ran to look, we found the cigar box lying flat and, putting an ear to it, we could hear faint stirrings. Then we slipped a piece of cardboard underneath and flipped it over to contain the culprit. And each morning, for the next week or so, Papa made a detour on his way to the IRT.

Hanging out an upstairs window, I watched him walk, in his overcoat and hat, up toward Park Avenue, carrying the cigar box and holding the cardboard lid in place. The armory on the other side of Park stabled police horses and there, at the big side entrance, getting up close to the gap beneath the gate, Papa would bend down and open the cigar box. What better place for a mouse than amidst all that good straw and grain?

This procedure repeated itself so often that Papa became suspicious. He now believed, he said, that he was releasing the same mouse each morning. We wondered how the daring little rodent managed to cross Park Avenue without being hit, and marveled at its determination.

When good times happened with Papa, I wanted to speak of them to my friends at school. Once in the crowded pupils' staircase, as we were shuffling and shoving our way up to class, I recounted something funny and dear that Papa had done, laughing a little and shaking my head as if to say, "What won't he do next?" My classmate Chantal wheeled around, glaring at me. "You told us that before! You don't have to keep telling us what a wonderful father you have." I burned with shame, caught showing off for what wasn't even true. Though the pathetic little incident I'd recounted had actually occurred, I hadn't told the entire truth. On top of that, she thought I was boasting — to her, who had lost her father so young she couldn't even remember him. She never knew there were times I almost envied her for that.

I was coming to terms with the fact that I had inherited none of Mama's beauty. Before the mirror, I pulled at my colorless, uncooperative hair, tilted my head this way and that to see which angle showed the face not quite so long, the jaw — with its crooked, crowded teeth uncorrected by braces — not quite so big. It was Papa's face, and even more it was Daidee's: the same Saxon coloring, the Habsburg jaw.

Still, Mama dreamed for me a girlhood like her own: rounds of parties filled with gay banter and beaux lining up at the doorstep. She also supposed that I would only escape our circumstances by securing a husband — preferably one who was handsome, kind, and very rich.

Behind old hat boxes on the top shelf of Mama's closet I found a set of beige-pink pamphlets, embossed with violets. They were instruction manuals from 1920, entitled *The Art of Attracting Men*. Nothing on Earth could have interested me more. Chantal and I pored over them, committing key points to memory. Use every guile and opportunity to appear fragile, adorably helpless, for men like to feel strong and protective. At all costs, and especially by means of your sweet, silly dependence upon them, encourage their own self-regard. Wear filmy fabrics and, upon occasion, faint. Here a concrete example was provided: if you see a mouse, stand on a chair and scream, then, if a man is nearby to catch you, faint. Chantal and I tried putting wet blotting paper in the soles of our shoes, to draw the blood down to our feet and help us faint.

Chantal hardly needed those lessons, she was so pretty and had her long-term goal so clearly in mind: to marry one of the richest men in the Western world. On our very first afternoon of dancing class at the Plaza Hotel, the boys swarmed around her like bees. I was astonished at that because I didn't consider her very clever and because Mama had put so much effort into my own appearance. But Chantal was clever enough to wear a straight dark dress and to pin a gardenia in her hair, just below the ear, as if it were kissing her face, and even I could barely take my eyes off her.

Mama's hopes for me were set on those tea dances at the Plaza. After calling on Mrs. Bloss to talk her into quietly waiving the year's fee, Mama scrimped to buy me a dress at a wholesale barn in the garment district. When she was faced with the actual expenditure, so many practical considerations intervened — such as how long the dress would last me and in how many different circumstances — that I ended up with a slightly oversized pink flannel shirtwaist dress that would have been excellent for a lifetime as a schoolteacher.

I felt as if I were going into battle each time I rode down on the bus through the light-twinkling Manhattan dusk, walked in under the Art-Deco glass canopies to the strains of string music wafting from the Palm Court, and refastened my garter belt and stockings in the ladies' room. The major challenge was finding something to say to the boys who asked me to dance. It was not enough to attract their attention; I had to sustain it. That was the girl's job, and she seemed to do it by pretending she was having the time of her life —

chattering away, laughing, and tossing her head — so more boys would cut in, wanting to be included in all that mirth.

How different from being with my brothers, who didn't count, or the boys at the Lycée, who teased you all the time and whom you just had to ignore. How different also from the passionate intensities I was encountering in the tragedies of Racine, where Phèdre burned in her love for Hippolytus like a moth in the flame. Here, under all the frills and music, the whole enterprise felt more like a cold-blooded game in which you could only advance by securing the attentions of a boy, whether you could stand him or not. My face and mind went stiff from boredom and the effort to please.

Fortunately, since I wasn't pretty or clever enough to succeed at the game on its own terms, I discovered another book from Mama's childhood that allowed me to step through it. Dating from before the First World War, it told of a young woman invited to a party in a New York mansion. Ignored, and embarrassed by her own isolation, she wandered among the potted palms until she was approached by a mysterious aged gentleman who had been observing her. He told her he had a secret that could save her from the excruciation of not being popular. And true enough, it freed her from the paralyzing grip of self-consciousness. The secret he gave her was simple: "Everybody's lonely."

With this mantra in my mind, my attention shifted right away. It was no longer exclusively focused upon my own performance. I relaxed. The boys I'd been endeavoring to enthrall were not pawns in a game but real people that I could care about, at least a little bit, because, at some level, they were lonely too.

At the Lycée Madame Davide was taking us into the seventeenth century, *le grand siècle*. The dark passions of religious warfare were tamed now by the growing power of the monarchy and brought to order by the rule of reason. We learned how order and reason unfolded together through attention to form, and how they fashioned a culture of *élégance disciplinée*. I loved it the way I loved plane geometry, for the confidence bred of repeatable precision. What had been sweeter to me, after all, than to demonstrate again and again the reliability of the Pythagorean theorem?

Now René Descartes demonstrated that the same sweet powers of analysis could be applied to our own identity and existence. *"Avec un courage héroique de l'esprit,"* I wrote in one of my weekly papers for Madame Davide, he pursued logic to determine truth, walked step by step from the simpler to the more complex, moving in a straight line, just as you should do when *"perdu dans la forêt.*" That is how Descartes got so clear about things, and he demon-strated his clarity by making an absolute distinction between self and world, mind and matter. That distinction was fine by me. It felt freeing and invigor-ating, like an autumn wind stripping the trees of their dead leaves.

Descartes freed himself by taking nothing for granted; he doubted every-thing, Madame Davide said. He depended on nothing but his own mind. Although at that moment Jacques was reaching over to doodle on my note-book, I was able to catch a glimpse of Descartes' triumphant reasoning: *Je pense donc je suis*; I think, therefore I am. But I didn't apply this axiom to the cen-tral challenge of my own life until a few weeks later.

That insight occurred as I walked up 95th Street. I was heading home in the late afternoon, an hour or two before Papa would return from his office, when my mind lit up with cool and sudden clarity: "I hate, therefore I am." The logic, as impeccable as Descartes', flooded me with an immediate sense of relief. At last I knew, undeniably, that I truly existed in my own right. And I did so by hating. I had finally found my *moi profond*.

Hating can feel pure and clean. It is hard to sustain, however, when the object shifts and the issues at hand dissolve in ambiguities. Again I was in Mama's room, absorbing her distress and trying in vain to console her as she wept into her hands. This time her grief baffled me. Papa wanted to leave her for his sec-retary Mildred, she sobbed. He was asking for a divorce — and oh, no, no, she could not agree. The rejection and the loss of face were clearly too great for her. I was dumbfounded to see Mama closing the door on her own freedom when it was offered to her at last. Although now I understood why she had begun working at Papa's office, I could understand nothing else — nothing about the kind of happiness my mother wanted, or the value she set upon it.

My love for this woman and my need for her remained undiminished, but they were tortured now by something I could not allow myself to name. I was unable to acknowledge the judgments rising within me — judgment of her for clinging to the source of her suffering, and of myself for feeling that. In the process, I surrendered both my capacity and my desire to make sense of things.

That spring I went out into the streets of Manhattan. Though I remained obedient to the demands of the Lycée, with its heavy daily loads of homework, I sought distance from the house, and on Saturdays I wandered through the city alone. I walked for miles, not knowing where I was going or what I was looking for. I walked down littered, derelict streets; into churches and out again; into libraries and museums — never staying more than a moment. I moved through traffic like a sleepwalker, stood at crosswalks staring at buildings and passers-by, delivery trucks, fire hydrants. If a bus pulled up in front of me, its doors wheezing open, I might step on, without glancing at its route or destination, and ride for a while before lurching out at some unfamiliar street corner to resume the walking. I was fifteen and three-quarter years old and all I knew was that I was ready to walk straight into the isolation and meaninglessness I had feared. Weary of the hatred that had so recently defined and exhilarated me, I walked as if I were trying to wipe myself off on the city, like a piece of phlegm.

After a while a pattern emerged: same bus stop, same bus, same trajectory across the north end of Central Park on 110th Street. I would find myself getting off at Amsterdam Avenue and mounting the wide steps of the Cathedral of St. John the Divine. There under the dim, high arches I wandered for hours, moving randomly through shadows and narrow shafts of light and entering slowly, one by one, the chapels surrounding the apse. The generous immensities of that huge, unfinished structure soothed me. They surrounded me with mystery, received the turmoil and the aching emptiness I carried inside me.

V-E Day arrived. Outside, the city was exuberantly celebrating the allies' triumph in Europe and the unconditional surrender of the enemy. Here, in the vast and dusky interior of St. John's, I simply touched things. Hands are good for that. I placed my palms against the coolness of stone, the way I placed them on Spotty's flanks. I felt with my fingers the grain of worked wood, traced the intricacies of the carving on pulpit and choir screen. I did not seek symbolic meanings in the figures, the cross, the cup. That they had been made was enough, by hands like mine. I fingered the texture of altar cloths and the bronze roughness of sculpted saints, as if I could touch through them the soul of Montaigne with his earnestness, or of Phèdre who burned with passion, or Ron who burned from duty, or all the young *Kameraden* who believed, I hoped, that they had died for some purpose. In the dim, unfinished spaces of the Cathedral, their disparate lives seemed to weave together and fashion a kind of belonging that seemed somehow to hold me. If "everybody's lonely," maybe everybody belongs as well. I could feel the connections reaching out through space and back through time.

The mind's appetite returned. I could almost taste all I wanted to learn and understand. It was as if Montaigne's tower had become as big as my world. And that felt right because the time had come to decide about college.

By the end of *Seconde* I had completed the academic equivalent of an American high school education, which would allow me to move directly into an American college if I chose to. And it was my choice; this was my country, after all. But, barely sixteen, I didn't feel ready. Should I stay on at the Lycée for the *Classe de Première* and then enter college as a sophomore? Or, after doing *Première*, should I slip back to start as a college freshman? It was time to consult with Papa. It was he, after all, who had insisted on me getting a Lycée education.

College for me would not cost Papa any more than he paid for Harty at Yale, I knew that. Like my brother I was at the top of my class, and from my grades on scholastic aptitude tests and from interviews that Mama had arranged for me at the Vassar and Wellesley Clubs, it seemed reasonable to count on substantial scholarships. Sitting up late at the dining room table, poring through college catalogues and forms, Mama and I figured it out together: with stipends and loans and student jobs on and off campus, I could make it on less than five hundred dollars. If Papa wanted to wait a year before making that kind of expenditure, fine — that seemed reasonable enough.

As I waited for the best moment to approach my father, I was not as anxious as usual. All the previous times I'd had to talk to him about money — for shoes, say, or books — there was this falling sensation in my stomach, and my sphincter muscles tightened in fear, as if I might soil myself. But I did not feel that way now, because just thinking about college made me feel older and more self-assured — especially with these calculations that showed how much I could do for myself.

The meeting, when it happened, was fairly brief — the talking part, that is. "College?" Papa seemed genuinely surprised. "When did I say I would send you to college?" Then he repeated the question slowly, as if interrogating me in front of a jury. "When ... did you ... ever ... hear me say ... that I ... would send ... you ... to college?" I had no answer. He had hoped, he said, that I would be grateful enough for the fine education he had already provided me not to hound him with further demands. "Papa. Papa, please ..." I started, but I knew that no pleading would avail. There was utter finality in the words with which he cut me short: "Joanna, there is no money for you to go to college. You will not raise the matter again."

As I registered his words, I didn't want discussion either. A wildness took hold of me. It picked me up and threw me headfirst against the most solid object I could find. This is what I remember: how I started to scream, wordlessly, in a high, shrill keening; how I flung myself over and over again, with all my might, against the living room walls; how it was my head that I battered against them. I did not hit my father. I hit myself — as hard as I could — as if to dash out my brains against those confining walls.

Unmoved, my father withdrew and climbed the stairs to his room. Mama, who had been with us all along, did not try to hold me. But she later whispered to me: "We'll find a way." And she saw to it that we did.

3

The Cross

By the close of that school year I had turned sixteen and decided to return in the fall to the Lycée for the *Classe de Première*. Meanwhile, I began the summer at a week-long conference for Presbyterian young people. My friend Iris from Sunday school at Fifth Avenue Church had gone to the previous year's conference and insisted I come with her this time. She said I would love it and probably meet some cute boys, too.

Church was a steady and unquestioned part of my growing up. In addition to summertimes around my grandfather's and great-grandfather's churches, our weekly attendance in New York ensured that by sixteen I was pretty thoroughly imbued with Protestant Christianity. The hymns and prayers and Bible readings had grown as familiar as the alternation of day and night, or the need for three meals a day. The familiarity was reassuring to me, as were even the moments of boredom, of relaxed and wandering mind when the talking went on too long.

As a family we undertook no excursions, except for sitting in the dark together at occasional French movies of Papa's choice and the Translux newsreel theatre in Grand Central Station where he'd been given a free Sunday afternoon pass. By going to church we accompanied each other into a dimension that extended beyond the frustrations of our airless life together. It was a wider country with its own stories, songs, and rituals; and it provided continuity, too. I didn't really expect it to do more than that — to transform our lives, for example, or to be coherent with what I was learning at the Lycée.

When Papa decided that we should attend the Fifth Avenue Presbyterian Church, after hearing on the radio the excellent preaching there, I was unenthusiastic. I wished we could stay on at our neighborhood church on 91st Street, where I had friends. "Fifth Avenue," way down on the corner of 55th Street, was an imposingly somber pile of brownstone holding its own amidst luxury hotels and stores like Tiffany's and Bergdorf Goodman's. The congregation was older and more affluent; the overall effect was of dark wood, dark furs, well-coifed silver hair, kindly ushers moving smoothly as if on wheels, the fragrance of corsages and subtle perfumes.

We always sat in the same pew down in front to the right, close under the pulpit, where the floor dipped and slanted up again like the hull of a ship. All heavily crafted and carved of mellowed oak, the big oval sanctuary was not beautiful like Gothic-style churches I'd seen, or spare and light-filled like Ouie's. It was capaciously comfortable, though, the way it curved around like a great wooden ark. It was also like the sounding box of a giant cello, the way it filled and resonated with the organ's music and the singing of the people, with favorite hymns like "Holy, Holy, Holy" and "All Creatures of our God and King." It felt then as if we were sailing through seas of vast, familiar sound that surrounded us and came from inside us, too.

I especially liked St. Francis' hymn "All Creatures" because we sang then to the wonders I loved most, addressing them directly with lots of hallelujahs. "Thou burning sun with golden gleam, thou silver moon with gentler beam, hallelujah! ... thou rushing wind that art so strong, ye clouds that sail in heaven along, hallelujah!" The church's dusky interior and the city that confined me receded, as we evoked what I had pleasured in all summer long. Then I knew it was all still there, an enduring reality that was somehow inseparable from me.

During the early war years, when radio reports were full of U-boat attacks on allied convoys sinking troops who had just passed through New York on their way to battle, we often sang "Hear us when we cry to Thee for those in peril on the sea." This moved me greatly — not so much because of any faith I had in intercessory prayer, but because the simple, sober recognition of suffering, the act of naming the danger and holding it in our hearts, felt right to me and somehow useful.

If the church sanctuary was like a boat, Dr. Bonnell's pulpit was where you'd find the tiller. Presbyterians treasure the Word — that's why pulpit, not altar, is the central focus. Coming from the Lycée, where utter respect was accorded to mental construction, I felt at home with that focus and made little effort to harmonize the concepts of those two separate worlds. John Sutherland Bonnell was certainly as eloquent as a Descartes or a Voltaire, and more benevolent. A tall, patrician Canadian preacher, he delivered his liberal Protestant theology in a persuasively intelligent and gracious manner. His prayers invoked a God whose presence — like a warm, enveloping mind — became real then to me as well. I could feel it holding me, holding us all.

Like Jesus, and all the other preachers I had heard, our minister called this presence "Father". That didn't bother me. Already from Ouie and from books I'd read, I sensed what that word could mean — steady mountain, sheltering tree. It didn't occur to me to try to match these qualities with Papa's, or to take that troubled, tyrannical man as an exemplar of fatherhood.

Dr. Bonnell's sermons were as fine as his prayers. They seemed often so relevant to our own lives, so witty at moments and moving at others, that Mama and I liked to sit side by side so we could nudge each other, and to remember them together afterwards. I recall a sermon he preached about self-worth, about how you must respect yourself as a precious child of God and not automatically put yourself in the wrong. "Even a stopped clock is right two times a day," he said. Mama and I just crowed over that; Papa blamed her so consistently for everything, he'd not let her be right even once in a day. Since she had the habit of assuming that anyone as brainy and articulate as Papa must know what he's talking about, I would often remind her of Dr. Bonnell's saying — and we'd laugh. But it wasn't really funny to me. The way Papa denied having said things and insisted that they were figments of Mama's imagination made me worry a lot that she would lose trust in her own mind. I had seen Charles Boyer do the same kind of thing to Ingrid Bergman in the movie *Gaslight* — convince her that she was crazy. So I had the chilling sense that it could really happen, and was relieved when Mama turned to our minister for counseling. That she was actually talking to someone besides me — and deriving some benefit and backbone from it — made me love Dr. Bonnell even more. And it added to my lightheartedness at escaping the family to go to the youth conference.

At the summery campus of Blair Academy, the New Jersey boarding school the Presbyterians used for the week, I loved the independence that was suddenly mine. I immediately felt not older for it but younger, as carefree, almost, as the other teenagers seemed to be. Just as Iris had expected, I enjoyed the late night talks and laughter in the girls' dorm, the easy conversations with boys around meals and classes. "See! Didn't I tell you?" she teased, when an earnest, sweet-looking fellow with coal-black hair began watching for me and saving the seat beside him.

What Iris hadn't mentioned were the morning Quiet Times, which I liked just as much. For thirty minutes before breakfast you were expected to go off by yourself for prayer and reflection, to sit under a tree or on the open lawn with the Bible reading for the day. The reading and the praying were not obligatory, only the silence was — a silence filled with bird song and listening. You have to get still and pay attention if you want to pray, and that act of stilling makes spaciousness inside. It seemed luxurious to me that this stillness was actually structured into the day's schedule. Scattered across the campus, we were all doing it at the same time, simultaneously alone and together, undistracted by worries about appearing antisocial or missing out on something. When I heard Iris grumble about Quiet Time — "It's the one thing I can't stand here" — I was amazed, for I loved it the way I loved the maple tree and Montaigne's tower.

One of our teachers that week was an Air Force chaplain just back from the war in Europe. Mustached and solidly built, he wore no uniform and would have looked like a business man if he hadn't been so raw and serious. Each morning in the sunny classroom full of teenagers he paced back and forth, no notes in his hand, turning frequently to look into our faces, as if the words he wanted were in our eyes. Those words were not mellow or soothing, like Dr. Bonnell's, or full of certitude, like my Lycée teachers'. It seemed the war had stripped him of the comfortable ideas that make life easier for people.

He didn't bring us stories about the patriotism and faith of the flyers he served as chaplain; instead he brought us a way of looking at things that are hard to look at. And they weren't so much the horrors of war as the kind of world that makes war possible — the way we treat each other, the injustices and betrayals within our own society. He spoke of poverty and prejudice, the war profiteering, the squalor in migrant worker camps and Indian reservations.

Whatever he had to say about the kind of God who could be there for us, in spite of the mess we'd made of our world, riveted me. For that kind of God was free from our own pride and wishful thinking. He (and God was certainly a He, at that point) was exempt from having to be on our side — even on the winning side, whatever that might mean. He was a God who showed us the hells we make for ourselves and each other, and who meets us there. "The crucifixion of Jesus didn't happen just once, two thousand years ago," the chaplain said, "it is happening today. You and I are part of it."

Carefully, thoroughly, like the good Lycée student I was, I took notes in my notebook — and felt a shuddering inside me deeper than the fears and resentments of my life at home. Papa's tyranny, Mama's humiliations, Harty's withdrawal were only immediate instances within a far larger panorama of cruelty and suffering. It included the faces I had seen in my wanderings through

New York, and all who had passed through on their way to war, and the names read out on Papa's short-wave during the blackouts. If we are connected enough to belong to each other, as I had sensed on those Saturdays in the cathedral, then we're connected enough to hurt each other — a lot.

Now the chaplain was saying words I had first heard from my grandmother Daidee when she explained the funny name of her Inasmuch Group: "Jesus said, 'Inasmuch as ye have done unto the least of these my brethren, ye have done unto me.'" So, I reflected, when you're feeding the hungry and housing the homeless, it's like you're giving food and shelter to Jesus himself. Now the chaplain confronted us with what Jesus had gone on to say, challenging us to look not so much at our occasional acts of compassion as at our more habitual indifference:

> I was hungry and you gave me no food; I was thirsty and
> you gave me no drink; I was a stranger and you took me
> not in; naked and you clothed me not; sick and in prison
> and you visited me not. And those who heard him said:
> Lord when did we ever see you hungry or thirsty, a
> stranger or sick or imprisoned, and did not minister unto
> you? Then Jesus said, Inasmuch as you did it not unto
> the least of these, you did it not unto me.

By that logic, I could see that we all were there with Jesus at the end, doing our bit to put him on the cross. We were Pontius Pilate washing our hands to avoid involvement; we were the crowd watching, and the Roman soldiers hammering in the nails.

It was the next to last day of our week at Blair. Slipping away from the others, I fled for solitude to the far side of the campus. My throat and chest were so constricted they ached. The guilt I felt was not for hating Papa — which seemed too natural and inevitable to get upset about — but for what I let that hatred do to me. I let it close me in. That resentful self-enclosure was ultimately such a denial of life that it made me an accomplice to the world's suffering. We were *all* involved; there was no way to stand on the sidelines, although Montaigne in his tower had imagined he could. And if this were so — as the almost intolerable pressure on my heart seemed to confirm — then how do we ever get free from our complicity? No judgment of God's could be greater than my own right then and there. I could not imagine how to live with it.

I asked for a moment alone with the chaplain, and the next morning during Quiet Time he met me in the Blair chapel. I wanted to know how to go on living with the knowledge that if Jesus was being crucified every day, I was letting it happen. My words stumbled over each other.

The chaplain leaned forward, listening intently. After he paused to draw a deep breath, his response was immediate. It cut through the impasse I was caught in, carved open a space I could walk through. "Look!" he said, pointing above the altar. "Look up, the cross is empty. He's not still nailed on it, he is down here at your side." And he quoted the verse where Jesus says: "'Lo, I am with you always.' It's the risen Christ who says that, Joanna, and he is risen into the openness of your own heart."

Then the chaplain was saying words from the Communion Service: "This is my body, broken for you, Joanna. This is my blood, shed for you." The phrases from the Last Supper I'd heard so often suddenly filled with new meaning — an acceptance so deep that my mind could hardly grasp it. If I had let Jesus' crucifixion become real to me, then I could receive as well the hugeness of his trust in life: "This is my body."

That night, our last at Blair, an outdoor service was held. We carried lighted candles up the hillside behind the gym; they brightened as the darkness deepened, until they were all that I could see of us — just those long, bobbing, flickering lines of light gradually converging toward the top of the hill. Endlessly we sang, "We are climbing Jacob's ladder." I wondered: was I moving back through time with shadowy companions I had always known, or forward with them into the future? The fulfillment I felt was not about getting anywhere; it was in the going itself, through the darkness together, step by step.

As we came down at last to street lights and conversation, I caught sight of the black-haired boy waiting to accompany me across the campus, then saw a girl from my dorm hang back beside him so that he'd walk with her instead. "I'll show *her*," I thought, instantly competitive. The impulse felt so small and tacky I wanted to shrug it off. So I did, grinning at them both as I passed them, striding out ahead on my own. At that moment I needed nothing more to bring me closer to the heart of things.

I rode back to New York with Iris. Before her chauffeur-driven car dropped me at Bleak House, I thumbed back to a reading from earlier in the week. It was Psalm 139:

> Whither shall I go from thy spirit? or whither shall I flee
> from thy presence? If I ascend up into heaven, thou art
> there; if I make my bed in hell, behold, thou art there.

> If I take the wings of the morning, and dwell in
> the uttermost parts of the sea; even there shall
> thy hand lead me, and thy right hand shall hold me.

To "take the wings of morning" — Quiet Time was like that. I vowed to continue the practice daily. The very next day I shared it with my mother, sitting in a shaft of sun amidst half-packed suitcases bound for the farm. I could hardly wait till we were alone together. "Oh, Mama. What they've been saying about God, it's true, he's as real as you or me. And what happened with Jesus and the disciples is happening right now." As I recounted for her my discoveries at Blair, she sat as still as a statue, those brown eyes never wavering from my face.

Then I learned from her that Papa, who had come to depend on her help at the office, had only this morning, the day before our departure for summer on the farm, announced that she could not go. He would release her only if I took her place at the office. As I absorbed this information, I knew that I would have to confront him. Instantly the old, cold fear of him gripped me. Having been away — light years away — I could feel it more clearly now, like something distinct and even separable from me. "I'm sorry, Papa," I said that evening, "but I'm not staying in New York right now. Mama's not staying either. Later in the summer we will talk about my working for you."

The fear, as always, made me feel a little sick to my stomach; but now there was also a tiny island of calm. It consisted, in part, of my cool assessment that, having refused to help me go to college, Papa had little to hold over me now. It also grew from something warmer, a certainty fanned by words I had just read over again, so they would be fresh in my mind.

> For I am persuaded that neither death nor life nor angels
> nor principalities nor powers nor things present
> nor things to come, nor height nor depth
> nor any other creature
> shall be able to separate us from the love of God,
> which is in Christ Jesus our Lord.

In the months and years to come, I could count on this passage from Paul's letter to the Romans to bolster my courage. But no principality or power was as hard to face up to as my own father. Whether he actually smiled on that particular June evening I do not recall. Maybe I am now just imagining the warm flash in those pale blue eyes as they glanced at me quickly, taking care not to betray his surprise, or his pride.

When I returned to the farm that summer of 1945, I couldn't know that it would be sold before the year's end. The picking jobs were good in the orchards and tomato fields. For the first time I worked in peaches too, discovering how their fuzz sticks to arms and face and makes you itch.

One day in early August I walked through the shed door into the kitchen and found everyone gathered there because of some news. I heard a name I'd never heard before: Hiroshima. It seemed that America had built a new, incredibly massive kind of bomb — and we had gone and used it. There was the smell of milk, warm from the cow. And there was this sudden feeling of an unaccountable weight, as if something had dropped on *our* country, too. There was no clear reason then for the sense of foreboding, no way to explain what I sensed only with my body — that we had done something unnecessary and irrevocable that would change us forever.

Even when V-J Day followed the next week, with sirens and celebrations and the farmboys setting off firecrackers, there was this feeling in me of something unaccounted for. It felt like a menace that came from inside us and that we would have to turn to and face someday. But there was no language for this feeling, no rationale, so it sank below words, below thought.

That fall began my last year at the Lycée and at home, for Mama and I had decided I was going to college. That prospect became more likely as Wellesley College promised me generous scholarships; and then Mama's step-grandmother gave me the last five hundred dollars I needed. Meanwhile, school and family took less of my attention than before; I spent hours around Fifth Avenue church and at Presbyterian headquarters downtown with new friends my age.

When I heard news accounts of the suffering in Europe in the bitter cold winter following the war, I wished we could send some warm clothes to families there. Much to my amazement that turned out to be rather easy. All you had to do was hold the idea in your mind and tell it to people — first to one, then to another, then to whole groups. Assume that they care. As the clothing drive got underway, I faced larger audiences. At first I felt nervous as a public speaker but then remembered those words God said through Jesus: "I am with you always." When I remembered them, I could really feel his presence thrumming in me, like the circulation of the blood, except it was circulating out into the world as well, right through the listening people. I discovered that talking to people in groups can help you believe more in what you're saying.

I got a lot of practice in that the following summer of 1946, before I went off to Wellesley. For two months I took part in a Presbyterian program called the Youth Caravan. We were all of college age; at seventeen, I was the youngest of the lot. After a short, intensive training, we dispersed in teams that moved from one church community to another, working in each for a week at a time. For that week the life of the church was turned over to us; we led worship services, taught Vacation Bible School, organized programs and picnics for all ages. It was daunting to be given so much responsibility, in strange settings and among grown people we'd never met before. My own team of four was assigned to rural Maryland and moved through a series of farm communities along Chesapeake Bay.

It was like being part of a traveling circus or roadshow — the high-spirited teamwork as you hit a new town, adapt to new people, improvise to new challenges, each member supporting the others and doing what he or she can do best. While others on my team used their talents working with the choir or negotiating with church elders, I found myself in the pulpit — and though I trembled every time, I loved it.

Whether by lamplight in an old country church or in a dew-fresh morning service out of doors, I always ended up talking about the cross, as I had come to understand it at Blair. I spoke of the fears and defeats that seem inseparable from our lives, and of the grace that can happen when we stop denying our pain and let it reveal our connection with God and with each other.

The first time I preached, it was evening in a full country church. I was trying so hard to remember what I wanted to say that I studiously ignored the movements beginning to sweep the congregation. It looked like wind blowing over a field of grain, the way people's heads sank and rose in waves. I feared I would lose my train of thought if I stopped to figure out what was happening, so I kept plodding ahead even after I saw the bat. From out of the rafters or through an open window it had entered the sanctuary and was swooping back and forth over the pews. Bravely I went on with my sermon — knowing, all the while, that this bravery was a kind of stupidity. I wasn't confident enough to be flexible: to stop and acknowledge people's discomfort, to bring the incident into laughter, or even to use it to help me say what I wanted to say. Only in hindsight did I learn from that little calamity; I vowed to relax and be more present with the people who were good enough to listen to me.

Soon I could speak while looking directly into the faces before me. I learned to see those Maryland farmers, tradespeople, families, and children not as strangers, but as fellow journeyers who in their hearts desired a wider, deeper life, just as I did. I felt both emptied and exalted by that knowledge, and I believed it was God's power that freed me to speak so well.

My team-mate Ben often responded quizzically, giving me wry, almost compassionate looks. "That was great, Jo," he said, rumpling my hair after one of my sermons, "but watch it, honey. You can get a little carried away sometimes." I hated being told I was getting carried away.

"Ben, don't you feel it too, the cloud of witnesses, right here with us?" That image from Paul's letter to the Hebrews was potent for me: "Seeing how we are compassed about by so great a cloud of witnesses, we can lay aside every weight…." The cloud included all who had gone before us on the journey: Paul himself, Joan of Arc, the ancestors. I felt sometimes as if the same power that filled them filled me.

"Yeah, sure," Ben said, giving me a quick hug, "but the folks that came out tonight just want to feel *you* being here, ordinary you in ordinary Barkersville." He had perceived the almost mythic inflation that could seize me and was trying to shake me loose from it without ridiculing me.

At summer's end Mama saw me off at Grand Central as I boarded the train for a college campus I had never seen. Her step-grandmother Aunt Harriet from Los Angeles, whose $500 made it all possible, was on hand as well. She had bought me an outfit for going to an Ivy League college: an unobjectionable gray flannel suit and a matching pillbox hat that perched precariously over my forehead. "Wear it," she commanded, seeing me blanch at the cost. "Wear only expensive dresses, even if you have just one. No one sees what you keep in your closet." She also insisted that I use her crease-free method for packing: roll up each item of clothing in tissue paper, like a sausage.

As the train pulled out, I waved at Mama through the sooty windows, and she, standing there so beautiful in the dim light of the underground platform, kept waving too. What I felt most of all was my heart breaking. How could I abandon her like this, prey to Papa's moods and commands, without me there to turn to?

I discovered after a while that I'd boarded the wrong train. Changing at Hartford and again at Worcester, I finally reached the suburban station named Wellesley. By the time I lugged my bags up the long street to my freshman house, the pillbox hat shoved to the back of my head, it was well after dark.

A Christian college in the Midwest had offered me a full scholarship and I had been tempted to accept, knowing that it would nourish my dreams of a church vocation. But Mama, with unflagging persistence, kept urging me to choose Wellesley. She believed that I would find a more cosmopolitan array of friends there, and a wider scope for the mind. "That's where you belong, Nana," she kept saying, "among the best;" and she reminded me that my great-aunt Bess Rogers had taught art history there for thirty years.

Now that I had actually arrived — with the carillon bells ringing out across the campus — I felt excitement and anticipation. On the way to my first class I walked under a Gothic archway and looked up to read the college motto carved in stone above me: *Non ministrari, sed ministrare.* Not to be ministered unto, but to minister. I felt at home with that understanding of a life's purpose.

4

Walking Out

IN THE LATE WINTER OF 1950, my senior year at Wellesley, Professor Ferdinand Denbeaux called me to his office in the Biblical History Department. As I walked over in the gray afternoon from my job at the musicology library, I wondered what was on his mind. Except for council meetings of the all-campus religious organization, which he served as faculty advisor and I as student president, we had seen little of each other all year — no personal conversations that I could recall. That in itself was odd, considering that we had been friends since I came to college and that he was now chair of the department in which I was majoring. It occurred to me, as I skirted piles of dirty snow, that I had been avoiding him. That wasn't too surprising, given how weary I had been growing of the study of religion.

Of all the professors in the department, Denbeaux was the one I liked and respected the most, and the one I felt knew me the best, right from the start. My very first week at Wellesley, I attended a fireside gathering at his house and felt him watching me with benevolent eyes as I tangled with a couple of born-again Christians. They were a minority of two within a largely secular college class, but they wanted to capture the Christian flag — to define the terms in which we talked about faith. With earnest complacency and no trace of lipstick, they said they were redeemed by Jesus because he had "died for our sins"; he'd paid with his blood the debt we owe to God. It sounded like a watch being redeemed from the pawnbroker. This notion of atonement, as some settling of accounts in a cosmic ledger, struck me as silly. When I argued that the cross only "saves" through what it challenges us to know about ourselves, my two fundamentalist classmates looked at me blankly. But I sensed there was one who knew precisely what I was trying to say. Hulking tall and heavy-jowled by the fireplace, he was relighting his pipe. Behind his brooding Old Testament eyes was an intensity that seemed to match mine. "I look forward to having you in class," he said to me at the end of the evening. "Be sure to get assigned to my section of the sophomore course."

I had to wait a year for Biblical History 101; it was the introductory course in Old and New Testaments required of all sophomores, and the first course I was allowed to take in the department. "Bible," as it was popularly called, was the department where all courses in religion were concentrated, and in the 1940s that was limited almost entirely to the Judeo-Christian tradition. Having finagled my way into Denbeaux's class, I found it engrossing, even electrifying. I felt as if I'd been waiting all my life to walk into this particular landscape with this particular guide. He looked, as I quipped to a friend, like Orson Welles in the role of an Old Testament prophet — Amos perhaps, or Jeremiah. He didn't get us bogged down in arcane details of documentary sources, which befogged our other professors' courses; he did not want them to obscure for us the unfolding drama of a people's search for meaning.

World War II, from which we'd just emerged, made this search for meaning seem all the more urgent. Despite the Allied victory, it was a spiritually shattering cataclysm; the Holocaust and the massive bombings revealed new dimensions of moral culpability. I was stirred by Denbeaux's ability to look straight into this abyss and to eschew all easy answers in developing a theological response. It was a tough-minded response: rejecting the vague optimism of nineteenth-century religious liberalism, it stressed the human capacity for evil and the absolute necessity for rigorous moral choice, whatever the odds. I liked Denbeaux's courage and clarity and soon learned that what I was imbibing from him was a new, post-war theology called "neo-orthodoxy." It was being articulated, on both sides of the Atlantic, by the likes of Karl Barth and Reinhold Niebuhr. I responded wholeheartedly, at first.

In deciding to major in Biblical History, I went against the express advice of my avuncular advisor from the Presbyterian Board of Foreign Missions. Expecting me to serve eventually as a missionary, the board had made a small but important contribution toward my tuition costs. So I had reason to listen to Herrick Young when he visited Wellesley, staying with his friend Mildred McAfee Horton, our college president. When I shared with him my excitement over Denbeaux's course, he leaned back from President Horton's breakfast table and smiled and sighed and shook his head. "Wait until your graduate studies before doing theology, that'll be soon enough. For now, broaden out, explore, have a good time."

That made no sense to me. What was a "good time," if you separated it from having a meaningful purpose in life? From my first weeks at Wellesley I had felt sorry for the girls who did not have a clear idea of just where they were headed and what they were going to do with their lives. To not know, to wait around for directions, seemed vapid and rudderless. So despite Herrick Young's advice, I made up my own mind and went ahead to major in Biblical History.

As the semesters rolled by, my friendship with Denbeaux deepened. His course on Christian existentialism challenged me to look critically at the social and political context of my life and to question the comfortable assumptions I had inherited from my Republican family. By then I'd become involved with the Student Christian Movement in New England, a lively bunch that introduced me first-hand to issues of economic and racial justice. At one of our conferences I met Herb King, a towering, eloquent Black preacher from Grace Congregational Church in Harlem, and at another I came to know Jim Robinson, pastor of Harlem's Church of the Shepherd, which ran programs in West Africa. Both of these wise and open-hearted men blessed me with their friendship — and whenever I was home in New York, I enjoyed stepping into the world their churches opened to me.

Each time I returned to Wellesley I would make a beeline for Denbeaux's office to talk about the people and issues I had encountered. I told him about my involvement with Kirkridge, a Protestant lay monastic center in Pennsylvania. Inspired by the Iona community in Scotland, it embodied a strong social conscience, as suggested by one of its mottoes: "Picket and Pray." And before I left to spend a summer as a junior warden at the Connecticut state reformatory for women, I had consulted with him about the value of working there and living among the inmates. But somehow in my senior year we had seen each other only in large meetings.

As I climbed the steps of Green Hall and headed for the department offices, I wished I had time to brace myself with a cup of coffee. Miss Hitchcock, the music librarian, had just barraged me with reproaches that left me smarting. She was upset that I hadn't shown up for my Monday shift and that I hadn't arranged for a substitute either. I had gone skiing with friends up on Hogback Mountain, and the snow was so good I'd made a long weekend of it. "I tried to phone you," I said to her. It was a lie, and she knew it. She was surprisingly furious, considering that the musicology library was virtually empty on

Monday mornings. "I am especially disappointed in *you*, of all people, Miss Rogers. I am shocked that the head of Chapel should behave so irresponsibly."

As I walked down the hall to the Biblical History department, I dreaded facing one more judgment. Yet when I entered Denbeaux's office, all that registered was that I had missed that place, missed him. I looked at that giant of a man unfolding himself from his chair to greet me, and resigned myself at that moment to loving him forever. His gloomy exterior had always seemed just a cloak for his passion for humanity, a passion that confronted the depths and insisted that they yield transcendent meaning. That was why, from the very beginning, I'd trusted him so. Again I felt a pang of regret that he wasn't teaching the senior seminar in this, my senior year.

"Well, how are things going?" he asked, leaning back in his chair as he looked at me. "Fine." I made small talk about the busyness of the final semester. I felt surprisingly guarded and turned to look at the spatter of rain on the window. Denbeaux was excellent at allowing silence to build, and stubbornly I let him do it. I studied the rain, hoping it was snowing at higher elevations; otherwise ski conditions would be shot.

"I wondered if there was something you wanted to talk about," he said. "It's been a long time. I'm imagining that something is troubling you." Another silence while I wondered what I could possibly say. "I don't want to pry into your personal life, Jo." That's true, I reflected, he never had. "But," he went on, "are things all right at home?"

"Everything's fine at home," I said. "My parents just got a divorce."

"Oh, I'm terribly sorry!" He responded with shock and genuine concern. Divorce, in 1950, was not yet a common occurrence. "Well, that explains it," he said, sounding almost relieved. "I can imagine you're deeply distressed."

I looked at him and almost laughed. "Mr. Denbeaux, you have no idea how good this is." And I felt a glow of well-being just thinking of how, when the time had come, my mother had simply walked out. She'd inherited a small bequest, just enough to enable her to strike out on her own. One morning when Papa had gone on ahead to the office, she took the bags she had secretly packed and walked out.

The hardest thing for her was leaving Ouie and Daidee. She loved them and could hardly bear to leave them at Bleak House, at the mercy of their son, who could scarcely pass the time of day with them. Maybe it was dear Dr. Bonnell who gave her the shove to save her own life. She secured a divorce in Florida and then returned to Manhattan, to the last apartment we'd lived in before moving to the house. There she was near enough to see my grandparents frequently, when Papa was not at home.

I could hardly expect Denbeaux, or anyone else on campus except my closest friends, to realize what an enormous relief this was for me — to be able to go to bed at night and get up in the morning knowing my mother was free. It wasn't easy for her at first, going to secretarial school to learn shorthand and touch typing with girls even younger than me, but she landed a good job in the office of a friend of mine at the Presbyterian Board of Foreign Missions. She was her own woman now, able to enjoy her own gaiety and glamour. It was wonderful to behold.

"And your plans after graduation?" Denbeaux was asking, still watching me. "Will you be off to join Doctor Schweitzer in Africa?" He had heard me holding forth about meeting the great theologian and medical missionary the previous summer in New York. On Albert Schweitzer's first visit to America I'd been asked to serve for a day as his interpreter. It was a short encounter, but warm and strong, and we had been corresponding since then.

"No. Not for a while, anyway." I explained that I had applied for a Fulbright scholarship to France, to study French colonial policies in Africa. I said I thought it was a good idea to do that before proceeding with any plans for missionary service. *Those* plans, which had once so fired me, were becoming increasingly unreal, but I didn't know how to admit this to myself — let alone to Denbeaux or the Board of Foreign Missions.

Suddenly the professor stood up, moved around the room, leaned against the window sill. "Jo, I asked you to come see me because there is some concern on the part of the faculty who've had you in class this year. They tell me ... No, let me ask *you*: have you noticed what you have been doing this year in all your classes in the department?" I looked at him blankly. After a pause he said, "From the reports I receive, you are either yawning or arguing."

As a matter of fact, I had *not* noticed. Arguing or yawning — well, that was not surprising to hear. At least Denbeaux was kind enough not to mention what was happening to my grades. I rubbed my forehead, jaw, mouth, then looked at him quietly and nodded. He sat again, and we both listened to the rain, beating harder now against the window. How could I begin to tell Denbeaux, when I barely knew myself, what was happening in my studies of religion? I didn't want to acknowledge the dullness creeping over me, the resentment gnawing at my mind.

With painstaking care Denbeaux emptied and refilled his pipe; I watched each slow and separate movement as if it were the story of my life. How could I have ended up like this in my final semester at Wellesley, when I'd done everything I could have expected of myself? I had stood up for my faith as best I could. I had made Phi Beta Kappa in my junior year. I had chosen courses like New Testament Greek and labor economics instead of poetry and art and dance. I had become a campus leader.

Maybe I had tried too hard. With the kind of training I'd received at the Lycée, I could turn my mind to anything and absorb it unquestioningly, like a sponge. But what I absorbed in the Biblical History department, especially from Denbeaux himself, was the mindset of neo-orthodoxy. The brilliantly theorizing theologians had taken their toll on me. Rudolf Bultmann had "demythologized" my Christian faith, making propositions and explanations more important than the numinous immediacy of God's presence. Karl Barth and Reinhold Niebuhr had reduced faith to stringent dichotomies, the either-or of moral choice. While I appreciated the importance they accorded to the cross, I began to feel confined by the narrowness, the exclusivity with which they set it against the world and all that was natural and instinctive.

Feelings of mystical connection, yearnings to merge with God or nature, were viewed as intellectually sloppy and morally dangerous. That assumption had become so ingrained in me that I barely realized the toll it took. If I questioned it, I felt silly and adolescent — and would be reminded: "Look what nature mysticism led to in Hitler's Germany!"

By my senior year, neo-orthodox theology and its unrelenting dialectics had begun to weary me. Seeking a respite, I walked down sometimes to the Quaker Meeting in Wellesley village and sat in the simple sufficiency of its silence.

That listening silence seemed to have no place in the Christianity I was studying; indeed, whole dimensions of life seemed to be left out. Sunrise and the smell of wet soil were left out, and the way my body felt when I kissed Tony driving back from Harvard, and the leaping joy in my legs as I danced in the spring pageant to Khachaturian's *Scythian Suite*. As a matter of fact, most of humanity was left out.

Still, I tried to keep on going, seeing no alternative to my chosen path. I did not confront my own resistance until one fall morning at Kirkridge. I loved going to that retreat center in the Pocono mountains, with its mission of reclaiming a contemplative tradition within Protestantism. On my bunk, in the silent hour before breakfast, I sat up in my sleeping bag to pray. I hadn't observed Quiet Time for a long while and thought, "Ah! now at last, here in this monastic setting, I will pray again." But as I tried to do so, a terrible refusal took hold of me. I found myself utterly unable to commune with what God had become for me. The enveloping presence I had once known and trusted, as spacious and comforting as the maple tree, had turned into something else. A jealous, righteous judge was blocking the light that had spangled through the leaves. He was breathing down my neck, crowding me, sealing me in. It felt like being trapped in the legendary trunk that haunted me as a child. Yet my refusal to pray brought no freedom; it only triggered a sense of hopelessness. I had hit a monumental dead end.

That experience of spiritual claustrophobia abated; it had to. I was the newly elected president of Chapel and I had public religious duties to perform. I kept hoping that the buoyancy and conviction that had once filled my days with grace would come back. I could not easily relinquish the vocation that had for so long been the organizing principle of my life. It had been both the wind at my back and the horizon that beckoned. But now it began to feel like a burden, even a trap, and half-consciously I hoped to be rescued from it. Incapable of saying "no" to the life purpose I had espoused, I drifted numbly, as if waiting for some *force majeure* to intervene — some man perhaps who would sweep me off my feet, anything to free me from the burden of self-knowledge and choice.

Still patiently probing, Denbeaux was querying me on my courses in the department. "I imagine that you're finding the senior seminar a little ... trying."

"Early church history is ... hard for me to really get into," I said lamely, wishing I dared tell him the truth. The truth was I *hated* it, I couldn't bear it, it made me sick. But I didn't want to erode his respect for me any more than I already had.

Early church history, as it was presented in our senior seminar, was largely a record of squabbling, stubborn men. Whether as ascetics aiming to reject the world or as theologians fighting to define the faith, they seemed hounded by ambition. To subdue the hated hungers of their bodies, the hermits fled to the desert. When I read of their battles with their own prurient visions, I felt something fundamental to life being soiled in their pathetic efforts to be "pure" and "perfect." As to the theologians, they all seemed trapped in arcane and hairsplitting argumentation, driven by a remorseless, exhausting need to be right. What a dispiriting spectacle. To have to poke around in the Councils of

Chalcedon and Nicaea, the Arian and Athanasian controversies, the Pelagian and Gnostic heresies — as if any of it *mattered* — was almost more than I could stand.

For dry, endless hours I'd sit over ancient texts — Clement of Alexandria, Origen, Irenaeus — fearing I'd suffocate in the dusty treatises and slapping myself to stay awake while I pictured my classmates sailing out toward new intellectual horizons, invigorated by their senior theses in this culminating moment of our college careers.

I still knew, however, what mental excitement felt like. I was taking a course in international politics, and *that* was fascinating — especially the senior research paper I was writing on Indochina. In the former French colony, familiar to me from my studies at the Lycée, a war was going on. I heard myself tell Denbeaux what I was discovering about Ho Chi Minh. The poet leader, beloved of his people, was a nationalist, caught in the polarizing currents of the Cold War. "Any native movement that rejects colonialism is now branded as Soviet-controlled," I was saying with a little burst of energy. "The French betrayed Ho Chi Minh."

Denbeaux exhaled heavily. "You're distressed about the French in Asia. But we are not talking about the French in Asia, we are talking about you here at Wellesley, a senior major in Biblical History. Joanna Rogers, that promising, passionate mind, who's always had to believe in what she studies. And now for some reason she's dodging the very faith at the core of her life. She's fighting it."

He was standing again, facing the window, his words so charged he had to look away from me. Denbeaux, more than anyone, knew that I was not in this field of study just out of intellectual curiosity. Since I was unable to convey the spiritual desert I was in, my apparent indifference mystified him. "For some reason, you're fighting it," he repeated.

"I'm just fighting for it to make sense."

"Well, stop." He turned to look at me, anger and frustration in his eyes. "It will be an endless struggle; the resistant mind is never satisfied, never placated. Stop fighting, Jo!" He didn't say it in a comforting way, but as if he wanted to shake me. "Anyway, who's asking you to hang on to Christianity? Look, if you want to be an atheist, go ahead and be one."

His words, I realized at once, were a gambit. He was jerking the rug out from under me so that I would fall back into the arms of the faith I once had. "If you want to be an atheist, go ahead."

But I chose to take his words at face value. For a long moment I stared at him, speechless with amazement. Of course, I didn't need to be an *atheist*. I had no interest in acquiring another label or defending another position. But the idea that I could simply loosen my grip on Christianity, relinquish it even, had never occurred to me. Why not? Perhaps I *could* just walk out, as Mama had finally done. Open the door and walk out. I hardly dared believe that such freedom could be mine for the taking. "Oh," I breathed, "yes, of course."

From nearby Founders Hall the six o'clock carillon began to chime; I would be late for my waitressing job if I didn't hurry. I gathered my books and stood up. Denbeaux's dear face looked so stunned I wanted to touch it, put my lips to it. "Thank you," I said, smiling up at him, dazed and almost helpless with relief. "I guess that is what I'll have to do."

THE HOLE IN THE CENTER

5

The Cold War

I WALKED OUT OF DENBEAUX'S OFFICE RELIEVED, but disoriented. Claiming my freedom pulled the linchpin from my life. My commitment to a Christian vocation had formed the core of my identity and self-worth since I was sixteen. Its loss left a hole inside me, even as I celebrated Commencement with my Wellesley classmates and sailed for Europe — in fulfillment of dreams I had nourished since entering the Lycée.

The Fulbright scholarship had come through with its gift of a year's study in France, all expenses paid. When I applied for it the previous fall, I was excited by my course in international politics and my research on the war in Indochina. I figured I would go study the growth of nationalism in French colonies, reasoning that it would help prepare me for the missionary work I had been heading toward for so long. At that time I had not yet admitted my loss of interest in that goal. But now I had walked out on the Christian faith and, unhampered by any religious mission, I was free to follow, for their own sake, the political dramas of the postwar world.

The trouble was that these great dramas did not fill — and maybe could not fill — the space inside me once occupied by God and God's intentions for my life. In some innermost dimension I felt at sea, without a rudder.

While that was painful, it was also interesting, in a bleak sort of way. In my efforts to become an atheist, I was reading French existentialists. Camus and Sartre certainly showed how loss of meaning and direction was a characteristic feature of the world. Perhaps it was necessary to my growing up into a clear-eyed person of brave and honest intellect.

These ponderings were hardly constant though. When you are twenty-one and on your own in Europe, there is plenty to divert you from existential angst. And so I practiced giving myself to the beauty of the moment.

In early October the trees turn yellow along the Seine and their leaves, when the sun shines through them, are like translucent coins. The Fulbright orientation week in Paris was over, and in another day I would head south to Bordeaux to begin my studies at its Institut de Sciences Politiques. I erased that prospect from my mind as I walked the embankments for hours, gazing at the river, the occasional barge, the shimmering leaves.

A looping ribbon of white appeared in the blue. I caught sight of the tiny plane, slowly climbing the hill of an "l," then stopped to watch as it rounded an "a." A figure in blue coveralls, holding a fishing pole, watched too — his face, like mine, tipped back to the sun. *"On dirait que c'est un écolier qui fait ses leçons d'écriture,"* I commented. That could be a schoolboy practicing his writing lessons. *"Oui, et il a le grand ciel pour son cahier!"* And for his practice book he has the whole sky, said the workman in blue with a breathtaking smile, and now I saw how young he was, even younger than I. We laughed, as if to thank each other for so simple a moment of delight, and I walked on.

Crossing over a bridge, I stopped to lean over and watch the river from above. Words of a popular song, a love song to the Seine, hummed through my mind. *Elle coule, coule, coule, autour de ses quais fleuris; elle roule, roule, roule de Montmartre jusqu'à Passy.* The Seine is flowing, flowing, flowing along her flowered banks. If I could only be like that, flowing into the future, not agonizing about my life's work, not feeling lost and failed. But the Seine is held by the course she carves, between banks that she defines. What held me? Without a defining purpose — without a faith — did it matter in the slightest what I chose to do? The question repeated itself inside me as I leaned on the stone railing and closed my eyes to keep from crying. Suddenly I realized what I was doing: I was praying again. How absurd. I was a failure even as an atheist.

In conservative, bourgeois Bordeaux, you hardly counted unless you were, as they said, *dans les blés ou le vin* — in wheat or wine — and kept a villa in the nearby sea resort of Arcachon. But I forgave the Bordelais their snobbishness because it did not apply to me. As an American in those early post-war years — an American educated in *French* — I was almost exotic. A viscount's family took me under its wing and I experienced, at last, the dizzy social whirl my mother had always wanted for me, dancing till dawn in country châteaux. My one "basic black," purchased with Aunt Harriet's advice in mind, was more than adequate for most occasions. And when I got home at six in the morning in the viscount's car or on the back of my fellow student Philippe's motorcycle, no scolding awaited me. Instead of Papa raging in his bathrobe, there were giggles and gossip and a bowl of café au lait sent up from the kitchen. The large Bordelais family with whom I boarded delighted in such goings on: what else, after all, is youth for?

One morning at sunrise, returning from a distant party, collapsed happily against Philippe's back, the fresh wind whipping my hair and clearing my head, I persuaded him to take a side road. We stopped at the château of Michel de Montaigne. The tower was right there, squat and half-hidden behind its spray of trees. Lighting a cigarette to demonstrate his boredom, Philippe wondered why I'd wanted to come when it was too early to get in; he would bring me back another time. "This is enough," I said, touching the weathered stones. "I just want to see that it's real."

As I was dismayed to discover, Bordeaux' Institut de Sciences Politiques, to which the Fulbright office had assigned me, turned out to offer no courses relating to my stated interest: the growth of nationalism in French colonies. "Ne vous gênez pas, mademoiselle," smiled its director, the noted political scientist Maurice Duverger, "I have another plan in mind for you." It was research on the French Communist Party. For his next book, he needed a chronology of communist electoral and trade union strategies. "An understanding of international communism, and how it operates through local parties, will be essential to your future work in any colonial or post-colonial area." I hadn't a clue how to go about such research, so I took my time getting started on it and meanwhile attended classes.

The course in Marxist theory was taught by a short, intense professor who looked a little like Lenin. Sociologist and philosopher Jacques Ellul was to have more impact on me than any French mind of the century. What caught my attention was not his fiercely precise articulation of Marx's theory of surplus value, but an aside he made in his first lecture. He observed that the greatest problem facing our civilization did not stem from the conflict between Soviet socialism and free enterprise capitalism, but underlay them both. It was the power acquired by technology. Efficiency comes to eclipse all other values, he argued, shaping the choices we make and the purposes for which we live. What is technically possible takes on its own momentum, compelling us to use it.

My mind flew back five years to the time of Hiroshima, to the way I'd felt in the farm kitchen when I walked in to the news of the bomb. I recalled the sickening sense that we had created something we would be unable to control. Straight after the lecture, I followed Ellul to his office. "Teach me," I said — and that year in Bordeaux, he did.

Jacques Ellul was then in the process of writing his ground-breaking book called *La Technique*, or *Technological Society*, as its English edition would be called. With Cartesian clarity he demonstrated how our choices, our behaviors, and our politics are shaped by the tools we use; he showed how, in industrial society, the character of society reflects the logic of the machine. As corporations resist any purposes beyond their own profits and growth, he observed, they produce a standardized mass culture, a kind of "psychological collectivization" where freedom and originality of mind are ever more endangered.

Ellul's arguments were persuasive, remorseless. More than once I asked him in despair, "But what should we do about it? What can we do?" And Ellul would chide me: "You Americans are so impatient, you seek solutions before you've studied the problem. You must fully comprehend the problem first."

When I tried to do just that, comprehend this *problème numéro un,* as he called it, it seemed like a black cloud advancing slowly from the horizon. It doesn't cover the sun yet, but it is encroaching, and I wished people would all look at it together. I talked about it over that Christmas of 1950, when I gathered with old and new friends in the highest village in Europe: Obergurgl in the Tyrol.

Evenings, when we came in from the ski slopes and lounged by the fire, I shared my fascination with Ellul's thinking. "Sounds like you've been reading Frankenstein," said John from the States, now a Rhodes scholar at Oxford. He ridiculed the idea that the creations of science could ever rob us of free will, or even democratic process.

"It's more like Frankenstein in reverse," I said. "It's not about machines that imitate humans, but humans that act like machines. And this will change the face of history."

"What's changing the face of history is Soviet totalitarianism", said Hans, a medical student from Vienna. "It's dangerous to forget that as the lamps of freedom are being extinguished across Europe and the entire world. You won't be free to discuss your far-fetched philosophic concerns if we don't manage to contain the Russians." He had lived for five years with the Soviet occupation of his city.

Others chimed in to remind me of the stark realities of the Cold War: the blockade of Berlin, the stifling of democracy in Eastern Europe, the purges following Tito's defection, and now the Soviet-backed troops pouring into South Korea. I saw their point, and actually felt some relief in agreeing that Soviet communism was a more pressing challenge than the implications of technology. It was easier to think about.

Back in Bordeaux, when I wasn't partying, I applied myself to the research for Professor Duverger. I traced the tactics of the French Communist Party, which, like its counterpart in Italy, was an integral part of the Cominform, the far-reaching International ruled from the Kremlin. I learned how Moscow's agents managed to maintain and extend control, how the communist ideals of local party members were cynically, often brutally, subverted. Many of the brave *maquisards*, or partisans, whom my heart had reached out to during the war as they resisted the Nazi occupation, had now become steely-eyed communist party hacks — or, if they refused, were blackmailed, disappeared, perhaps into some distant gulag. A chilling pattern emerged, which made clear that the totalitarianism we thought we had vanquished in Nazi Germany was resurfacing in a different guise. The grimaces of Hitler had faded into Stalin's closed, implacable features.

If I needed a holy war to join, it was the war against Soviet communism. If I needed a faith to espouse, it was faith in democracy. But even that did not promise to fill my inner emptiness, and I had no taste for a crusade. Having survived early church history, I was a little weary of struggles between Right and Wrong, Good and Evil. They reminded me of living with Mama and Papa. Mama had walked out of that polarity, but I didn't know how to walk out of this one.

By late spring I had almost completed my research for Duverger and had learned as much from Ellul as I could absorb, reading what he told me to read and joining the small coterie of students who met with him on Sundays. One Sunday, after a May rain, we all took a walk through the open grasses of the Landes, the delta country of the Gironde river. The marshes smelled strong, almost rank. Under the full-bellied skies, so much was quickening, coming to life, stirring in the mud, it made me restless. The little professor and his gaunt students walked on as if oblivious to the caress of the air and the odors and croakings from the ripening ooze. They were discussing the dynamics of tech-nological society — which were essentially hopeless. They were walking so slowly and talking so much, I wanted to scream.

The next morning, in a travel agent's window, I saw a poster of North Africa and a sign: "Students Half Price." It took me two minutes to decide. "No one will know where I am, no one at home, no one at Sciences Po. I can disappear into the world." And I did, for a while, in Casablanca, Marrakech, Tangiers — and the world entered me as well.

I had walked New York and Paris in search of myself, but here in Marrakech I was walking inside my own body. The sandstone tower of the Koutoubia was the color of warm flesh against the throbbing blue of sky. It steadied me like a familiar gesture, as I rounded it to enter the great square that kept drawing me back: Djemaa el F'naa, the place of madness. In its blazing, cacophonous expanse and the shadowed winding lanes of the souks beyond, I wandered until that teeming, filthy, fragrant, kaleidoscopic world felt inseparable from my own being. This larger body of mine was loud. It reverberated not with cars or machinery, but with hawkers yelling and selling their wares, with goats bleating, with bells and drums and the singsong whine of storytellers. It blend-ed into a thousand smells — jasmine, urine, camel, cardamom — and offered to the touch a thousand textures, from the rough woven wool rubbing by me in the crowd to the cool wet tiles of a corner fountain. Here, in the heart of the dryness of desert, like music, like laughter, water splashed, trickled, gleamed in rivulets over tile, over stone, over hammered copper and henna-painted hands. This wetness seemed to spring from the secret well of my own being, for I had been in the arms of my lover. I had given myself to him — the twin, the waiting one, whose face I had tried so long to imagine. And I knew I would open my body to his again, as I would meet him again and again in different faces and forms. The song of life was mine now.

I possessed no means of making sense of what I had done. I was appalled by, and marveled at, the fact that I should walk off the plane in Casablanca, turn to the smiling banter of a fellow passenger, and within two hours be in bed with him. I marveled even more at what our lovemaking had revealed about the universe. Over the years I had come to believe that news about the nature of reality came solely through the mind, in the shape of pow-erfully moving ideas. And now, totally independent of my views and judg-ments, this revelation, this breaking open, this falling through — into what?

What were these currents and vortices that drew me down into them, as if everything else I've ever done were just dried sticks drifting on the surface of life?

My head rang with scolding voices. They sounded shocked and chagrined, as Mama would surely be. Whenever I had asked her about the act of love, she seemed to view it with embarrassment. These voices were my Presbyterian ancestors too, scornful of my weakness, my depravity. They even sounded like *me*: my inner guardian of personal integrity was horrified at what I was risking. I was frightened of wrecking my life by getting pregnant — and in any case, having to hide a whole dimension of me, as if ashamed.

So I left Pal in Casablanca and headed to the desert to pull myself together, to resume my independence, to think of other things. However, each waking moment — while squeezing into a bus full of Bedouins or relaxing with mint tea on a Marrakech rooftop — I relived what had happened, evoking sensations that did not lose their power. How bold and patient and full of laughter he was, this free-spending Hungarian-American some fifteen years older than I. How swift and inevitable each step we made was, after that first grin at the baggage counter. How blandly he offered me the use of his hotel bath, then calmly walked in to help me soap up. How careful he was to let everything seem ordinary and unforced — reading the *Herald Tribune* and starting the crossword puzzle — until the slow hilarity of lovemaking took over.

What happened then felt so primordial, and so important somehow for the ongoing order of things, that I imagined at moments whole populations gathered below our window beating drums and cymbals. Clearly, this physical call and response was the primary phenomenon of the cosmos. How else do the planets swing so steadily in orbit, how else do the starfish attach to their rocks? Here the wildness inside me and the tenderness that tore me were married. Hence the laughter and the languor; yet at the edges, there was terror too — of the lies and the longing that waited in the wings. It fit my sense of life's seriousness that there should be this outlawed and irrefusable dimension.

Wandering through Marrakech, letting its aromas and clamor register in every cell, I began to be glad that this initiation had happened solely on its own terms, unburdened by social roles. None of society's expectations to meet, none of its domestic burdens to assume. Just pure encounter — just Pal, my stocky, black-eyed gypsy lover. And I knew it wasn't over. Like a string of beads, our meetings that spring and summer spilled over North Africa and Europe: Tangier, Madrid, Frankfurt, Berlin, Amsterdam. His business errands took him many places and were always laid aside for me. Once near the end, in a Calvinist fit of conscience, I fled after breakfast, without a trace, only to call him that night from another city, another country, frantic that he might have moved on. But he caught my message and followed me to Amsterdam. There, one last time, our ritual unfolded again: Pal pulling me across yet another hotel lobby with that grin of his, the Hungarian gypsy musicians he always managed to find to play by our supper table, then in the room the token attempt at a crossword puzzle. "We need a five-letter quadruped starting with E. Come on now, where are you hiding it?"

I would have stayed in Europe at the end of my Fulbright year, but Mama drew me back. In her letters she sounded so desperate for me that I declined a job with UNESCO in Paris and booked my passage home. Since childhood I had imagined I was essential to my mother's life. I was not, of course — certainly not now, in her active, pleasurable life four years after the divorce. As I learned when I got off the boat, her pleas had been essentially rhetorical — unthinking expressions of her attachment to me. "I just wanted to see my little girl again" — that was all it boiled down to. I was stunned by the loss I had incurred in taking my mother seriously. I realized how little she understood my desire to work in the world. Mama would not have asked either of my brothers to drop everything and come home to her, but then — to be honest — they would never have acceded, even if she had.

On my return from Europe I saw Papa, too — not at Bleak House, but for lunch near his office, even a supper at the Yale Club. I prepared myself each time, vowing to retain the sweet sense of personal sufficiency that I'd come to know overseas. I wanted to remain, in my *own* eyes if not his, the woman I had experienced myself to be — alive and glad, not frightened, not closed. But all my enthusiasms and wide-flung interests shriveled in his presence, and all my ideas felt like sham. *Ideas?* His lectures dwelt tirelessly on cigarettes and alcohol and sexual promiscuity. Silently I'd turn the glass of ginger ale in my fingers, watch the bubbles rise to the surface, the drink go flat.

Still something had changed in my regard for him. There was a gratitude that I never found air time to express. It was for his challenge to me in the summer of my sophomore year, when I worked at the Connecticut Women's Reformatory. At nineteen, to live with the inmates and supervise their work in the fields was a difficult and often scary experience for me. Such deep, unaccustomed fatigue came upon me that I decided to cut my commitment short and take a fortnight's vacation before going back to college. Hearing of this, Papa, who never — ever — left Manhattan, journeyed up to talk with me.

He pointed out that fatigue has many sources. It could be due to ill-health, and in this case I would have every right to cancel my commitment to the reformatory. It could also, possibly, stem from my not wanting to be there. In that case, I had no excuse to leave. "I don't want a quitter for a daughter," he said.

I stayed. The last weeks weren't hard at all — perhaps because of the fierce self-respect that my father had challenged me to find. And throughout the years to come, I often silently thanked him. I was glad I had a father who cared enough about his daughter that he did not want her to be a quitter.

Now, having reconnected with Papa and having seen how good Mama's life had become, I went to Washington.

Thanks to my work in Bordeaux on the French Communist Party, the Central Intelligence Agency had developed an interest in me. And thanks to what that research had taught me about Soviet tactics, I accepted their invitation when an intermediary — the gracious, silver-haired aunt of a friend — sounded me out. Where else, she asked, could I better use my new knowledge — which, incidentally, I had acquired at government expense? Back then, in late 1951, it was a politically correct outfit that I was invited to join. World War II heroes from the fabled OSS (Office of Strategic Services), like Wild Bill Donovan and William Sloane Coffin, and idealists like world federalist Cord Meyer were people I could identify with.

We recruits were in the hands of a dozen trainers, drawn both from "the shop" and from military branches of intelligence to oversee this new agency venture, the Career Officer Training Program. It was inspired by the rather classy British model for training spies and at moments had the flavor of an extremely intense house party on an English estate. In this pioneer American version, twenty of us — including three other women — were the first guinea pigs. For three packed months, in preparation for service to our country and the "Free World," we were pummeled with information and taken into the labyrinths of the "intelligence community," all the while being scrutinized and subjected to batteries of tests.

The culture of secrecy to which I was immediately introduced appealed to both my curiosity and my vanity. I liked belonging to a small elite that knew more than other people. Our trainers sermonized exhaustively on the privilege and responsibility of handling classified materials, and I saw how swiftly this bred in us a sense of self-importance. We liked to believe that the information we handled, which was obtained at great cost through devious means, was completely unknown to the wider public, and our possession of it cast an aura upon us, at least in our own eyes. I viewed with condescension those who were limited to what they could learn through overt channels. "Oh, he's just in State!" I laughed, belittling the opinions of a cultural affairs officer in the State Department.

An enduring lesson I derived from my two and a half years in the CIA is how easy it is to feel elite and aloof by virtue of the secrets one possesses. Having personally suffered the self-delusion that secrecy breeds, I acquired not only skepticism. I came away with a wry kind of compassion for those who are trained to hide what they know and who come to believe that what is concealed is truer than what is not. I would remember this often in the future, in dealings with the nuclear industry as well as in encounters with religious groups where esoteric teachings are held as privileged information.

Another abiding lesson concerns the conditioning of mind. Those who fall prey to their own professional training — like the policemen who pepper-sprayed me in the 1999 WTO demonstrations in Seattle — are harder to condemn when I remember the persuasiveness of my CIA tutors. They spared no effort in teaching us to be "tough-minded" and convinced us that toughmindedness was a sign of excellence, maturity, and readiness to defend the "Free World." We were rated on how well we could demonstrate that virtue, and were respected accordingly.

When at the end of my Career Officer Training Program a final batch of written and oral psychological tests was administered, I handled them like a good Lycée student, striving for clarity and consistency in letting the teachers know that their lessons had been well learned. A team of three interpreted the results for each trainee. Mine included Colonel Caprelli, an affable, corpulent Army intelligence officer who took a special interest in me. Summing up my results, he said: "So you see, this means you've ranked at the top for moral flexibility in the line of duty."

"You mean," I said, "I'd sell my own grandmother?" "Yes," he said, beaming at me. He could barely contain his pride. "Now look at this, Rogers. These parameters here indicate a candidate's aptitude for paramilitary operations. They demonstrate that out of the entire cohort you are the best suited to be dropped behind enemy lines." Well, why not? I felt rather pleased with myself.

Despite these test results, I did not move into "cloak and dagger" operations but spent the rest of my brief career in intelligence working in more overt programs. They were essentially cultural activities conducted through journals, broadcasts, and conferences where the only secret was the source of funding. The early postwar years witnessed remarkable success on the part of Kremlin-directed communists in infiltrating and taking over cultural and youth organizations in Europe and the Third World. The office I now joined provided support to students and intellectuals who resisted Soviet control.

It required discernment and restraint to support a foreign association, publishing house, or trade union without imposing your own government's agenda. Watching my mentors in this office of the agency, I soon saw that you couldn't do this work unless you tried to take freedom seriously — and were unafraid of being called idealistic. Arguments would erupt at times when clandestine services wanted to use our local contacts as spies; and I admired my colleagues who defended their integrity with tough talk. "Keep your frigging hands off these students [or writers]," they would say. "Whether you like it or not, this is a free group, not a front — and they'll make up their own goddamned minds. Creating fronts is the Soviet game, not ours — should you care to remember what this Cold War is all about."

Recalling the pressures the French Communist Party exerted on its members, I knew that it took courage to voice disillusionment with Soviet socialism. These dissidents and their networks needed support, but without any contaminating connection to the U.S., which was already emerging, in the eyes of many around the world, as a blundering bully with knee-jerk anticommunist reactions.

In June 1953, with total absorption and aching hearts, we clustered in our offices tracking the people's uprising in Eastern Germany, and then the crackdown that followed, the isolation of Berlin, the building of the Wall. I was glad that we refused to let go of the fragile threads that linked us to those on the other side. I could picture them there being sealed off brick by brick, and I wanted — via the air waves and through smuggled books passed hand to hand — to reach them and tell them we were all still part of the same world. I could not bear to think of our brothers and sisters in Eastern Europe and the USSR being entombed beyond the reach of supportive voices. We would tap on the wall, we would stay connected. This drama — the attempt to penetrate the barriers erected by the Cold War — set the context of my life for the rest of the 1950s.

The urgency of that drama relieved me somehow of having to deal with what was waiting in the wings — something bigger, scarier, harder to think about. I confronted it, though, one spring morning in the agency screening room. The first footage of the first tests of our hydrogen bomb over the Eniwetok Atoll was classified then, shown only to the brass — an unusual privilege for the likes of me to see. Projected silently in black and white, a multi-storied fountaining of cloud boiled ever higher into the stratosphere, over tiny black chips far below, battleships on the surface of the sea. Edward Teller had had his way in Los Alamos. We had our thermonuclear bomb now; it was part of our arsenal, part of our lives. After the screening, as agency officials chatted briefly before dispersing to resume their day's work, I stood on the steps in the sunshine, waiting for my world to reassemble itself. I felt stupid and sick and unprepared. There it was again, the same chilling foreboding that had come over me in the farm kitchen with the news of Hiroshima, the same sense of an irrevocable shift of fate, like a shudder in the ground beneath my feet. I knew what Jacques Ellul would say, and he'd be right: our technology had turned demonic and we were all becoming its victims. Beyond the Soviets loomed this specter, and I wondered how soon the time would come when we would have to face it together.

6

The Wheel

ONE HOT JULY EVENING, my first summer in Washington, Fran Macy showed up at my door and took me swimming at the Georgetown public pool, then for crab cakes at a dilapidated bar on Wisconsin Avenue. We had met very briefly in our college years, when he was at Wesleyan University and then in Harvard's graduate program in Soviet studies. Mutual friends in the New England Student Christian Movement had tried back then to call our attention to each other, but without much success. Apart from my thinking that he had to be very manly to get away with a name like Fran, he had seemed a bit too handsome and untroubled for the likes of me, and I a bit too earnest for his tastes — but then, before those crab cakes, we had never really talked. Once we started, there was no stopping.

I had a nine o'clock date that night, who was waiting in his sports car as Fran and I ambled up, engrossed in conversation. We stopped in mid-sentence as Fran, with utter courtesy, leaned down to open the car door for me — it was a gleaming MG, close to the ground. We both knew the interruption was temporary. Five months later we became engaged and five months after that — in May 1953 — we married.

From the start I found pleasure in Fran's company, and a kind of liberation, too. I loved his body and I loved his mind; in both I found freedom to relish my world. He never used his maleness as a shield. Thoughts and feelings became clearer to me when shared with him. We courted during the presidential campaign of 1952. Packing the *New York Times* along with our picnic basket, we would drive into the Blue Ridge mountains, reading aloud to each other the speeches of Adlai Stevenson, delighting in his wit and the elegance of his moral wisdom.

While my undergraduate years had been largely taken up with theology, Fran's had focused on public affairs. A summer in Eastern Europe watching the takeover of Czechoslovakia motivated him to study the realities of the Soviet regime and to prepare for a life in international affairs. As he learned the Russian language, he fell in love with the literature and culture of the Russian people and identified deeply with their travail under Stalinism. We liked to look at the world together.

We also liked to be quiet together. Fran introduced me to the classical music he loved and took me farther than I'd gone before into the natural world. From the time he was four, his large family had taken him along on extended canoe trips through the inland waters of Ontario, and now he took *me* camping. I drank in the starlight and the dawn, the smells of pine and wood smoke, but most of all the wordless way our bodies moved around each other, pulling up the canoe, making camp, feeding the fire. There the world beyond the reach of the talking mind came into focus, pressing upon us its full and intricate presence, and at such times I wanted only that — together to pour our hushed attention upon each jewel-like piece of Earth and to receive what it disclosed.

When we decided to marry, we were eager to tell Herb King, minister of Harlem's Grace Congregational Church. Having known each of us separately in the Student Christian Movement, he would be delighted, we thought, to learn of our plans. We informed him over a spaghetti dinner in Greenwich Village. At one point during the meal, Herb put down his fork and looked at us both. "Cherubs," he said, "I have one prayer for you." We listened carefully, our eyes upon his brown face gleaming in the candlelight. He said: "It is this. May you ever see the other as a stranger."

The next Sunday Herb preached a sermon that amplified his prayer for us; it was on the spiritual necessity of not being fooled by familiarity. It's easy to assume you know all about a person, especially someone with whom you share your daily life — and that very assumption stifles the wonder, dulls your perceptions of that person's extraordinariness. Herb's charge to us has reverberated over the last four and a half decades, recurring now and again as a little jolt of surprise when we see each other — even in our own house. "Who's this? Who just walked into my life?"

I needed Herb's prayer because although I had always wanted to marry and have a family, it turned out to be harder than I expected. It was hard to commit myself, not just to another person, but to socially prescribed roles and responsibilities — especially as they were defined in the early 1950s. I encountered aspects of myself that I had never suspected, except perhaps in that grim childhood afternoon when I accidentally locked myself into the attic crawl space. The person who sometimes surfaced now, fearful of being trapped, did not scream her lungs out like that seven-year-old; instead she seethed with impatience, erupted in sarcasm and anger. The morning I physically struck out at Fran, hitting him as he showered, we looked at each other stunned. Who was this madwoman?

These outbursts frightened and shamed me. I wondered if a congenital flaw was now revealing itself and I was somehow turning into my father, whose rages I had so feared. After all, I was the only one who had shouted back at him; my mother and brothers were never roused to anger. As for the Macy clan, I gathered that no one ever said a cross word. Harmony had reigned in Fran's childhood, so he was shocked and confused. His silence infuriated me, as if by retreating he was abandoning me to the awful darkness that now welled up from the hole inside me — that emptiness left by my lost faith, that lack I had never managed to fill. Though I had known hard and painful times growing up, I had never considered myself a bad person; but now I found no alternative but moral self-condemnation.

But we persevered, Fran and I. We knew how to have good times, good friends; laughter helped, and the gladness of our bodies together, and the challenge and congeniality of my work at the agency.

One morning in bed in Mama's apartment, I awoke to a new awareness and tried to describe it to Fran. We were in New York that weekend because down the street at Bleak House, Ouie, at ninety, was dying. As I swam to consciousness along the warm, familiar coast of Fran's body, I realized that a feature of my life that had been with me for as long as I could remember had disappeared: my fear of Papa. Like a steady background sound you notice only when it ceases, this fear had, I sensed now, been unremittingly present through all the years and places I had lived. "It's gone," I said into the hollow of Fran's shoulder. "The fear of Papa has gone from me. I didn't know how constant it's been, but it's lifted now."

We think our first child was conceived on that weekend of Ouie's death. When he was born, we named him for my grandfather, the Christ-bearer: Christopher Lewis.

We had finally located a doctor who practiced natural childbirth, and even before the cord was cut, Chris turned and held my gaze. Throughout the first night I sang to him of all that we would do together. But the year and a half that followed were hard. The episodic desperation I had known in early marriage grew more intense. The changes in our lives were abrupt and wholesale: Fran went to work for the New York office of a Russian-language radio station beaming into the Soviet Union; I quit my agency job; we found a rental in upper Westchester. In the blink of an eye everything had changed, from a stimulating life in Washington to a cottage in the woods outside a suburban town full of strangers. I felt suddenly as walled off from the world as the dissidents we tried to reach behind the Iron Curtain, or the doomed ones in the gulags.

Nothing had prepared me for the isolation and exhaustion in which I found myself as a young mother. In the mid 1950s, with that decade's unshadowed enthusiasm for the nuclear family, my role was idealized by the culture at large — and no one back then, eight years before Betty Friedan broke the silence, named the suffering this role entailed. For all the value Wellesley had placed on a life of public service, I had caught no suggestion that this would be difficult to balance with raising a family, no mention of postpartum depression, no advice for maintaining sanity. Without a women's movement to offer cultural perspective and emotional support, I could only understand my own responses in terms of personal failure — and increasingly, as month followed month after Christopher's birth, of personal craziness.

From dawn until dark Fran disappeared into Manhattan, an hour's commute away. *His* life was still on track. He had a job, with a title to it, and purpose, dignity, pay; he had adults with whom to engage and use his brains. By some gross oversight, I did not. I could not even name what I did between the time I stuffed baby into car to drive Fran to the train at dawn and my reinsertion of same baby into car to drive again to the station after sunset. To persuade myself that I was accomplishing something — that I even existed — I tried making lists: washing up, nursing, cleaning, laundry-washing, nursing, laundry-hanging-to-dry, eating, shopping, nursing, cooking…. There was no one to help. There was no one even to be with, who did not make me want to scream, for sitting at the kitchen table of another housewife, while babies fussed and toddlers stuck jammy fingers in my face, made me feel even more that I was buried alive. I envied Fran and hated him, then hated myself even more. In self-punishment and a terrible rage to break free, I pushed my hand through a windowpane. I did it in the middle of the night, as I paced in desperation — when I knew I wouldn't bleed to death because Fran was there, quietly sleeping in our bedroom with the Mexican furniture we had bought on our honeymoon.

For a split second it felt wonderful: splintering of glass, cold air rushing in, sharp pain in forearm, surge of blood. Waiting to be stitched up in the emergency room, I answered the medic's questions matter-of-factly: "I put my hand through the window." It didn't dawn on me that I was crying for help. No one heard me anyway, except for Fran, who redoubled his efforts to get assigned to the radio's Munich office, knowing that life overseas, with the stimulation and household help it promised, would be easier for me. Meanwhile it occurred to no one, least of all to me, that I might obtain psychological help. So I helped myself the best I could.

I decided to work my brain like a muscle. Between housework, child care, and errands, I managed to carve out of each day two hour-long periods just for myself. 9:30 Algebra, 10:30 Greek. I craved clarity and precision of mind, unblurred by emotion. My years at the Lycée now stood me in good stead; I was glad for companions like Descartes.

One morning in early June, I raised my head from the old Greek grammar book, stopping mid-phrase. Smells of sun-warmed soil and late lilac were coming through the open window, and sounds too: birdsong, bees, and a run of hums and chuckles from the playpen on the screen porch. All around me life was happening. I could open to it now because I again had structure to my days and a working mind.

By the following spring, in 1956, we were living in Europe. Fran had succeeded in transferring to Radio Liberty's program center and transmitting station in Munich, and that beautiful, war-scarred Bavarian city became our home for the next four and a half years. The adventures it offered were available to me because, given the local economy, I had my pick of household help and was never without an Annie or Liesl to handle meals and help care for Chris — and, after a while, his brother Jack. There were the Alps nearby to hike and ski, classes at the university in art history and German, and the poignantly intense exile culture of the radio station itself.

Staffed by refugees and broadcasting in seventeen languages of the Soviet Union, from Russian to Kalmuk, Radio Liberty beamed its round-the-clock programs of uncensored world news and culture through the Iron Curtain. Its broadcasts were heavily jammed by Soviet transmitters but still audible enough, to judge from smuggled messages and the defectors who made their way to the doors of the radio station. My life in Munich was not separated from Fran's work, as it had been in suburban America, and over lunch at the station and supper at our house I came to know these passionate people of the USSR. I learned how brave they were, and how cranky and competitive they could become in the rootlessness of exile.

With the Alps so near, I began to ski again — and along with the exhilaration of it, there was now a whole new method to learn. The week-long courses in Davos and Arosa provided by the university sport club were intense and high-hearted. I loved it all: heading out at dawn with my fellow students, climbing uphill on skis to warm the muscles and practice turns before the lifts started, then letting loose on the kilometers-long run from the peaks, down ridges and slopes, through farmyards and over footbridges in the lightfilled, colorshifting air — never stopping till sunset, when we wove right through the center of town, past the fancy hotels, back to our hostel, where soon we were eating, laughing, and singing at long wooden tables. It was like being part of a flock of birds, letting the skill and the daring of the others ignite my own. I liked to forget that I was the only foreigner and the only married person, and let myself imagine that this youth I was living was my own, and forever.

The downhill method breaking through in the mid-fifties, called the "new Arlberg," involved a shift of weight and use of gravity that were counter-intuitive. Instead of letting the momentum of each turn pull you around toward the slope, you swiveled your hips and shoulders to keep facing down-hill. Throwing all your weight onto the downhill ski, you leaned out from the mountain into the emptiness of air. It felt very risky at first, but that outward thrust into the void — "tossing yourself to the devil," I called it — created a dynamic of its own that held you in balance. You couldn't be *sure* it would happen each time, but it always did — if you trusted it. That was the challenge and the exhilaration of it, that wild trusting.

I was reminded of my experience in natural childbirth with Chris. When I had managed not to contract against the pain, it had moved through me, bearably, doing what it needed to do. I had felt then that I was in the hands of something greater than myself, and could surrender to it. In skiing I did not surrender so much as interact, as the world rose to meet me and raced under me, dropping away, then pulling close — like two bodies playing together.

Two days after Christmas of 1957, in the basement of the university of Munich's Frauenklinik, our second son, Jack, was born. I tried to practice what I had learned during Chris's birth, tried to remind myself that everything was all right and would unfold naturally, but no one was there to help me remember. Instead of Fran, who was banned from the delivery room, and the doctor, who was late, there were an aproned midwife, two silent nuns in white coifs, and terrible, ripping pain. Herr Professor Doktor Sedlmayer only showed up after the birth: *"O, gnädige Frau Macy, ich bin schon da."* Seeing that I had torn, he administered a hefty dose of ether before sewing me up. In principle, I knew that the anesthetic was not necessary, that a natural numbing would kick in, but the birth had hurt so much I was glad to go unconscious for a while. *"Danke schön, danke, aber Sie brauchen mir nicht so viel zu geben,"* I said as I inhaled lungfulls of the thick sweetish smell, determined to go under speaking correct German.

I am lifted up, high over the world, which is so far below I that cannot see it. Yet I am also at the heart of the world, and a giant wheel is turning — and the manner of its turning is the secret of all things. I am on it, spread-eagled across its spokes, my head near its open center. Sometimes it seems I could *be* the wheel, I'm so inseparable from it. I feel the spokes shudder through my body with alternating and intensifying sensations.

I am warm and the warmth is pleasant, and with my wanting of it, the warmth increases. It grows hotter, then hotter still, as the wheel turns like a giant dial. Just at the utter limit of my capacity to bear it, the spoke of extreme heat passes through me, and I begin slowly to slide into its opposite.

The relief is exquisite. Oh, this coolness is now my home, my refuge, and here I'll stay. But as I try to cling to the freshness, the wheel keeps turning and chill deepens into raw cold. It penetrates every cell of my being until I am congealed in ice, a freezing grip that at its nadir, by the very pressure of its gripping, gives way to a slow, inexorable melting into warmth. Oh, here I'll stay in this blessed warmth, my haven and true nature.

Now heat is experienced as movement, as an agitation of the molecules — and I feel that this vigorous freedom of motion is all I've ever wanted, all that I must be and have. But gradually, with my desire for it, the movement accelerates, speeding up more and more to the point of frenzy. Just when I am about to explode into a myriad insanely vibrating particles, when all my desperation is for stillness and solidity at any price, the agonizing limit of that condition passes on through me, and I start to subside into the next segment of the wheel, settling into consolidating firmness, into stasis — the alternative to motion, and its prerequisite.

Endlessly, helplessly, I turn on the rack of the turning wheel. As its spokes move through my body, each sensation gives birth to its opposite, first with welcome relief, then with slowly intensifying pain. Each polarity I experience is different, yet similar. The opposition of the heat and cold is present in the contrasts of motion and stasis, and also in those of freedom and order, passion and reason. In my flesh I feel the cold rule of logic turn into the fires of the mushroom cloud, which then congeals into iron-clad security. From the deadening grip of the police state, life returns as the warmth of erotic passion, which, as I succumb to it more and more, tears me limb from limb with its ecstasy, until I welcome with deepest thanks the cool sweet touch of reason, before it freezes me again in immobility. Each of the opposites becomes intolerable without the other. Each, when clung to, gives rise to its antipode.

Bearable life occurs only at the point of balance, and that point, so fleeting and fragile, is won only through a terrible openness, through allowing the pain to pass through. Other than that, no god, no self, no safety. There is only the turning of the wheel, and the hole in the center that allows it to turn. I accept, as if I have always known, the inevitability and accuracy of what now is revealed. But I am frightened and pray for ignorance.

Mercifully at last, Fran's face comes into view, small, at a great distance, and I focus on it with all my might, that it might transport me back into the comfort and blindness of ordinary life. And it does.

"Wer sind Sie eigentlich?" I kept asking the midwife, licking my lips to let the words through. "Who are you really?" Herr Professor Doktor Sedlmayer had disappeared. I was sure that she, who had been there from the beginning and now steadied me with her hands, her face hovering over me, was my guide between worlds. Surely she held the key to the door that had swung open. I knew she had existed from the beginning of time, and I insisted on knowing her true identity.

But all she said, in German, was, "It's a boy."

The Bavarian wallpaper in Christopher's room, along the central seam of its widest expanse, was coming unglued. Bored with naps at three years old, Chris had begun peeling it back. He pulled off the tight-figured print just a little at a time, so that his work would not be too noticeable. By the time I returned from the hospital, the hole was larger than Chris himself.

One morning when he was in kindergarten and Baby Jack asleep in the bassinet by my bed, our housemaid Liesl and I took a quiet moment to survey the damage. Now the area of exposed plaster reached higher than my shoulder and extended more than a meter at its widest point. "Perhaps Christopher wishes to deface the room he will share with his Brüderchen?" queried Liesl, looking at me sagaciously. I'd been talking to her about the emotional challenges that the baby presented to Chris, and I was grateful she had refrained from scolding him.

"Hmm, maybe. It's also kind of fun to do," I said, fingering a loose edge of the wallpaper and uncovering another centimeter of plaster. Soon we were both absentmindedly pulling off tiny shreds, as we discussed what to do. "To bring in workmen to repaper the room will cause such a mess," Liesl reflected. Yes, I agreed, "and it would undo all of Chris's work."

I fetched my watercolors from the back of a closet, spread newspaper on the floor, and that afternoon Chris and I began. On the denuded plaster a road snaked through flowering fields and hills, climbing into lavender mountains. Farms appeared with pigs and carts, and castles on the heights. Elephants flew out of trees. On the day I added a door frame to enclose the vista — its windowed panels invitingly swung open — Chris demurred. He preferred no limits to the country we'd created; but the doorway, I argued, made it more realistic.

Meanwhile, around us, the daily life of our household ran on. Liesl married, Annie came in her stead, Baby Jack moved into his brother's room, Russian émigrés smoked and argued around our dining table. Yet, busy as I was, and tired as I was with a baby to nurse and now a siege of mononucleosis to pace myself through, this ordinary life felt different to me. My experience under ether had not dimmed by one iota. In a way that I could not explain, even to myself, the turning wheel betokened an order at the heart of reality. It erased my fear of the hole inside me. Even as I complained about my illness and all the things to do, there was this strange gaiety — like skiing steep, leaning into the void. If a hole appears, just walk through it, see what's on the other side. You'll never be lost because this emptiness is central to life, figured into the nature of things.

FALLING IN LOVE WITH MY WORLD

7

Turning South

WE RETURNED TO WASHINGTON in the late summer of 1960 when Fran joined the Russian desk of Voice of America. After six years away, it was good to be back, especially in the excitement of John F. Kennedy's presidential campaign. I listened to him debate Richard Nixon while I painted and papered Chris's and Jack's rooms in the house we had just bought on Lowell Street. I didn't know which made me happier — to have a candidate of such wit and discernment or to have this house and neighborhood to settle into with my family.

The three-story white clapboard, with wide porch and deep backyard, won our hearts the minute we saw it. It was built before the First World War and, like the neighborhood itself — tree-shaded streets, good for kickball and hopscotch, front porches with rockers and swings — evoked small-town America. Yet it was close to the center of things: a few blocks from the embassies, a few minutes' drive to the State Department, a pleasant walk to the Washington Zoo. After the election, many members of Kennedy's administration moved in around us, and you could hardly take out the trash without discussing some new government policy. The area's most dramatic feature, the huge Gothic pile of the National Cathedral, rose just a block away. Its vast interior, often filled with music and always with colored light from the stained-glass, became an extension of our lives, as did the winding walks and gardens of the cathedral close.

For the next quarter-century the Lowell Street house would serve as our home base. Though we would leave for years at a time, it remained an anchor, and a haven to welcome us back.

Now Peggy joined us — named for my mother and looking like her too. *"A daughter?!"* We hardly dared believe it. To convince Fran, who in 1961 was still excluded from the delivery room, the nurse had to unswaddle the baby. This time young motherhood in America did not spell total drudgery and isolation. Thanks to the neighborhood's playgroups and collaborative shopping schemes and thanks to the young women from Munich who came "au pair" to help me, there was plenty of support.

John Kennedy's administration was called the "New Frontier," and that seemed apt, because so many possibilities opened before us in the kinds of people and the kinds of ideas that were now taken seriously. Many of our mentors and old friends came to Washington now to take part in government: some were elected, like John Brademas, who became a Congressman on his third try after Oxford, and some were appointed, like Fran's brother John Macy, who was called in as the president's personnel advisor. I relished the wit and elegance of the New Frontier, including the sheer style of a First Lady my own age. But the most potent magic of that period called Camelot was the intellectual ferment. Standing on the sunbright snow before the Capitol, Chris on Fran's shoulders, we watched the inauguration and smiled at each other when we heard the summons: "Ask not what your country can do for you, ask what you can do for your country." When Kennedy proposed a "Peace Corps" for voluntary assistance to new nations, I thought, "This is just what I would have joined after college, if it had existed ten years ago."

By 1960 the Civil Rights Movement was spreading; after Germany's homogeneity, it felt good to be home again in a multiracial society and to talk late into the night with our Black friends about the bold new tactics of nonviolence. Until then the lessons of Gandhi's struggle had seemed remote to me, best suited to saints and Hindus. Now, as I watched film clips of college students at lunch counter sit-ins in Greensboro, North Carolina, I saw that Americans, too, were capable of nonviolence.

Our nation's capital was still a southern town, with magnolias, swamp smells from Foggy Bottom, and — despite a large Black middle class — racial segregation in housing, hotels, theatres, restaurants. I soon found myself involved on behalf of Africans, whose new presence in Washington served as context and pretext for my own civil rights work. By now the wave of African nationalism, which had fascinated me ten years earlier, had brought forth new nations — twelve in 1960 alone, including Ghana, Ivory Coast, Guinea, Nigeria, Madagascar. These countries were sending not only students to attend American universities, but also diplomats to establish embassies. And when they arrived in the capital of the United States, they found Washington's best facilities and properties tacitly reserved for Whites only.

Within weeks I was running an informal service out of our house. Three file boxes of index cards stood on my desk: one for the Africans' housing needs; one for leads on rentals and sales ("Don't answer the ads yourself, just let me look for you"); the third for hospitality. Listed on the cards in that third box were American families ready to entertain Africans. I had discovered that even in the long-established Black embassies, like those of Ethiopia and Liberia, diplomats could complete a whole tour of duty without ever entering a White American home. To fill that third box with cards, I spoke in local churches and clubs. It wasn't hard to persuade people of the rewards they would reap from "adopting" an African friend or family. And I knew that in the process they, as hosts, would learn more about racial realities in their own country.

Eventually, to continue the work I had begun in my home, I was given a title, a salary, and a desk in the State Department's Office of Protocol. By then, in 1962, the Kennedy administration was ready to push for a fair housing ordinance in the District of Columbia, and the experience and contacts I had accumulated were useful. My job was the first part-time, flex-time position I knew of in the State Department — twenty-four hours a week at my own choosing. It was as productive, I began to suspect, as many a full-time job — and it was lively. I enjoyed the colorful diplomatic receptions at embassies I had helped to get located, and especially the friendships. Because they had gone through the same Lycée education as I — and had done so as outsiders, like me — diplomats from francophone Africa did not censor themselves in my presence. A young Algerian ambassador who had grown up in a revolutionary movement or a Senegalese First Secretary schooled in Paris felt free to think out loud with me about the ideological and cultural conflicts they felt. I recalled how these very concerns had gripped me when I went to France as a Fulbright scholar a dozen years earlier; blocked from pursuing them then, I had become engrossed in the Cold War. Now, after a decade of feeling for cracks in the Iron Curtain, it felt good to redirect my attention southward, to turn my face to the sun.

Shifting from his broadcasting work in the U.S. Information Service, Fran began journeying inside the USSR, taking over the first exhibits on American culture and technology. With Khrushchev in power and initiating a "de-Stalinization" campaign as well as announcing amnesty for political prisoners, a new era seemed to be dawning. Fran moved from city to city with his traveling circus: displays on transportation technology and young Russian-speaking

Americans as guides. In every city — from Kiev to Stalingrad — long lines formed before dawn. Thousands of Soviet citizens moved through the halls, avid to study each item, and, most of all, eager to talk to the Americans. They were hungry for contact.

In late spring 1964, when Fran came home from a four-month journey behind the Iron Curtain, the children and I made our own show to welcome him, with popcorn and lemonade and calliope music. We seated him and his mother under a sun umbrella in the backyard in front of the jungle gym of swings and ladders, which we had decorated with streamers and balloons. I was the barker and master of ceremonies. Nine-and-a-half-year-old Chris performed breathtaking feats, culminating in a leap from the high horizontal ladder to the tire suspended from the choke cherry tree. Jack, at six, was junior acrobat and senior lion-tamer. His ferocious but eventually obedient African lion was two-and-a-half-year-old Peggy, whiskered and maned and dragging a tail of stuffed stocking.

When the performance finally wound down and Mom Macy shepherded the children to supper and bed, I took her seat beside Fran. Contemplating the jungle gym, we reviewed the choice that faced us. Fran had returned with the offer of a position in the U.S. Embassy in Moscow. It promised influence and could advance him many rungs up the ladder toward the top public affairs post, and maybe some day an ambassadorship. At the same time an old roommate from Harvard had approached him with an interesting proposal. Would Fran like to help run the Peace Corps program in India?

Sitting together in the Washington twilight, the barker's black mustache still smeared on my lip, we considered these offers. Was it crazy to drop Russian affairs, to which Fran had given fifteen years, and go out to Asia to serve a bunch of young American volunteers? What did we know about India anyway?

Well, not much, but we *did* know that Fran had loved working with his young American exhibit guides, helping them to function in a foreign culture and to engage the local people. And we also knew that living in the Moscow Embassy compound, with its wiretaps and KGB guards, would isolate us from the Russian people.

We recalled our excitement at reading the social thinker Robert Theobald's views: that the new nations of the South could learn from the mistakes we made in the North, avoid our costly excesses, and leapfrog over the worst aspects of industrialism. That seemed relevant too.

As we talked, I watched the jungle gym. Between its upright ladders, whose rungs stayed rigid one above the other, the swings were swaying in the evening breeze.

By early August of that year, 1964, we'd found tenants for Lowell Street. Fran took off for New Delhi and I followed soon after with the three children, ready to make India our home for the next two years. We circled down into Delhi through the towering, multi-storied cumulus of the monsoon.

In the torrential rains, streets disappeared into puddles the size of lakes. Urban waifs earned coins by wading into them up to their knees, their waists, their shoulders, so that drivers could judge their depth. Black rain streaks ate into modern cement façades until the buildings resembled ruins rotting back into the soil. Indoors and out, smells of wet plaster and mold blended with those of incense, curry, urine. So we could stretch our legs, Fran released us into the mud and blazing din of a neighborhood fair near Nizamuddin's tomb. Within the frames of rickety Ferris wheels, half-naked men climbed and swung to make them turn. We had come braced for poverty and squalor, but not for this outlandish, throbbing excitement. In terms of sensory onslaught, India was Marrakech squared. Even over tea in the ease of the hotel garden, we were besieged by peddlers and fortune tellers, deafened by crows, dizzied by darting, wheeling flocks of parakeets — and once, from out of nowhere, there was a swift, dark assault, like a blanket being snapped in my face. It was a kite stealing the toast I was lifting to my mouth.

In the 1960s, India was a rewarding place for Peace Corps volunteers to work, thanks to the Block Development Scheme. It was ambitiously designed to invigorate rural communities, but it often didn't work because of a gap between civil servants and the local villagers. The American volunteer, when well-assigned, could step into this gap and serve as a bridge, helping people at the grassroots use their own government's programs, and also helping civil servants stay abreast of local needs.

In those years, staff spouses were encouraged to participate in Peace Corps work. I was not viewed as just an appendage, or an adornment for the receptions and cocktail parties that were de rigueur for the wives of foreign service officers. To the extent that I was ready and willing, I could be part of the team providing support to the volunteers. I certainly was *willing*, preferring hot dusty jeep rides into rural India to air-conditioned receptions. And I was *ready*, as soon as the children were engrossed in their school routines and the necessary servants were hired and happy.

We needed three servants, for caste and custom restricted their roles: the cook wouldn't clean, the bearer wouldn't cook or go to market, and neither of them would take any responsibility for the children — that was the job of the ayah or nursemaid. Our team of three, once they decided they could work with each other and with us, made it easy to share our home with convalescing volunteers, who became hero figures to our children and developed their own relationships with each of them.

Our first long-term guest, recovering from hepatitis, was a shy, lanky Boston-Irish boy in whom Peggy — at three — developed a maternal interest. As soon as she was fetched home from her nursery school at midday on the handlebar seat of our cook's bicycle, she would run to Tim's bed to see what he needed and to hear more of his adventures.

"Rats on the *door*??" Tim was describing the monsoon season in his village when he had first fallen ill. Severe flooding had driven snakes and rats out into the open. "Yeah, they wanted a dry place, too. Tried to get in, but I had this screen door, see, which kept them out. So the rats just climbed up the screen, dozens of them, blocking the light, hanging there looking at me." "Oooh," said Peggy wide-eyed and shivering. "Then what'd you do?" "I was too sick to get up off my charpoi, so I threw things at them, sandals, books. But those big old rats didn't budge." "Oooh, then what'd you do?" "I just lay there and stared back at them." And Peggy stared too, upon Tim, in pity and adoration. "I think you need your lunch now," she said, smoothing his rumpled sheet.

Now and again I visited volunteers at their sites, from poultry projects in desert villages of Rajasthan to clinics amid the paddy fields of Mysore.

Jeff, one of the "poultry" volunteers, put his head to the floor to adjust the flame of his kerosene burner. He was cooking some rice and dal, while regaling me with his triumph of the week. He had persuaded a government officer to make a local visit. "I actually got him to walk inside a chicken house, can you believe it? I figured if he saw the sick hens with his own eyes, he might finally do the damn paperwork and hit the department in Jaipur for the medicines he promised. Can you find the privy in the dark? Here, take my flashlight."

I knew my way. Outside under the stars I filled my lungs with the sharp, chill air; it got cold as soon as the sun went down. Jeff's tiny quarters outside Bikaner seemed swallowed up in the vast blackness of the desert night. I imagined his loneliness here, and it moved up close to me like a presence. Straight off an American college campus, and here he was on his own, working all day long in village Hindi — and persevering. You could tell he was in his second year by his patience and humor. These qualities seemed as beautiful to me as the peacocks I had seen strutting on village walls, or the intensity of color in the Rajasthani turbans, purples and crimsons vivid enough to drink.

Though I didn't say so, the frugal simplicity in which the volunteers lived impressed me as much as the work they did. Sometimes they apologized for the stark conditions in which they received me. Then I would laugh, "This is something we are *all* going to have to learn — and you're way ahead of the rest of us on that score." I wanted to know the inner strengths that hardship revealed in these volunteers because I assumed that sooner or later we would all need to find them. For I didn't think that the overblown lifestyle of the industrialized West would last for long.

My love for India grew. My habitual impatience — with having to wait hours for a connection, an appointment, a motor repair — began to abate as each moment presented its own panorama of humanity. I could lose myself in watching. I understood how the Peace Corps doctor's young wife wanted to disappear into it — and she did one day, just walked out with nothing more than the cotton sari she had taken to wearing, releasing herself into the throngs of peddlers and sadhus and beggars and cows, not to be found again for months. I envied her a little and realized that I too wanted to lose myself in the embrace of Mother India.

When an errand took me near Old Delhi and its teeming bazaars, I made time to park the car near the Ajmeri Gate and wandered in, threading my way through the crowded streets and alleyways. My goal was the Jama Masjid, the Great Mosque, whose sandstone mass and marbled minarets rise over the sordid clutter of shops and rickshaws. In those years before Moslem militancy closed it to infidels, I could enter at any hour and feel its welcome — feel at ease, as if returning to a world where I had once belonged. Sometimes I took the children with me.

We climb the high steep steps and leave our sandals in the dim passage of the gateway. I love the moment when the vast marble court opens out before us. It is a plate held up to the heavens, like an offering, and when we walk out onto it, we are part of that offering. Jack starts running, drunk on space, sending pigeons wheeling overhead. We sit by the shallow bathing pool, splash water on our cheeks and foreheads, watch how the minarets move against the passing clouds. We talk about the relics guarded here, the hair of the beard of the prophet and his sandal, nestled in dried rose petals. Chris hangs back in the shadows of the gateway, then joins us looking, startlingly, like the children of Old Delhi's streets. His eyes are painted with kohl. Now Jack and I do it too. We squat and squint as the bearded old vendor leans over us, applying a deft black lick of his antimony pencil along the lower lashes. "See," says Jack, dancing back into the blazing courtyard, "it 'tects the eyes, like sunglasses."

8

The Tibetans

THE DRIVE FROM DELHI TO DHARAMSALA took twelve hours and only one dented fender, where I tangled with a bullock cart near Ludhiana. It was early March, 1965, two months short of my thirty-sixth birthday. I was at the wheel, which was why I'd been invited to come along on this adventure. It had been organized by Terry, the vivacious Peace Corps secretary, as a farewell gift to herself, and she had arranged everything: the loan of one of the big blue Chevrolet Carry-Alls, the company of some of her favorite volunteers, and — "I still can't believe it came through," she crowed — an audience with the Dalai Lama of Tibet. "I just need someone to help me drive, since the volunteers aren't allowed to, and to be honest I'm a little nervous with the big vehicles. Are you up for it?" I certainly was.

It was a major occasion, Tibetan New Year, Terry explained, "and there'll be thousands of refugees coming to Dharamsala to be near the Dalai Lama and get his blessing." So an hour before dawn on the second of March, stuffed into the Carry-All with packs and bedrolls, mountain boots, cases of coke and beer for our volunteer hosts — and out of the darkness behind me Jon "The Nose" Nyberg playing his harmonica — nine of us headed north to cross the Punjab and welcome the Year of the Wood Snake.

Two of us had read *My Land and My People*, His Holiness' account of his life up until his escape to India in 1959 at the age of 24. We briefed the others about how the emanation of Chenrezi, *bodhisattva* of compassion, was found in a peasant family and raised with pomp and mystery in the Potala palace, and how at fifteen he was confronted with the Chinese invasion and, nine years later, to save his people bloodshed, fled over the Himalayas. Dottie and Jon Nyberg, who worked in a TB sanitarium, had their own stories about Tibetans. Coming down from their high world without natural immunities, the refugees succumbed easily to the diseases of the Indian plains. As patients in the sanitarium, they were remarkable at handling pain, and also irrepressible. Even right out of surgery, with tubes draining his lungs, one monk hid a litter of kittens under his bed; another climbed out the window and up a tree for a view of the land.

We inched through the traffic of Pathankote, the railhead for Kangra valley, then, turning to the northeast, came on the mountains fast. Suddenly we were in a different, glistening world; the late sun washed over liquid green terraces of new barley and wheat, glinting on lavender slate roofs and, beyond them, high snows against the deep northern sky. Up ahead, on a spur of the Himalayan foothills with its back to the Daula Dhar range, was Dharamsala.

As the road climbed and twisted, I saw them for the first time: figures in Tibetan dress turned and waved, laughing as we drove by. Some greeted us from piles of rocks, where they labored with picks and mallets. Their broad grins of greeting startled us, for we had grown accustomed to the stolidity of Indian faces. Six more miles of hairpin turns and we pulled up onto the narrow ridge of McLeod Ganj, where I unbent my fingers from the wheel and we climbed out. Here, between ramshackle houses and a drop-off onto treetops and roofs, stretched a world of Tibetans. They had no shops then, just tarps spread on the ground for their wares — plastic combs, bronze Buddhas. Around them, throngs moved in a steady murmur of greetings and gossip. By the pump a woman in embroidered boots filled her pail, a bare-armed *lama* washed. Except for a Parsee from Bombay who kept the general store, no one else lived there.

I wandered about the bazaar, fingering turquoise beads and fur-trimmed hats, but all I seemed to see was that smile. From ruddy, weathered Central Asian faces, crinkling eyes laughed straight into mine. They are smiling at me, I thought to myself in disbelief. It is not I who have been forced from my homeland, seen my loved ones and teachers tortured, killed. It is not I who have trekked out of the far heights to sicken in the heat and see more of my brothers and sisters die. Not I who now labor in road gangs breaking rocks — my culture, my tradition, lying in pieces around me like the boulders being broken into stones, the stones into gravel. Yet *I* am the one they are smiling at, as if to reassure *me*, as if to tell me that at the heart of it all and in this moment there is joy.

Two hours to the northeast up Kangra valley, we descended upon a household of four volunteers; I already felt linked to one of them, named Logan, who had stayed with us in Delhi. Our hosts were disgusted that we had drunk up the entire case of coke we had intended for them, but the beer was still intact and we all settled in. The foursome was engaged in creating a teachers' training camp, but Logan seemed more excited about something else entirely.

"I've found this encampment near here — a group of refugees from Kham in Eastern Tibet." They were squatting in a tea estate outside Banoori, he explained, and he had been spending more and more time with them. "They've invited us to come tomorrow to their New Year's *puja* — their rituals of prayer. Want to come?"

By six the next morning I was following Logan down a footpath winding through tea bushes. Tall poles came into view, slanting against the dawn sky, their full length fluttering with prayer flags. A conch shell sounded, then the deeper voice of horns, and cymbals clashing. The summons issued from a large, mudwalled tent; the puja had begun. Maroon-robed figures greeted us and ushered us inside; we bent to enter. As I sat on a leopard skin that was stiff with age, the deep-throated chanting of monks thrummed through my whole body. It seemed to erase time and all the incidental features of my life. Centuries of certainty were present in that chanting, as if no displacement had occurred, as if each instrument and ritual object had not been carried so far and at such cost to foreign soil.

After an hour, as the puja continued, we were beckoned out to rooms in a nearby shed, where, with mounds of fresh New Year's pastry, Tibetan tea awaited us. It was my first taste of that salty, buttery beverage. I sipped it cautiously and watched the lay people through the door. They were circumambulating the puja tent, spinning prayer wheels, murmuring mantras, and when they peered in at us, the older ones displayed their tongues in an ancient form of greeting.

Logan was briefing me: the community belonged to the *Drukpa* or Dragon tradition of the Kargyu lineage. Its leader, a certain Khamtrul Rinpoche, was away at the moment giving teachings to the royal family of Bhutan. *Rinpoche*, which means Precious One, is the honorific title for a reincarnated lama. It was thanks to Khamtrul Rinpoche, a great *Dharma* master, that these lay people and monks had managed to stay together. This was rare, for life in exile tended to fragment the refugees — scattering them into road gangs, monasteries, orphanages, disrupting the age-old symbiosis between the laity and the monastics. This absent Khamtrul Rinpoche had also managed to bring out Tibetan *togdens*, or *yogis*, perhaps the only ones in exile. They had already arrested my attention with their distinctive white and red robes and big topknots of uncut, matted hair. I gathered that they were repositories of the most esoteric practices of this ancient stream of Tibetan Buddhism.

"My best friends here," Logan said, "are younger rinpoches called *tulkus*. Each has his own monastery back in Tibet, but now in exile they're completing their higher studies under Khamtrul Rinpoche, who's like their spiritual father." He looked past me now, his face lighting up. "Good morning, Choegyal Rinpoche. Tashi deleg! I brought my friend Joanna." I turned to see a skinny, maroon-robed figure in the doorway. His eyes were large and luminous, his smile shy; in his hands he held a sheet of paper. It was a watercolor he had just painted. "Choegyal is the only one who speaks any English. He learned it from a British hippie who hung out here before I came along — so he interprets for me with Khamtrul Rinpoche and the others."

Rising, I bowed. We met. It was in the painting he showed me that I seemed to see him first. No icon or deity, no stylized lotus, just a landscape: green treeless hills, herds of sheep and yaks, the low, dark tent of a nomad family. This was the land and the people he had left behind at thirteen. "I paint it for remembering," he said. As we talked, I calculated: at nineteen, he could be a younger brother to me. I did not suspect that our lives would be linked from then on. I had no reason to imagine that twenty-two years later he would take me with him into that same green landscape in Kham. When we said goodbye that New Year's morning, he placed the watercolor in my hands — and it has hung in our home in all the places my family and I have lived.

"I'll be back," I said. "And when I come see you again, I want to bring Fran, my husband." Ah, that would be impossible, they would not be there. Choegyal seemed embarrassed to tell me why, as if speaking of their misfortune would cloud the pleasure of our meeting. It seemed that the plantation owners had accused the refugees of destroying tea bushes and, after fining them heavily, were about to evict them. They had to move off by the end of the month. Not to worry, Choegyal said, touching my hand. His gesture wanted to reassure me that this band would manage somehow to stay together, just as they had throughout their long exodus, through the snow-blinding passes and the border towns where they got separated and found each other again.

Now, as we wound our way back to the road, I understood: Logan wanted to change his Peace Corps assignment and work with these refugees full-time. "They're artists, as you saw, and I want to help them find a place to live and start up a handicraft business. With an economic base, they can stay together as a community."

Logan realized that he would need not only Fran's agreement but his active intervention with the Indian government, which explicitly forbade U.S. Peace Corps involvement with the Tibetans. The situation looked pretty cut and dried: there was no way this could happen. Yet Logan was grinning in anticipation. "It's going to be great working with these Khampas! It's going to work out, just you wait."

On the day of our audience with the Dalai Lama the sun laughed from the snow peaks and the glinting streams. Heading back to Dharamsala, with four more bodies crowded in, the Carry-All rang with harmonica music and song — "Chenrezi-baby, here we come" and even "Hello Dalai!" On a high, wooded hillside above McLeod Ganj, by the entrance to His Holiness' residence, Indian police officers stood guard, rifles erect against the flowering rhododendrons. Two lamas, a secretary and an interpreter, led us into the compound and around to the front of a bungalow facing out over the distant plains. I expected *some* degree of pomp from the days of the Potala, some arcane ceremoniousness befitting the emanation of Chenrezi, Gyatso, ocean of wisdom. But as we rounded the house, I simply saw across the grass a single figure. In plain monk's robes, his back turned to us, he leaned over a wire fence, peering at something down the mountainside. He looked so alone that my first response was a desire to weep.

One by one, with great solemnity and the gestures we had practiced, we presented and received back again the white ceremonial scarves we had brought. The thirty-year-old who accepted this homage had a twinkle in his eye and, after the scarf routine, gave each of us a very firm Western handshake. We talked about the Peace Corps and about his people, Logan and I betraying our eagerness to connect the two subjects. His Holiness spoke mostly of the book he was preparing on Buddhist philosophy, but throughout the half-hour my attention was more on the person than on his words. The photographs I had seen of him, bland and bespectacled, hadn't prepared me for the charged beauty he conveyed. The voice was vigorous, its timbre deep and resonant. This person needed no pomp. His authority was unmistakable, graced by alert, expectant stillness. No wonder they called him *kundun*, presence. The presence of Tibet. That is what the thousands of refugees came here to find, for to be *in* that presence was, in some real way, to be home.

As we passed through the gateway after taking our leave, an adornment overhead caught my eye. I turned to look up at it, stopping still. A large, eight-spoked wheel, flanked by kneeling deer, stood upright against the sky. "That's the *Dharma Chakra*," said Logan, "the Wheel of the Dharma. Very sacred symbol."

"Yeah, I know," I murmured. I had read somewhere that when the Buddha taught, he was said to be turning the wheel, with the spokes representing the Eightfold Path. But something else, a fiercer, more intimate knowing, rose from within my body. The memory of the great wheel on which I had hung and turned had never dimmed in the seven years since the ether experience at Jack's birth. It had let me glimpse a vast, underlying order that connected and made sense of all things, and left me with the hope that I might some day be able to understand. Now in India, among the Tibetans, I encountered it again. Had the Dharma been in store for me all along? This time, instead of fear, I felt only awe and promise.

That season back in Delhi I met Freda Bedi.

I remember the moment I opened the door, how she stood there in her maroon robes graciously greeting me, as if somehow I, and not she, were the guest. There was a Peace Corps-related matter to discuss, and Fran had invited her for lunch. She was an English woman in her early fifties, a Cambridge graduate who had married a Sikh and made India her home. And she seemed to the manner born. I loved the way that touch of the Raj blended, so paradoxically and superbly, with the monk's garb she wore. Although she was no taller than I, and almost as slender then, her presence always seemed huge to me, as calm and unstoppable as a ship in full sail. I sensed that her warm but majestically unruffled demeanor could see her through anything and was not surprised when I learned later that she had been the first British *satyagrahi* to be jailed with Gandhi and, after independence, had coordinated social services for Prime Minister Nehru. When the exodus from Tibet began, she visited the refugee camps and soon resigned her post to devote herself full-time to Tibet in exile.

The Tibetans who knew her called her "Mummy," as soon I would, too. A few years after we met, she was ordained as a nun and shaved her head, acquiring the name Karma Khechog Palmo. She went to live in the great monastery of Rumtek in Sikkim alongside His Holiness the sixteenth Karmapa, head of the Kargyu lineage.

"Did you become a Buddhist after meeting the Tibetans?" I asked her. No, she had turned to the Dharma many years earlier, taking instruction in the Theravada or Southern school of Buddhism and going to Burma to practice under the Venerable Mahasi Sayadaw. There in Rangoon the ancient practice of *satipatthana,* now widely known as *vipassana,* had been resurrected in the early twentieth century. Many came to train under the great teacher, in an arduously strict months-long course. Freda Bedi later described to me a kind of enlightenment experience she had there. Once when she walked out of the monastic training center onto the streets of Rangoon, there was suddenly no distinction between self and other. Everything — each being and object — was bathed in the same internal and liberating light.

One day in 1959, Nehru sent Freda to Tezpur near the border, where an Indian government train awaited the Dalai Lama, who had just escaped the Chinese. She saw him standing on the platform. And that was it. She had found her spiritual home. Now her life was in constant service to the Vajrayana, or Tibetan Buddhism, and those born into it. Unlike many Western Dharma enthusiasts, Freda displayed as deep a regard for each man, woman, and child of Tibet — no matter how impoverished, filthy, or sick — as for the most exalted teachers.

To help preserve the tradition she had come to respect so profoundly, she worked to establish sites of instruction and practice, like the two nunneries she set up not far from Dharamsala in the Kangra district. The apple of her eye was her Young Lamas' Home School, recently moved from New Delhi to a big, old mountaintop villa called Kailash above the hill-station of Dalhousie. There, young tulkus she had found in the refugee camps could continue their training under traditional teachers. To help them survive in exile and serve their people, tutors also taught them Hindi and English, geography, math.

The school at Kailash was the topic she wished to pursue with Fran. A Peace Corps volunteer to teach English to the young tulkus (but not Indian-English, with its idiosyncrasies of vocabulary and intonation) to prepare them to take the Dharma into the modern world — that was precisely what was needed now. She was aware that the government of India was being a bit difficult about all this, but surely in such a good cause…. Fran and I looked at each other and laughed. "You're getting it from all sides," I told him, for I had already been after him to try to transfer Logan to work with Khamtrul Rinpoche's group.

"I shall speak to my friend Mr. B. in the cabinet," Freda smiled. "I already know the volunteer I want; his name is Ray. When, do you think, we can expect him?"

In that moment I viewed her with a satisfaction almost equal to her own. Yes, I could learn a lot from this woman. Confidence, for one thing — the marriage of serenity with sheer nerve.

By the end of our lunch, Fran had assured her he would do what he could, and *she* had invited the whole family up to Dalhousie when school let out. "You must all come to Kailash then, to get out of the heat. May and June are unbearable in Delhi. I know just the place for you — a lovely old cottage a short walk from our school, four or five rooms, I think, with lovely views. Just bring your cook along to buy food; it's a mile uphill from the topmost bazaar." As she left, she turned to me and said, "By the way, I have an idea for Khamtrul Rinpoche's group. There are some abandoned houses in lower Dalhousie that should do fine with a little repair. I will see what I can do about a loan; I think His Holiness will be glad to help."

Driving up through the Punjab in the furnace heat of June, we stopped at irrigation pumps and bucket wells to soak dish towels and put them over our noses and mouths. Until they dried within minutes, they provided some refreshing lungfulls to the three children and me and Tomis, our cook. Three hours beyond Pathankote, on steep Himalayan foothills, rose Dalhousie, our destination. It harbored not only the Young Lamas' Home School at Kailash in its higher reaches, but also now, lower down, the community from Kham, recently resettled from the tea estate. There I would encounter Khamtrul Rinpoche at last, but I have no recollection of our first meeting and I wouldn't know, till the time came to leave him, how rare a space he would occupy in my mind, my life.

The layout of Dalhousie seemed perpendicular: three rings, each higher than the last and linked by steep roads and crisscrossing paths, looked out over the plains of Punjab to the South and allowed, as we climbed, glimpses of hidden valleys to the west and north. Its geography imprinted itself on my soul, resurfacing in my dreams for years after I'd left India. The dreams were always of seeking Khamtrul Rinpoche, of climbing the mountain paths up steep inclines, around half-familiar bends through trees and along drop-offs, then up some more across the brow of a hill to where he would always be waiting, with his people, his broad face turned toward me in a smile. Sometimes I got lost, or diverted by some maddening errand. When we finally met, the dream would end, with that fulfillment.

In actuality the hikes to Khamtrul Rinpoche and his community that summer were downhill, not up. Kailash, Mummy's Young Lamas' Home School, perched above the highest ring, and our cottage even higher than that, while the assortment of old houses where the Khampas were quartered lay a good hour's walk below, on paths pitching down from the bus station bazaar. My days were divided between those two settings. Mornings and middays I enjoyed hillside picnics and rambles with the children. After lunch I left them napping, reading or playing games under Tomis the cook's watchful eye, and trekked down to visit the Khampa lamas and the newly forming Tibetan Craft Community for the Propagation of the Dharma.

Logan had fancied a snappier name. "At least a name that's not such a mouthful, Rinpoche! How about Khampa Krafts?" But Khamtrul Rinpoche was imperturbable. "You see, it's all for Dharma, isn't it?" said Choegyal, still serving as interpreter.

When his reassignment had finally been negotiated, Logan moved in with the community, taking quarters up-slope from the makeshift monastery. He had unpacked his books, bedroll, and portable typewriter in a bare room next to some of the yogis. "They're going at prayers all night. I doubt if they sleep, and now I don't either," he said cheerfully. He seemed to know everyone by name and have some special connection with each, including the many children. At this point there were about three hundred monks and laypeople in residence — it was hard to get an exact count. They included a remarkable number of painters, sculptors, woodcarvers, weavers, mask makers, dancers, for the ancient ritual arts were strong in the Drukpa Kargyu lineage. Logan was determined that these arts be turned to economic as well as religious use.

New production plans sprouted: traditional scroll paintings or *tangkas* mounted on brocade, watercolors of folk scenes on handmade paper, thick-napped carpets vivid with vegetable dyes. The intricately carved woodblocks used for prayer flags would be sold as art objects in their own right, with handles for hanging on walls. Logan made it easier for me to participate in these plans, for I knew he was tireless in helping to carry them out — from hammering out letters to badgering government offices in Delhi for refugee rations, export licenses, loans for looms and wool.

My afternoons with the lamas were devoted to those plans, with no time left for learning Dharma, the teachings of the Buddha. With all the rinpoches had on their minds and hands, as they cared for the ritual life and physical survival of their community, I couldn't imagine interrupting them with requests for teachings. But the lessons came anyway, in unexpected ways.

Mummy, now in residence at Kailash, taught a Dharma class for her handful of Western volunteers. Chris, nearly ten by then, came along with me. "So countless are all sentient beings," Mummy said one day, "and so many their births through time, that each at some point was your mother." She explained a practice for developing compassion: view each person you meet as your mother in a former life.

I played with the idea as I walked to Khamtrul Rinpoche's community down the narrow, winding road. The astronomical number of lifetimes Mummy's words evoked boggled my mind — yet the intent of this quaint practice, for all its farfetched fantasy, moved me. What a pity, I thought, that this was not a practice I could use, since reincarnation hardly figured in my belief system. Then I paused on the path as the figure of a coolie approached.

Coolies, or load-bearing laborers, were a familiar sight on the roads of Dalhousie, and the most heavily laden of all were those who struggled up the mountain with mammoth logs on their backs. They were low-caste mountain folk whose bent, gaunt forms were dwarfed by their burdens, many yards long. I had become accustomed to the sight of them, as well as to the consternation that it triggered in me. I would usually look away in discomfort, and pass by, my mind muttering judgments about the kind of social and economic system that so exploited its own population.

But this particular afternoon I stood stock-still. I watched the slight, bandy-legged figure move slowly uphill toward me, negotiating his burden — the trunk of a cedar — around the bend. Backing up to prop the rear of the log against the bank, to ease the weight of it, the coolie paused to catch his breath. "Namaste," I said softly, and stepped hesitantly toward him.

I wanted to see his face. But he was still strapped under his log, and I would have had to crouch down under it to look up at his features — which I ached now to see. What face did she now wear, this dear one who had long ago mothered me? My heart trembled with gladness and distress. I wanted to touch that dark, half-glimpsed cheek and meet those lidded eyes bent to the ground. I wanted to undo and rearrange the straps so that I might share her burden up the mountain. Whether out of respect or embarrassment, I did not do that. I simply stood five feet away and drank in every feature of that form — the grizzled chin, the rag turban, the gnarled hands grasping the forward overhang of log.

The routine comments of my internal social scientist were stilled. What appeared now before me was not an oppressed class or an indictment of an economic system so much as a unique and incomparably precious being. My mother. My child. A dozen questions rose urgently in my mind. Where was she headed? When would he reach home? Would there be loved ones to greet him, and a good meal to eat? Was rest in store, and quiet talk?

When the coolie heaved the log off the bank to balance its weight on his back again and to proceed uphill, I headed on down the mountain path. I had done nothing to change his life, or to betray my discovery of our relationship. But the Dalhousie afternoon seemed to shine in a different light; the furnishings of my mind were rearranged. How odd, I thought, that I did not need to believe in reincarnation in order for that to happen.

In those afternoons, when I arrived at Khamtrul Rinpoche's cottage, I usually found the tulkus and Logan occupied around the large tea table. The room with its altar, tangkas, and photos looked as if the lamas had been settled in for years, not weeks. Khamtrul Rinpoche would have a stretched canvas propped at his side on which, with his customary equanimity, he painted, as we drank our tea and discussed the next craft project. His big, round face exuded a serene confidence that our deliberations would bear fruit, as certainly as the Buddha forms on his canvas would take form under the fine sable brush in his hand. Behind him tall, handsome Bonpa Tulku hovered, as silently watchful as a butler. Bonpa Tulku had accompanied and served his teacher since Khamtrul Rinpoche and he were brought as children to the great and glorious monastic center of Khampagar — and it was Khampagar in exile, along with its surrounding lay community, that they were seeking now to re-establish. Choegyal Tulku, who was already becoming my friend for life, might be sorting through sheets of watercolors or carpet designs with Logan, while his Dharma brother, Dorzong Tulku — the same age as he and, like him, the abbot of his own monastery back in Tibet — might be contemplating the large antique typewriter. It frequently broke down, and Dorzong would then survey it in silence, as if he could learn how to repair it by meditating on it — which he repeatedly seemed able to do.

One afternoon a fly fell into my tea. This was, of course, a minor occurrence. After ten months in India I considered myself to be unperturbed by insects — ants in the sugar bin, spiders in the windows, even scorpions in my shoes in the morning. Still, as I lifted my cup, I must have betrayed disturbance by my facial expression or a small grunt.

Choegyal leaned forward in sympathy and consternation. "What is the matter?"

"Oh, nothing," I said. "It's nothing — just a fly in my tea." I laughed lightly to convey my acceptance and composure. I did not want him to suppose that mere insects were a problem for me; after all, I was a seasoned India wallah, relatively free of Western phobias and attachments to modern sanitation.

Choegyal crooned softly, in apparent commiseration with my plight. "Oh, oh, a fly in the tea." "It's no problem," I reiterated, smiling at him reassuringly. But he continued to focus great concern on my cup. Rising from his chair, he leaned over and inserted his finger into my tea. With great care he lifted out the offending fly — and then exited from the room. The conversation at the table resumed. Logan and I were discussing procurement of the high altitude yak wool Khamtrul Rinpoche desired for carpet production.

When Choegyal reentered the cottage he was beaming. "He is going to be all right," he told me quietly. He explained how he had placed the fly on the leaf of a bush by the door, where the wings could dry. And the fly was still alive, because he began fanning his wings, and we could expect him to take flight soon.

The next lesson in compassion that I received from Choegyal was less light-hearted. I had been after him, as the only English speaker and the most confiding of the tulkus, to tell me some of his memories of the Chinese occupation of his homeland. It was clear to me by then that the lamas preferred not to talk about this subject, but I believed that the telling would help win support for their community. I envisaged an illustrated article for a popular periodical like the *National Geographic*, with some of the stunning photos Logan and I had taken of their faces and ancient rituals, their art, their poverty. In order to hook Western sympathies, such an article should, I figured, include the horrors from which these refugees had escaped.

I knew that Choegyal had been a mature thirteen-year-old when the Chinese invaded his monastery and that he had his own memories to tap of what they had done to his monks and lamas. I suspected a voyeuristic element in my eagerness to hear the ghastly tales — a voyeurism bred by the yellow journalism of Sunday supplements in my childhood and by the horror movies of arcane Chinese torture that Harty used to recount. Still, I knew that such tales would arrest the attention of Western readers and rally support for the Tibetan cause.

Only when I convinced Choegyal that sharing these memories with the Western public would aid the Tibetan refugees, did he begin to disclose some of the details of what he had seen and suffered. The stories came in snatches as we paused outside the carpet-making room or walked over to the monastery in its rough, temporary quarters. But the lesson I learned, one particular afternoon, was not about the human capacity for cruelty.

We were standing by the side of the road. The sunlight through the branches overhead flickered on his face and robes . He had just divulged what perhaps was the most painful of his memories — what the Chinese soldiers did to his monks in the great prayer hall while he, hidden by his teachers, watched from the mountainside above. As I gasped with shock and breathed hard to contain the grief and rage that exploded in me, Choegyal turned to look at me with eyes that shone with unshed tears.

"Poor Chinese," he said. "They make such bad *karma* for themselves."

9

Train To Pathankote

AS OUR SECOND YEAR IN INDIA UNFOLDED, friendship with the lamas deepened. Every few months I took the overnight train to Pathankote and the early bus up to Dalhousie, dropped my bag and bedroll in Logan's room, and spent a week with the community. Occasionally, school permitting, I took the children too, who grew accustomed to the third class coaches. Since four-year-old Peggy, like her brothers, preferred to climb to an upper berth, we would tie her in loosely from the waist to keep her from falling. Once I awoke to a slow pendulum movement near my face: it was my daughter swinging headfirst, like a bat, and still asleep. Another time, come morning, she was gone altogether — to be eventually discovered sitting on the distant berth of a Sikh gentleman, attending to the wrapping of his turban.

Sometimes the lamas came down to Delhi. With selected young monks in attendance, they filled our big ground floor flat with their presence — and soon were busy with their favorite toys. Dorzong was hockey champion, standing over the game's wooden stand as motionless as a statue, except for his wrists twisting the knobs to send the puck flying at lightning speed straight into the goal. Khamtrul Rinpoche liked "Blockhead" best, a coffee table game that consisted of erecting a tower with oddly shaped pieces of painted wood; under his steady gaze and hands the tower would grow to ever more improbable heights. One night the Tibetans appeared without warning just as we were sitting down to a supper of leftover spaghetti. Even for us the food was barely enough, but we squeezed the six monks around the table with us anyway — and I prayed. And we feasted. No one else seemed surprised that the serving bowl never emptied. We remember it as the night of the loaves and fishes.

The company of these Tibetans filled me with a kind of wild gladness. I felt increasingly drawn to the religion — or whatever it was — that had shaped their minds. I knew that Khamtrul Rinpoche was renowned as a master of the

Dharma. I also knew the demands on his time and attention, the long hours devoted to starting up the handcraft business, and the longer hours devoted to ritual and pastoral duties. So I did not ask him to give me instructions; I wanted to ease his burdens, not add to them.

In off hours, in a desultory fashion, I began to read. A stumbling block I immediately encountered was the Buddhist teaching on suffering. Right off the bat, smack!, was that First Noble Truth: life is *dukkha*, suffering. What a premise to build a religion on! It was not only unappealing, it was inaccurate as far as I was concerned. I had a *good* life. True, its hurts and anguish had been real enough, and the Cross of Jesus had taught me that they were not to be denied; but still I preferred to see them as incidental, unique to certain situations, not as the character of life itself, not as the basis of a religion. The puzzlement must have worked deep into my psyche, for one morning I awoke from a strange dream.

The dream spanned generations. Intricately convincing plots unfolded, like a series of Galsworthy novels. I was inside one character, then another, in their manifold, ongoing relations through turns of fate and social upheavals. A kindly, learned man, growing old in the hopeless love for his brother's wife, his childless daughter abandoning her life's work to care for him in his long last years — I was each in turn and many more, experiencing their passions and losses, their yearnings for fulfillment. Their illnesses and deaths were mine.

I awoke spent, and full. Wandering around our Delhi home in the early light I tried to recapture the details of the characters' relationships, the twists and turns of their lives, but already the specifics were receding. What remained was recognition. All I knew was that the story — the story of our living — was as much about suffering as it was about anything else. I could no more extricate life from suffering than take the eggs out of the batter, or lift the tapestry free from the warp on which it is woven.

We were all on hand in early April of 1966, when our Tibetan friends staged their lama dances for the first time in Dalhousie. It was easy to get caught up in the thrill and splendor of the dances, the high point of the community's year. I was glad to reach Dalhousie early, with the children — my three, and some of their schoolmates from Delhi. The suspense-filled preparations — the making of the masks, the monks' rehearsals, the last touches to the wildly ornate costumes — were even more engrossing than the final ritual performances themselves. Even in the harshest conditions of refugee life, Khamtrul

Rinpoche had insisted on the annual reenactment of these dances in honor of Padmasambhava, the great magician who had brought Buddhism to Tibet. This year once more he himself would take part, as dance master, in the famed Black Hat Dance. Logan knew which monks had been sick — some from chronic chest colds, some from the lingering effects of malnutrition — and ran about administering Bufferin tablets before they pulled on masks and heavy brocades for the exertions of the day.

Mummy, too, was there for the dances, all three days of them. Having watched for six straight hours, she was now resting in the garden of a friend's nearby villa. I knew just where she was, but as I started down the steep paved path below Khamtrul Rinpoche's cottage, I hesitated. The request I carried inside me that afternoon made me shy. Who was I to ask for so huge a thing? Yet Mummy's smile from her garden chair, as I knocked tentatively at the gate, dispelled all doubts. She seemed to know what was on my mind even before I asked, and to consider it the most natural thing in the world. "Yes, of course, my dear," she said, "I will be delighted. That is just the thing."

She had been waiting for me to ask, and wanted to start me off the way she had begun her own Dharma practice. For that a retreat was best. "You will want at least a week to settle into it; just let me know when. I will arrange a place for you in the nuns' hermitage." Sudden joy opened a boundless space in my chest. It seemed too good to be true, yet it was. "It's true," I sang in my mind, as I walked back up toward the dancing ground through strokes of late afternoon sun, "Ho ho, it's true, you lucky girl."

In May I journeyed back to Dalhousie to meet Mummy and enter meditation practice. The departure seemed a cinch — menus had been written, carpools and after-school activities arranged, promises secured from Fran to come straight home after work. Now it was just a question of getting me, my backpack, bedroll, and water jug onto the Pathankote Express before its ten p.m. departure from the Old Delhi station. The place was a madhouse; never had I seen such crowds. Half of north India's population had poured onto that one platform. Why had I been so cocky not to reserve at least a second-class berth? When the doors to the nearest third-class carriage finally opened, the crowd at each was ten or twenty bodies deep, each hell-bent on getting aboard. The crush pressed me so tight I could barely breathe. I feared suffocation, yet the surging push did not let me escape. My arm with the water jug, caught between coolies as they shoved ahead, seemed to get separated from me; I was sure I'd be dismembered. As I was rammed through the door, I started to panic; over the shouts and deafening din I heard someone screaming, realized it was I, and began to cry instead. Three-tiered wooden berths, running crossways, left only a narrow aisle. From the maelstrom of bodies, hands pushed me up, like jetsam tossed from the sea, onto a topmost shelf. Other hands threw my bag and bedroll. Weak with relief, drenched with sweat, I cowered there under the ceiling.

Directly beneath me a large, garrulous family unpacked an endless series of containers, thrust up redolent wads of rice, curry, melting banana. Accepting a chapatti, I drew up my feet and disappeared behind a book. I wanted to effect as total a withdrawal as possible while the lights still permitted me to read. I wanted to banish from my mind the last half-hour and erase the whole teeming carriageful of humanity, its jabber and clamor and smells. A pencil marked my place part way through the chapter on Buddhism in a paperback on world religions by Huston Smith. I proceeded to read. The subject was the Second Noble Truth, the cause of suffering, which is held to be *tanha* or craving. Grateful that I was able to concentrate at all, I reread a paragraph that yanked at my attention.

"Tanha is a specific form of desire, the desire to pull apart from the rest of life and seek fulfillment through those bottled-up segments of being we call our selves," I read. "It is the will to private fulfillment, the ego oozing like a secret sore...." Every few lines, to let the words sink in, I would lift my eyes, let my gaze wander down the packed coach. "We strap our faith and love and destiny to the puny burros of our separate selves which are certain to stumble and give out ... Prizing our egos, coddling them, we lock ourselves inside...."

My breathing deepened, each breath filling more of my body, as if to ground and steady me for a physical challenge. My mind stilled in wonder, for the thing that then occurred seemed outside its control. Suddenly I was no longer enclosed inside my own body, but I wasn't outside it either. It seemed to be silently exploding, expanding to the point where everything else was inside it too. Everything out there — each gesticulating, chewing, sleeping form; each crying baby and coughing heap of rags; and the flickering, swaying carriage itself — was as intimately my body as I. I had turned inside out, like a kernel of popcorn shaken over the fire. My interior was now on the outside, inextricably mixed with the rest of the world, and what I had tried to exclude was now at its core.

My mind, when it could think, repeated one thing: "Released into action. Now we can be released into action." The world from which I could not protect myself became a world I was free to enter — to be. The division between doing and being had evaporated; some primordial tension had dissolved — at least for the moment — letting self-righteousness and self-blame cancel each other out. The self was neither to be vaunted nor overcome, neither to be punished nor improved — it needed only to be seen through, like a bubble that would eventually pop.

The lights switched off and I stretched out on the wooden shelf as the swaying coach rattled northward to Pathankote. I let the experience hold me till dawn, let it slowly fade as I scrambled off the train and onto the bus, tasting it now and again as I hired a coolie in Dalhousie and made my way up the mountain to the Young Lamas' Home School and Mummy. I didn't fret at its going, because I didn't expect it to last. I was just glad for the glimpse — and the awe it left in its wake.

Freda Bedi had everything planned: I was to stay with her, right under her wing, for a day and a night, while she taught me the basics of the practice, and then she would take me even farther up the mountain to the hermitage of her Tibetan nuns in intensive retreat. She would visit me there twice during the remainder of the week to monitor my progress.

I had imagined that when I finally received serious Dharma teachings I would be given food for my mind: ideas and beliefs to chew over, digest, incorporate. But now, on the contrary, I was expected to empty my mind, or rather to clean it up and air it out, as I would a dusty, cluttered room. To this end Mummy set me to doing *satipatthana* meditation as it was taught by her first Buddhist teacher Mahasi Sayadaw of Rangoon. Now here in this Tibetan world, in the midst of colorful Vajrayana practices — monks and nuns doing visualizations and mantras and prostrations — she held me to the stark, mind-wracking simplicity of the Theravadan mindfulness method with which she herself had begun. For the first while, to assist my efforts, she gave me Nyanaponika Thera's book *The Heart of Buddhist Meditation*.

Bare Attention, without any editorial comment, was to be applied to every successive event of mind and body. To hold the attention steady, and to provide it a point of return when it wandered, the movements of breathing provided a focus. Simplest and most accessible were the movements of the abdomen: "rising" with the inbreath, "falling" with the outbreath. The process was one of simple, repeated noting. When thoughts or sensations intervened, these were to be noted as well, with Bare Attention: "Thinking, thinking … itching, itching … walking, walking…." Thus, for hour after hour in Mummy's sitting room, every sensation, every mental ramble was watched as keenly as a message from outer space. Voices and footsteps in the big busy house made it easier to concentrate, as if forcing me to create my own fierce island of intention and intensity.

I knew my time was short. I had this one precious week. Then would come all the preparations for the family's departure in less than two months, the mounting hullabaloo of packing and good-byes — for the orders had come, reassigning us to Peace Corps North Africa. To leave India at this point was a grief I could barely begin to face. So focus inward: rising, falling. Learn to catch the thought, and note it: "thinking," "remembering," "planning." Let each instant be noted, like the cars of a passing train.

It was maddening to realize how far I could be transported down the track before coming to my senses and jumping off the train to resume the role of alertly noting each passing coach. I imagined myself on a hillside over the tracks watching the endless freight train rumble by. Sometimes my image of the surging mind was that of a wave sweeping up on the beach; the trick was to focus awareness on the very edge of its advance as it churned and bubbled up onto the sand. It was not easy or restful, it took a lot of vigilance, but occasionally the focus stayed steady enough for an inner silence to well up, such as I had never known before. Brief as it was — a few seconds maybe? — that steadiness of mind seemed very real, and all I'd ever wanted.

The nun's hermitage to which Mummy now escorted me had been a British sahib's old villa perched up under the sky, above Dalhousie's weather. I was given a glassed-in porch with a bed and sitting cushion, with steps leading to an overgrown garden. Through the walls I could hear mutterings, the rattle of grain on dish, the swish and thump of prostrations — the nuns were deep in practice. I learned later they were doing *nundrel,* the foundational practice that included a hundred thousand prostrations, a hundred thousand mandala offerings (that was what the rattle was). At all hours of day and night their soft singsong hum came to me like the murmur of rain on roof or the rustle of wind through leaves. As I wrestled in grim silence with the wanderings of my mind, I sometimes envied them for having something active to *do*; but mostly I was grateful for their presence. Their efforts seemed companionable, supportive of my own.

The satipatthana grew more difficult. My mind was as slippery as an eel. Continually it escaped my grasp, slithered into memories and conjectures. It seemed addicted to reliving past events and rehearsing future ones; what was gone and what had not yet arrived drew it like a magnet. I was shocked and appalled to discover how little I stayed in the present moment — maybe five percent of the time? Had I always lived my life *in absentia?*

When Mummy came up after two days, I spoke of this, my voice rusty from disuse. "I am so dispersed! I am amazed at how inattentive and lazy I am!" She cut me short: "Stop saying 'I' in that way when talking about your experience." She explained that using the first person pronoun to categorize yourself works like cement, anchoring passing feelings into a kind of permanence. It was more accurate, she pointed out, to say "judgment is happening" or "sloth is occurring" or "fears are arising." Her admonitions helped me recognize the burden of a solidified self, of its everlasting carping and goading — and the burden began to lift a little.

Desperation turned to heightened resolve. Here, you lucky girl, is a whole system designed to help you liberate yourself from the prison cell of ego. Here is a place of silent, loving people to protect and encourage you as you begin to dismantle it. "Oh blessings on the Dharma," I hummed to myself, then quickly noted: "thinking, thinking" and "excitement is happening." Even in delight the mind kept wanting to go off on its own, to slip out of the harness of Bare Attention. But that actually presented no problem: I was discovering that even lapses were grist for the mill — just more events to note, sooner or later, when the mind was reeled in.

The noting now speeded up, and as it did, the events themselves accelerated, until it seemed I was nothing more than an increasingly rapid flow of experiencing. As I held the flow in focus, that was all I seemed to be: a torrent of sensations and thoughts arising and fading away. Nothing else. At no point could I detect an experienc*er*, an identity or an "I" separate from the experienc*ing*. If there was a "self," it had to be that bubbling stream of happenings. This was scary; it was like the everlasting turning of the ether wheel. With no solid place to stand, to call my "own," I felt almost seasick. But it was also exhilarating, like skiing a steep slope, when you throw your weight away from the mountain.

To calm down, I paced in the tangled garden. I tried to note each step and the mini-movements within each step: lifting, shifting, placing, stepping. But the agitation persisted. Reentering the porch, I found by my cushion a tumbler of milk tea with a warm, tough chapatti — the kitchen nun had left me my supper. Ah, food would bring steadiness. Sitting … reaching … lifting … biting … chewing … swallowing.

After I had finished, the turbulence resumed in a new and awful way. Like a suitcase turned upside down to spill old socks and letters onto the floor, the mind began to disgorge the contents of its past — not stirring, memorable events, but total trivia. It was as if over the years I had tape-recorded the most absurd and forgettable of comments, and now accidentally pushed the play button. Voices in all timbres and tones assailed me, insanely repeating themselves: "Move to the back of the bus … Move to the back of the bus … Where did you put the keys? … Rinso white, Rinso bright … If I told you once, I told you a thousand times … Mais je n'ai pas la moindre idée … Hold still, that's a good girl now." I held my hands over my ears, I shouted to drown the voices out, I recited the Lord's Prayer and the 23rd Psalm; I cried. But nothing stopped the onslaught, until hours later by the glimmer of moon through the leaf-laced windows I sank, exhausted, into sleep.

The morning light brought a wry and empty calm: so this is the mind I had imagined was mine; here it is, just a cultural catch-all. This was the other side, the shadow side, of erasing the boundaries between me and my world, of opening to sheer experience. I felt humbled and scoured. No point in defending the precious self against the externalities of life if its crazy jumble was already inside me. A tenderness took hold — for myself, for the voices, for my people in this crazy time on Earth. It felt like abundance, embracing both our noble ideals and our daily absurdities; it felt like compassion. And a confidence came upon me that the tradition whose meditative practice had triggered this disorienting revelation, this psychic enema, could show how to stay in that fullness.

I felt a surge of intellectual appetite: to study the philosophy in which this meditative practice was grounded. Oh, to think I had a lifetime for such an exploration!

To my inner eye appeared a bridge, slightly arching, made of stone. I could see the separate rocks of which it was built, and I wanted to be one of them. Just one, that was enough, if only I could be part of that bridge between the thought-worlds of East and West, connecting the insights of the *Buddha Dharma* with the modern Western mind. What my role might be — at the podium of a college classroom? at a desk in a library tower? — was less clear to me than the conviction possessing me now: I would be a stone in the building of that bridge.

10

Africa

"I'LL MISS YOU, MY DEAR; but you have the practice now," Freda Bedi said as I took my leave of her in a cloud-swept Dalhousie monsoon. It was July 1966. "What a shame that you and Francis and your wonderful family are not going to a Buddhist country like Sri Lanka. But even in North Africa you, my dear, can keep to the practice. And when you finally return to the States, you will meet Trungpa — he will be going there after England, I believe; you will be in excellent hands." Mummy had often spoken of Chogyam Trungpa Rinpoche: how he had already been learning English from scraps of newspaper when she found him as a boy in a refugee camp, how she missed him since he had left, with her help, to study in England, and how great it would be when I'd meet him. "So I am sure that all will work out for the best. Just remember: you are held in the blessings of the Triple Gem."

Mummy's serene confidence encouraged my own; and I was too busy those last weeks and days in India to succumb to the grief of departure — until I knocked at Khamtrul Rinpoche's cottage to say good-bye to him. He was painting as usual, sitting tailor-fashion on his carpet-covered bed. I knelt beside it, speechless, my head against his arm, my eyes streaming. I was taken aback that I should display such emotion in the presence of a rinpoche. Compared to what the Tibetans had been stripped of, my own approaching loss was trivial, my sorrow little more than self-pity. But it did not *feel* trivial; it felt unbearable. I had the momentary impression that Rinpoche and I had been through this before, in other places, other times — and I didn't know if I had the strength to go through it once more.

Khamtrul Rinpoche smiled as he gazed on me, and we spoke about the future of the community. He reached for the length of turquoise silk he had gotten out to give me, murmured prayers of blessing. Then, pulling me up, he placed his great round forehead against mine, as I'd seen him do to other lamas. I felt my distress being received into the vast spaciousness that he was, and beginning to dissipate there.

Tunisia, until its independence seven years earlier, in 1959, had been colonized by the French. Like me, it entered the modern world with its native tongue and ways plastered over with those of classical France. Cultural leaders and government officials, drawing on a Lycée education similar to mine, found it easier to relate to me than to most Americans — which was gratifying. Tunisia's recent past was familiar to me too, both from *leçons de géographie* about France's prized overseas possessions and from my later research on North African independence movements. I had followed the career of Habib Bourguiba, the spunky leader of Tunisia's nationalist party, the Neo-Destour. I saw in him, as I did in Tito, a model of how the stale abstractions of Marxist ideology could be rejected in favor of local self-rule. Now I arrived to find him ensconced as President Bourguiba, and even met him in person — for that kind of access is one of the rewards of being posted to a small country.

These rewards left me almost savagely indifferent. I bent my efforts to finding a house and schools and friends for the children as well as to keeping up a front as the new Peace Corps director's wife, entertaining Tunisians and volunteers. But my insides felt dead. The exquisite Tunisian landscape and villages, the charm of its almost Biblical scenes — all that seemed remote. It was hard to take in, and I didn't *want* to take it in. What was I doing here? What was I doing in this two-bit country hardly bigger than the Punjab? What was I doing in this place where nobody knew who I was? Fran still had a continuing identity: he had walked off the plane into familiar responsibilities and a respected public role; he could build on all he had done before. But the work I had found for myself in India — the Tibetan Craft Community, the profiles I had begun to write on Indian community organizers, the deepening explorations into Buddhism — was now ripped from my hands, like a half-woven tapestry from the loom, as if it were totally dispensable, worthless.

It would have helped to have a name for this anguish like "postpartum depression" or "post traumatic stress disorder." A name would have provided perspective on what was happening to my soul and revealed it as a natural psychological phenomenon rather than some personal neurosis. Maybe something like "radical discontinuity syndrome," or even "cultural miscarriage." Such a term would reflect the experience of countless spouses who are yanked from one country to another without the connecting thread of professional engagement.

Certain things helped. In the first couple of months, when we were waiting for a house and the children were already in school, I took long solitary walks across the hillsides behind the Tunis Hilton. Those hills are built over now, but then they were open, grassy, flowering. Shifting breezes — salty from the sea, spice-scented from the inland groves — ruffled my hair, dried the tears on my cheeks. They bore strands of smoke from shanty encampments down the slope, and snatches of laughter and guttural Arabic calls. One family, recognizing me as I passed on the crest of the hill, soon began drawing me in, the women laughing in welcome and fingering me lightly with their blue-tattooed hands — and I'd crouch on the woven mat, drinking their strong sweet tea, unable to converse and feeling oddly at ease because of that. At ease at last in just being a stranger.

The Dharma helped too. I did not manage to root myself in a regular sitting practice, but I would pull out Nyanaponika Thera's book for encouragement and apply myself for an hour, and now and again, in the midst of things, I would remember to return to the breath and the bare noting of what was arising in mind and body. To do that even briefly interrupted the mental rush. And it was always interesting, like stepping up on a footstool or even lying on the floor, because it gave an altered view of things.

I often picked up my tattered copy of *The Teachings of the Compassionate Buddha*, which had been provided in the Peace Corps India booklocker. I'd used it so much that its pages were loose, held together now with a rubber band. Among the *Mahayana* texts, I discovered a treasure, a poem of the third Chinese patriarch Seng T'san.

> The Perfect Way is only difficult for those who pick and
> choose; do not like, do not dislike; all will then be clear.
> Make a hairbreadth difference,
> and Heaven and Earth are set apart;
> If you want the truth to stand clear before you,
> never be for or against.

It was good to be reminded that I didn't need to approve of life's arrangements. My likes and dislikes did not change the ways things were, and often only got me in trouble. What a relief to recognize that! Seng T'san's lines suggested more than stoical resignation, more than a self-protective refusal to care about things. They evoked the quality of presence I had seen in the Tibetans and tasted in moments of satipatthana practice: a wide-open availability to immediate experience before the mind interposed its judgments.

Of particular help to me was a little book by Alan Watts, *The Wisdom of Insecurity*. It consisted essentially of one continuous meditation on the fluid nature of existence — on the absurdity of attempting to arrest or possess that flow and the suffering we fall into when we try to do just that. It reminded me of the experiences on the train to Pathankote and in the Dalhousie hermitage. It added something, too. While the satipatthana texts focused on the discovery of what we are *not* — a permanent self, separate from our experiencing — Watts' rhapsody focused on what we *are*: a constant flowing, like a river. We are *bhavasota*, a stream of being, the Buddha had said.

It took courage and a strong love of life to stand in that river of being and not try to dam it or seal it up. Years before, when we were leaving Munich, I used a private little hand gesture to help me with the sadness of leaving — an opening and spreading of the fingers, as if letting water run through. I could almost feel it. I could almost see it sparkling as it trickled and splashed through my hand in its constant leave-taking. When you try to contain the water and keep it "yours," it goes stagnant.

Meanwhile Tunisia was coming toward me. The sheer beauty of the land and culture pressed more insistently upon me. It was a sun-washed, ancient world, softer than India, alive with echoes of our own ancient history. The beaches and islands of Tunisia's wildly beautiful coast were within easy reach, offering more solitude than India's teeming, scruffy countryside. On weekends Fran and the children and I explored the blue and white villages, set up our tent in hidden coves, swam the azure waters of the Mediterranean. Our excursions took us inland to old Moorish cities and Roman ruins and Berber settlements — and beyond them to the Sahara and the lure of its windswept immensities. Facing the desert, I wanted to walk out and keep on walking, to be emptied and scoured clean by sun and singing grains of sand till I was more transparent than a crystal; I wanted to disappear into that limitless space.

The years in India had left us a bit gaunt and sallow from dysentery and the quinine against malaria. And ill-health had interrupted the month I scheduled on an Israeli kibbutz after leaving Delhi. I had hoped to ignite in the children a desire for collective living; I didn't want to go back to the nuclear family pattern when we eventually returned to the States. The *kibbutzniks* of Gesher Haziv received us warmly as short-term working members, but soon discovered that we were not well enough to be allowed to stay.

"We spent years getting rid of amoebic dysentery," they explained regretfully. "We can't afford to reinfect ourselves." And also there was the insect life in Peggy's mop of curls, a memento from our last long visit with the Tibetans. "Those aren't lice, they are only fleas," I protested, but the old kibbutz doctor had the last word. Extracting something from my daughter's hair and holding it aloft, he said, "Lice I know how to recognize; we had the same in Buchenwald."

Now the dry, clean air of Tunisia, its salt-cleansing waters, began to do wonders for our health. We fattened on couscous, olives, figs, fish, and the date and chocolate cake that was the pride of Khemais, our cook. Continual excursions and camping trips grew us brown and vigorous; we tasted of salt. No amount of sweeping could keep out the sand we tracked into the house.

Mornings I began wandering in the heart of Tunis. I drifted through the winding souks and ever again into the enormous, covered *Grand Marché*, feasting my eyes on its towering displays of fruit and flowers, dew-fresh as the morning, its marbled counters gleaming and slapping with rainbows of fish. Even here in the midst of raucous trade, exquisite care was taken to please the senses. Tunisia taught me how to relish its offerings to eye and nose and touch, how to receive beauty.

The Tunisians themselves — who had seemed so bland after India's all but Dionysian frenzy — began to delight me. At a crossroads of history, swept by one invasion after another — Phoenician, Roman, Arab, French, German — they still retained an almost voluptuous esthetic, and the mildness it bred in them. Of all the Muslim peoples I knew of, these men in their pastel jebbas, who daily tucked sprigs of fresh jasmine over their ears, were the least dogmatic in their religion, the least militant in their politics.

I wished for a survey course to help me understand them better, so in our second year I created one. I wanted others to love Tunisia as I was learning to. In a quick exuberance of meetings I drew together a small committee, designed an initial series of eight lectures, secured the Ambassador's sponsorship, and enlisted local scholars: historians, Arabists, anthropologists, political scientists. I called it "Tunisian Perspectives". In the role of impresario, I enjoyed every step of the process, from tracing the logo to setting up chairs in our roomy old house in Cité Jardin. The *Tunisian Digest* followed on the heels of this orientation course. In Tunisia in those years, there was no English-language news or commentary devoted to North African affairs; so I enlisted a politically astute partner, Adele Simmons, along with logistical support from the American Embassy, and started a biweekly newsletter for diplomats and business people.

The work was unpaid, of course, for as a Peace Corps dependent I could not earn money; but I thrived on the teamwork and the knowledge that I was of use. So the days were full and good, when toward the end of our second year it became clear we would be moving again.

Fran was asked to assume directorship of the Peace Corps program in Nigeria in the wake of the Biafran war. As we talked it over, we agreed that the transfer to that big turbulent West African country made sense. Though I hated to leave Tunisia by then, I took comfort in the fact that I had come to love it so well. I chose to believe that strong connection with a place made departure more bearable because then, in a way, you could take it with you — and the place itself might somehow bear the imprint of your love. As the poet Borges said, "You can only lose what you never had."

So I began my leave-taking — not the going-away parties, but the real and wordless good-byes to places I cherished. Two especially, Dougga and Zembra, had opened my senses: one to an ancient past and the other to the world beneath the sea. Now the open-heartedness of my farewells would keep these places present to me through the years to come.

Southward from Tunis, in open rolling countryside, lie the ruins of Dougga. The Roman city invites me to walk back almost two thousand years, and to pretend that nothing has intervened to still the ancestors' voices or to rob my eyes of what their eyes beheld. Chris and Jack and Peggy run ahead, out along the curving streets, calling to each other as they dive into doorways. Dwellings, temples, baths — some lie open, revealing their mosaics to the sky, others have stairways to climb, hidden rooms to explore.

I walk on toward my own destination. The limestone slabs are warm through the soles of my sandals, olive tree shadows flicker cool on my skin, the air smells of thyme. At the amphitheater, I climb halfway up the ledged embankment, take my seat, and look out across the stage below and through its open pillars. This will be here long after I leave. If I let it absorb me now — pressing my eyes and heart into it — I will be here too, when I am gone.

In the Roman days, walls several stories high enclosed the performance area and a roof of canvas shielded the seats, but I prefer it this way — broken open. I like it when the walls we build crumble to let us see the glory that's all around — these sweeps of land in shifting colors, these drifting flocks of cloud. It feels good to be cradled in time — vast stretches of time that enfold and hold our perpetual departures.

I must also say goodbye to the underwater world off Cap Bon. The seascape around the island of Zembra was declared a marine preserve just before we had arrived two years earlier. Back then, we made the crossing on a small fishing boat that tossed us and washed us in headlong waves as we clung to mast and gunwales; but today the launch is larger, steadier, for many other foreigners come now to snorkel and dive. Our friends Reggie and Jean-Claude, British and Belgian scuba diving instructors employed by the Ministry of Tourism to turn Zembra into a resort, are returning to open it for the new season; they invite me to come along. Having the place to ourselves, we can dive to our hearts' content, so I bring Chris along too, excusing him from school. Almost twelve, he is a skilled and tireless diver, and I can't bear him missing this, especially since he's so bored and sad in the classroom.

There is a lot of work to do — airing the buildings and getting the equipment in order — but Reggie and Jean-Claude are as eager to play as Chris and I, and every day we take time to explore — below the far cliffs and out to smaller, sun-baked islands forgotten by time. Beyond one of them, about thirty meters down, we come upon a treasure of Greek amphorae half-buried in the sand. When my tanks are empty — I use up my air faster than most — I paddle placidly on the surface, amidst the bubbles that rise from my companions below as they work to free the tapering pots. The bubbles expand as they ascend, till they're as big as dinner plates when they burst around me. It's like swimming in champagne.

On our last morning we head out at sunrise to dive off the dramatic promontory of Lantorcho, Reggie's favorite spot because of the deep rock pillars and the big manta rays and amberjack they harbor. I have never gone down so early. The slant of the sun's beams through the aquamarine waters creates an effect both mysterious and friendly. On previous dives here I had felt an edge of fear, some unknown treachery in the sudden depths, but not this morning. Now it feels like going to church — like entering St. John the Divine or Chartres, if you can imagine those huge sanctuaries rising within luminous waters. I feel welcomed, like a pilgrim in a sacred place that is not mine so much as theirs, these brother-sister beings, who in silver-shimmering colors glide like notes of music. I see Reggie converge with a giant ray and, in a silent choreography, grab hold, glide off. I am drawn to the schools of smaller fish, whose hundredfold beings move and turn as one, like flickering veils. Swimming over and around and through them, breathing air through my mouthpiece, its gurgle and suck loud in my ears, I also breathe their vast calm.

Through the face mask my eyes caress them. Privileged to enter this world so undisturbed by humans, I sense its dignity, its grace, its intelligence. In my heart runs a river of thanksgiving, and a prayer that says: Remember. "Remember always, the Buddha of the Fishes."

The reverence in me is not just mine; we all feel it. I can tell we do even though we can't talk. Spontaneously, Chris and I begin to make offerings. Like the Juggler of Notre Dame before the high altar of Our Lady or the devadasi dancers in a Hindu temple, we offer movement. We do it one at a time, for the others to see, so it is like a circus, too. First Chris swan-dives from an under-water rock high above me, headfirst and spiraling, to even out within an inch of the sandy floor. Then he watches as I swim up to follow suit; then he tries somersaults and I go next with wider loops and a reverse roll; then together we tumble, interweaving our bodies. Our virtuosity, as we continue, is extravagant, limitless. Never have we so daringly relished our weightlessness; all freedom is ours. Reggie and Jean-Claude finally herd us back to the anchored launch before our tanks run completely empty

Nigeria in 1968 was recovering from the Biafran civil war. Federal soldiers trickled back from the shattered eastern region to the national capital of Lagos in the west. The Peace Corps volunteers who had enlisted with the rebellious Ibos in the east, causing a diplomatic furor, had been retrieved and sent home. The Peace Corps program, limited now to the Yoruba region of the west and the Hausa land in the north, was diminished but still useful. Fran's job was delicate, requiring his considerable diplomatic skills. My own skills were devoted, just as they had been two years earlier and two years before that, to finding and furnishing a house, settling the children in routines of school and after-school activities, hiring help, making a home, meeting new faces, trying to remember names, showing up as the new Peace Corps director's wife.

I thought I had learned how to manage such transitions. I had yet to learn that each time the depression is worse — deeper, blacker, longer. Not only had I lost my life and work in Tunis, but now, in the late sixties, the role for staff wives in Peace Corps volunteer support was reduced, restricted to hospitality. Fran, to cheer me up, encouraged me to join him at a conference for volunteers in an upcountry Nigerian hotel; but when I got there, I hid in our room. I had to hide because I could not speak without crying. A sense of cumulative loss sent me tumbling headlong, like a loose elevator plunging down its shaft. It scraped the scabs off old wounds. It crashed me against all the blocks I had ever encountered in seeking a use for myself. As if I had never surmounted them or adjusted to them, these blocks bruised me again — Papa's refusal to help me go to college, my abandonment of a Christian vocation, the stupid waste of my time with the CIA, the claustrophobia of those first years of marriage and motherhood, the loss of my work with the Tibetan refugees and now of the programs I had started in Tunisia. Throughout, one thing was clear: for this wasting of my life I had only myself to blame.

On the bare floor of the hotel room, I lay hugging my knees and gasping. In the darkness I had fallen into, a yet darker figure towered, pointing its mocking finger at me. Looming over me, it looked fierce but insubstantial, like a vertical slash in the fabric of existence, like a stick for beating me, like an "I." Was it Papa? It felt like Papa; it seemed to exert the same humiliation. Or did it represent the ego, the punishing fiction I had almost seen through in Buddhist practice? Was my endless self-contempt but another form of self-attachment? I didn't know whether to fight back or let it wipe me out.

I remembered to breathe. To watch the breath and sensations only. "Breathing … breath rising, falling … throat hurting … chest hurting.…"

Gradually a shift occurred. Sensations replaced that looming mental figure. Simple, almost clinical curiosity arose, free of judgment and interpretation. "Oh, what is this feeling *really* like? Is this pain in my throat like a rock inside it or a rope tightening around it? Is the hurt in the heart more like being crushed by a weight or like being ripped apart?"

With these wonderings came a kind of distancing. The sheer act of sustaining attention seemed to work like a solvent — like pouring turpentine on a pair of garden shears jammed with rust. It loosened up the life inside me. It freed me a little from the old mocking voices because they were not the sensations happening *now*; they were only ideas. Right now there was simply hurting, not some separate thing *causing* hurt or *being* hurt. Or being a victim or an endless failure. Just pain. And the pain, when seen in its own right, changed. It changed into just one more interesting thing that was going on. Curiosity, once awakened, widened. Attention, once engaged, caught more sensations to feed on: the trickle of my own sweat in the sub-Saharan heat, its sweet, acrid smell, the liquid laughter of African voices on the road outside the hotel room.

West Africa's sounds and smells and textures pulled me in. If Tunisia was clear, open spaces of sea and desert, realm of the eye, Nigeria was close in, like jungle foliage, its shapes too near to be seen, a throbbing, almost shameless intimacy of touch and tang. The hollow, gulping rhythm of the talking drums seemed to beat from inside my bones. The seas we swam in off Lighthouse Beach were not for viewing their lucid inner vistas, but for tossing and tumbling in the wild surf, for being thrown on the gritty sand after careening in from the farthest breakers. All was for feeling and sensing: cool tile floors of our house on Ikoyi, the sea-ward side of Lagos; gleaming needles of sun through palm leaf thatching; smells of ripe cassava and bananas from the market village next door, its clamor and calls.

Chris and I gradually collected quite a menagerie for our family — from pythons to a pangolin — and those animals, too, I remember by touch. The deft little fingers of Lucy the blue-nosed monkey as she skittered up to groom us — she most loved Fran's chest. The velvety face of Claude, our young baboon, softer than the softest velvet, though his mane was growing in strong and bristly. These two and Snoopy, our Punjabi-bred dachshund, loved to race and leap, ambushing each other in endless, teasing games. In the cool of the evening we would sit out and watch: it was like going to the movies — the Marx brothers, say, or the Three Stooges. "Lucy's quicker, but Claude's smarter," Jack decided.

The pangolin, by the way, is a tree-climbing anteater, an armadillo with armored scales instead of rings — like the one in Kipling's *Just So Stories*, which we got out to read again. There was also the alligator, who was vicious and left alone under the garden tap, and the mice I bred to feed the royal pythons, and the little jennet, an exquisite striped kitten-creature with huge nocturnal eyes. She was so tame and yet so exotic-looking that I affected wearing her on my shoulder — moving oh so casually, head high, while aware that all eyes were upon me. I stopped doing that after the day in the lobby of the Ikoyi Hotel when I happened to glance down and see that she had shat over the front of my black linen dress.

In the rich, moist heat where all this unfolded, it began to seem almost enough just to be. But to finish climbing out of my depression and to be sure it didn't pull me back, I needed to work, to harness my energies to some worthwhile task, with other people, if possible. Immediately I said yes when invited to teach French at the university. And to connect more closely with the culture, I began interviewing the instructors there who were amending the classical British curriculum to include indigenous history. They wanted to reclaim for their professionally ambitious students a measure of pride in their West African heritage, and I wanted to see how they did it. I anticipated writing a monograph that would serve them in getting recognition and funding.

Recalling those interviews, I most remember how the sweat trickled down my belly and thighs as we talked, tickling me under my loose cotton dress, as if the heat itself were mixing me into these people. As if in opening the pores, it opened the heart as well, making everything intimate in a generalized eros of connection.

On Sunday mornings before we drove over the bridge to Victoria Island and took the launch out to Lighthouse Beach, I often attended a Friends Meeting. Held in a home, it was small: there were rarely more than a dozen people, all foreigners as I recall. Together we stilled and listened. The gathered silence provided me a kind of fueling station for the spirit, as did the words that arose spontaneously from that silence and, by their relevance and their restraint, seemed to deepen it. I did not do my satipatthana practice but rather simply sank — and kept sinking further — into deeper layers of waiting attention.

I found solace in the company of these men and women who were imbued with Quaker nonviolence and immersed in Quaker activism. I knew they shared my anguish over what was happening to my country, and in our world. There was ongoing grief within me over the assassinations of Martin Luther King and Bobby Kennedy the previous spring, and continuing horror over the accelerating war in Vietnam. From our last home leave, I carried television images of the 1968 Democratic Convention in Chicago and the police violence against young anti-war protestors in Grant Park; now Nixon was in the White House. Even as I opened to the lushness of Nigeria, this distress accompanied me.

One Sunday, Eugene — a modest, balding man recently arrived from a series of posts with the American Friends Service Committee — spoke into the waiting silence. His words were plain, almost groping, as he tried to express what he sensed at that moment in his mind and body: "The South African organizer in jail, the North Vietnamese girl under our bombs, the Russian teacher in a gulag, hungry, cold, lonely … I *feel* them. They are here inside my body, or maybe I am somehow in them."

As Gene spoke, his words became true for me as well. They had authority because they broke something open inside me. I saw Gene's mind — or some bigger mind of which he was a part — as a vast net, and all the lives he evoked were points in it, like knots in the webbing. I saw it as wealth. I knew that Gene could be understood in metaphorical terms, poetically expressing our human bondedness. Yet I took his words literally; they testified to some extraordinary potential within us. My heart expanded with pure possibility. First, there was the miracle that we should even be able to enter into the suffering of others. And then there was this inkling that in that entering something real could happen, something of enormous importance. All this transpired in the flicker of an instant, yet it opened a direction in which I wanted to move

After those Sunday morning meetings Fran and the children would pick me up, and with swimming gear and picnic basket we would catch the one o'clock launch straight across Lagos harbor to a far spit of land. Then we'd walk half a mile through beach vines and dune grass to Lighthouse Beach and the open sea. Jack, who had been physically timid in his early childhood, now gave himself to the surf. Laughing and careening on his bellyboard, he let himself be tossed and dunked and pummeled, then turned as always to share his joy with Peggy, showing her how to hang on, when to push off. Fran and Chris were usually way out, indistinguishable from the other dark heads bobbing beyond the breaking foam.

When the sun was setting, we walked back to the dock on the Lagos side. The return launch on Sunday nights was so crowded it seemed impossible that everyone could fit. You had to leap with daring to get a foothold on the bobbing boat, its low plank seats just inches over the water. In the shove to get aboard, I remembered the extended sensorium that Gene had evoked and tried to imagine I could feel the larger movement of which I was part. Was it possible to experience myself as a drop in the stream, a corpuscle in the artery, and to identify with the larger flow? Yes — my edges were softer, my pushing less aggressive. I felt myself being held in place by people I didn't even know. Their voices lowered in the darkness we traversed, beneath the lights of the tankers so far above us. Here by the slap and kiss of the black, glinting water there was just this hum and murmuring touch, the flare of laughter, the rub of skin on salty skin.

But when I hurried, I became a separate, pushy self tending to tune people out — like that Monday I ran into the bank. My car was double-parked, and I started dealing with the teller I knew, without waiting for him to finish chatting with a countryman who lounged against the counter. I guess I assumed that the two men, whose conversation I interrupted, were just passing the time of day. When I completed my quick business, I heard a wry, laughing comment at my shoulder. Something about "the imperious Mrs. Macy, always in a mad rush, barreling ahead of other people."

I turned to look into a face filled with genuine amusement. I had to laugh, too, but was doubly embarrassed now because I recognized the man. I had recently met Adekimba at an official function; he was director of some government information service. My instinctive response was to clap my hands over my mouth in shocked remorse, but my hands were full, so I did the odd thing of simply ducking my face against his chest. It lasted only a second or two, but the spontaneous act surprised us both. Kimba remembered it in the times to come. "Without stopping to think, you put your face just so," he recalled, taking my head to demonstrate, placing it below his shoulder. "It was so swift and trusting, like a child. And so clever of you too, giving the lie to what I'd said to tease you. That's an irresistible combination, you know — trust and cleverness."

Adekimba was a Yoruba. Like most of his university-trained countrymen, he had an accent and wit with a strong British flavor. When we were first introduced, I found him too charming to take seriously. The day after our encounter at the bank, he brought his son and daughter to meet Jack and Peggy since, at eleven and seven, they were the exact same ages. We were pleased that they got along with such alacrity. Kimba was devoting an extra measure of attention to his children because his wife, an Englishwoman I didn't recall meeting, was back in London completing a graduate nursing program. That late afternoon as we watched the children and each other, I did not see him as a dark-skinned Englishman, the kind of imitation colonial I had scoffed at in India, but as an embodiment of all that was drawing me into West Africa: the vitality, the quick humor, the almost languorous warmth and love of life. Soon he was more than that.

Like our children, Adekimba and I were the same age, born just a month apart. It amazed me to think that for nearly forty years we had been winding our way toward each other with no clue that the other existed, and with no terror that we might miss. We were both a little dizzy with gratitude — it almost eclipsed the pain that we soon knew was in store. For we knew that when the time came, our lives would close over and go on as before, our family arrangements unaltered. We were glad that for this brief spell our spouses were away a lot —

Fran often upcountry, Helen in London — and took care, as best as we could manage, not to embarrass them or cause them avoidable suffering.

One half of one year. But time, I discovered, is elastic. A laughing look of recognition can make you feel more seen and known than you have ever felt. A night together can wipe out years of not having each other. Refusing to waste one minute in self-pity, we became artists in not-clinging, turned transiency into exuberance. Moments can be stretched by full attention. I collected and strung them like beads on a rosary. Many were with family and friends. Many were of just going toward him: picking up the phone and grinning at the sound of his voice, walking down Bar Beach toward his offices, maneuvering the car over congested bridges on my way from the university. Some were of forays to parts of his early life he insisted I see. Some of those cherished moments I wasn't with him at all, but just taking his daughter on my lap, or diving into the Ikoyi pool thinking: this water is in Kimba's land, this water is Kimba, it is Kimba's body, I am diving into him. Most persistent in my memory were the moments in the privacy of his inner office. When we had managed to clear the time, he would order lunch or supper, lock the door, sit down to work, pass me some papers, reach under my dress.

I learned that government censorship was becoming an issue. I admired him for his ingenuity in avoiding it, his courage in refusing it; but he was quick to reject my tendency to idealize the role he played. He teased me for that, which annoyed me; I like to have heroes. "You are not to see me as a political category," he said, tracing with his finger the shape of my ear. "I want you to love me, even if I were the most corrupt and cowardly rake on earth, which I could well be." I protested: "But you aren't! Your integrity is beautiful, it matters to me." Then the teasing smile and the slow embrace — "Come show me my integrity," he murmured — as if my passion for him had nothing to do with the values on which I had built my life. He was infuriating. I felt safe with him.

He knew how to scold me, catching me quick when I got high-handed. In arrogance and directness I had met my match. I always hated to be kept waiting, and resorted to sarcasm when he was held up in a meeting. "Stop being so bloody-minded," he said calmly. "Please behave yourself." To my surprise and relief, my angers did not bother him.

One late morning I sat under the thatched overhang in our back garden and made lists. What I had suspected had come to pass: we would be leaving Nigeria, and in only six weeks. My monograph on recovering West Africa's heritage in university teaching had been tossed back on the table. I had tried to attend to it, but what use was it now, when I hadn't completed the interviews? When I had to leave anyway? My mind was rattled by thoughts of our impending departure and all that needed to be done. I succumbed to those thoughts and made lists. Different lists for different categories of things to do: the shipments to prepare, the gifts to buy, letters to Washington friends and schools and the Lowell Street tenants, homes to find for the animals.

The air was still and hot; Claude the baboon and Lucy the monkey were immobile in their respective trees, Snoopy panted at my feet. I glanced at my watch — an hour yet before Adekimba's chauffeur would pick me up. Each day's prospect of meeting, the newness of each encounter, always made the intervening tasks seem light as laughter; but now my hand with the pencil sank heavily to my lap. For once I allowed the dread to well up. I confronted a life in which I would no longer be able to see his face. No, not ever, nor run my thumb along the curves of that generous mouth, nor know that dark satiny body on mine; I would not even hear his voice. I would be doomed to effort, to crawling up the mountain alone — to *making* the mountain out of my own everlasting self-seriousness.

Looking into that abyss, I knew I could not bear it. Yet I also knew that I would go on living without Adekimba. That was the horror of it: that I would go on — mother, wife, citizen, scholar — without his laughter and his touch and his knowing of me. Not only that, but I would be separated from his land, his people. In the White and desiccated world to which I was returning I would forget what it was like because without smell and sound and taste and texture you cannot really remember. Without these — and Kimba — knitting me together I'd be dry as dry bones, scattered and reduced to my own arduous, piecemeal striving.

Of what use was the Dharma? The lines in Seng T'san's poem with which I had comforted myself in Tunisia — "do not like, do not dislike; all will then be clear" — were of no use at all. This wasn't about "liking," as if you could sit on the sidelines and make a choice. It was about coming home to the deepest currents of one's being. It was about surrendering to the authority of life's connection with itself.

Yes. And if that was so, how was I to go on? Was I *supposed* to go through the years with half myself missing? Of what possible use was it that I had known this safety and this passion? Perhaps there was nothing to take with me but a gaping hole.

As I sat there under the thatching, a face appeared to me. She was instantly familiar, as if I had known her — or been her. A weathered High Asian mountain face — Tibetan perhaps, or Mongolian — a little older than I, calm and rugged, with eyes that looked beyond me into far distances, and the barest hint of a smile. She could have been a nun, for her hair was cropped short. Just to behold her quieted and braced me, as did the words that came. Her lips did not move, but the words were hers nonetheless; her face was saying them straight into my heart: "It is an honor and a blessing to be granted so great a love."

I realized I had somehow known that all along, and the meaning of the words that followed as well: "Only in strength are you worthy of this honor, only in strength can you receive its blessing. Let this love blow through you like the High Asian wind blows through me; can you feel it? You have that strength because it is mine." The words were inseparable from the face, which even decades later I can still see — more clearly now than Adekimba's. They helped me as we approached our leave-taking. We stayed strong-hearted till the end.

"Tell me again, my darling. What precisely is this thing you are planning to do?" Adekimba had developed a need to picture, as exactly as he could, how I was occupied at every hour of the day. "It puts oxygen into my blood," he said, and he required a fairly detailed run-down each morning. With a large ocean between us and no prospects of our meeting again, that would soon be as absurd as it would be impossible; but still we knew that each would be trying to imagine the contours of the other's life. That would be easier for me to do than for him. I told him again my idea of graduate school, a doctorate in Buddhist studies. "And I'll walk the straight and narrow," I added with rueful resolve, "no more mad passionate affairs."

Adekimba was aghast. "Don't say that! What a frightful prospect! You'll make a dreadfully dull scholar. For sheer momentum you, of all people, need to love with all you have and all you are. It's like riding a bicycle; you need momentum to stay in balance."

He threw us a wonderful farewell party at his home, with throngs of mutual friends and high-life dancing and "small chop," as he called the bountiful food. I wore a smashing dress of Yoruba print that made me look as slender as a reed, and instead of crying I danced, for in these last moments his eyes were still upon me, and I could still turn at any moment and see him.

FASHIONING MY TOOLS

11

My Country, My Self

IN THE SUMMER OF 1969, after five years in India and Africa, I returned with my family to Washington D.C. We had changed a lot, my country and I. In contrast to the buoyant hopes of the Kennedy years, America was divided and embittered, torn both by racial strife and by rage over the Vietnam war. If my country seemed broken apart, I felt broken open — by the teachings of ancient India and by Africa's gift of a love I could not keep.

When I had left for overseas to our Peace Corps postings, I believed that the United States had something to offer the rest of the world. Now on my return I beheld the failure of the vision it had held even for itself. I saw the police patrolling streets still burned and boarded from race riots. I saw them arresting veterans in wheelchairs on the Capitol steps, while the war in Vietnam continued unabated. The hope I brought back for my people was not that we dispense far and wide our political forms and latest technologies, but that we learn how to learn from those with whom we share this world — from their beauty and their suffering and their own stores of wisdom.

"Glad to be back?" neighbors asked, and I answered with an honest "Yes." The depression that hit me on the heels of each move between Delhi and Tunis and Lagos spared me now, for I had reason to come home. It was more than returning the children to their native soil and their remembered home on Lowell Street, and more than being near my mother, struggling now with Parkinson's disease. The wider reason it was good to be home had to do with America's agony. I wanted to imagine that if I had been capable of loving so deeply what I knew I would lose forever, then somehow I could love my own country as well, even in the midst of its self-inflicted anguish.

While we were away, traffic-choked freeways had encircled Washington and high-rises had sprouted in the suburbs, but our in-town neighborhood had changed mercifully little. The familiar one-storied shops were still in place, and the only new feature on our skyline was the Cathedral's completed gothic tower, whose bells pealed out now over our days. Before we had begun to unpack, the boys were running off with Peggy in tow, reacquainting her with every nook and cranny of the cathedral close, the Bishop's Garden with its labyrinthine paths, the Children's Chapel she couldn't remember being christened in, the choir stalls where Fran would be singing again with the Choral Society. In the south aisle of the nave, where the sun cast slowly shifting pools of color, they could step into sapphire, bathe in flaming crimson. Come Thanksgiving we resumed the day's "traditional" game of Hares and Hounds I had started in Tunis, and local friends joined in. The hares, with whom I always ran, had a quarter-hour lead and marked their trail with slips of orange crepe paper, hastily but judiciously placed — on a lamppost here, a doorknob there. Fran always ran with the hounds, who bayed a lot as they picked up the scent, sometimes even in the cathedral itself, as they'd find a telltale orange strip tucked in the Bible on the pulpit or stuck on the ear of a marble saint.

We had acquired the habit of enjoying each others' company. "You know why, don't you?" Jack said years later, when we visited him in college. "It's all those years in India and Africa — no TV, no movies, no ongoing gang of friends — the good times were what we made together."

In his current Peace Corps job, Fran, who liked to think up new schemes, was helping devise two ventures: a kind of "reverse Peace Corps," where Tunisian community organizers would work in American cities, and a multilateral volunteer program under the aegis of the United Nations. I assumed he had suspected my love for Adekimba, but he behaved as though nothing had changed in our relationship — and that was true; our trust and pleasure in each other remained unaltered. An image came to me for this moment in our marriage: it was of Fran waiting for me at the turning of a trail, perhaps in the Blue Ridge mountains where we loved to camp. I have taken a detour, ventured up a side trail on my own, but now as I turn back I see him down the path, in his old jeans that unravel at the ankles and smell of wood smoke, the big pack on his shoulders. He is quietly taking in the view, waiting for me to join up with him again so we can proceed.

Some years later we would learn how to talk with each other about our loving other people — and it would be a relief when we did, clearing the heart, deepening the sense of alliance. But back then I was glad we did not discuss Adekimba. Like the maple tree or Spotty or my favorite ski run in the

Alps, Kimba was becoming part of me — no longer separate enough to think about much.

Within months of our return I took a part-time job with the Urban League, a venerable civil rights organization. What better way to catch up with the racial dramas in my country than to hire on as a speech writer for a Black politician?

The very act of distilling another person's thoughts and trying to convey another's views helped me glimpse the nonseparateness of things. It required, at least momentarily, that I shuck off the persona and perspective of a White woman and clothe my mind in the experiences of my Black compatriots. To do that wasn't hard. It struck me as a privilege. I loved the mental stretch and the sheer energy of curiosity, and I saw how easily, almost inevitably, curiosity turned into empathy. I fancied how fine it would be if every graduate of West Point or the War College were assigned the task of writing speeches for Ho Chi Minh. Or every FBI official an autobiography of a Black Panther. Why not, in fact, start earlier, in school, with every suburban fourth grader asked to describe the life of an inner city child, in the voice of that child?

In the speeches and articles I drafted I loved quoting the phrase "the inescapable network of mutuality." Those were the words of Martin Luther King Jr. from the Birmingham jail in 1963. "We are caught in an inescapable network of mutuality, tied in a single garment of destiny." Sometimes, instead of saying God, he used that phrase, and in a broadcast on Christmas Eve four months before his assassination, he expanded on it, saying, "This is the way our universe is structured. We aren't going to have peace on Earth until we recognize this basic fact of the interrelated structure of reality."

Dr. King's words reminded me of Eugene's back in the Lagos Friends Meeting — and of the interconnectedness that became so vivid to me as he evoked distant beings whose presence he felt. And Choegyal Rinpoche's compassion for his Chinese oppressors, did it not spring from that same "inescapable network of mutuality"?

Meanwhile, the war in Vietnam obsessed us all. Images of White men assaulting Southeast Asian villages with tanks and flame-throwers had been stamped on my mind for two decades — ever since my senior paper on France's war in Indochina. During our Peace Corps years overseas I had listened to my government talk about "containing world communism" in Southeast Asia and had watched it commit first "advisors," then, with the entire machinery of modern warfare, whole divisions, and soon hundreds of thousands of troops. In 1969 and 1970, our first years back in the States, Nixon had our planes drop as many tons of bombs on North Vietnam as we had unleashed in all of World War II; and now he and Kissinger were having us bomb Cambodia and Laos as well. The brutality and deceit that I had thought we were fighting in the Cold War were now our own.

But I returned not only to a lying government committed to a doomed war, I returned to a movement. Anti-war actions had expanded in our absence, reaching into every state and city. Fran and I, with the children, joined candlelit marches by the White House gates and mammoth rallies that turned the Mall into a sea of humanity intent on expressing its refusal of war. We believed in the power of that intention.

To bear witness against the war, some priests and lay people, along with an Anglican bishop from South Africa, prepared to enter the Pentagon and conduct a Eucharist service at the office of the Secretary of Defense. The idea was to celebrate the sacredness of life, to mourn the dead, and to pray for forgiveness. I decided to join them. We met at St. Stephens, an inner-city interracial church I attended and loved. Since the Buddha Dharma had entered my life, I could feel at home again in my own root tradition, not taking its dogmas literally and opening instead to the compassion at its core.

Gathering in the sanctuary with the other peace activists, we reviewed the day's plans: our entrance in ones and twos through the Pentagon's underground garage, our point of convergence on an inner concourse, the starting cue that the bishop would give, our rights when we were placed under arrest. Then we stopped talking and stood around the altar table, taking each others' hands. In that still moment I felt, along with my anger over the war and my fear of arrest, something stronger — solidarity with the men and women beside me.

Father Wendt, the rector, began to speak; he talked about the very solidarity I felt — and then extended it beyond our circle of protesters, even beyond those in our society who agreed with us. He told us to imagine that the hand we held was that of Melvin Laird, the Secretary of Defense. He also said something about our other hand holding a Vietnamese villager's, but Melvin Laird's was taking all my attention. Here was Nixon's henchman, moving in bland complacency to execute this disastrous war — and I had taken his hand. Even though he didn't know it, I had chosen to take his hand. It was just an ordinary human hand — which meant that it was also as *extra*ordinary and as vulnerable as every other hand, with all the little bones so delicately hinged, and the naked, sensitive palm and fingertips

My judgment of Melvin Laird and his ilk did not dissolve, but the fear and loathing seemed to leave me. As we entered his prohibited realm and staged our Eucharistic liturgy, I knew that our illegal action was for his sake too, and was supported at the deepest level by his — and our — irreducible humanity. The same seemed true for all the officers, aides, and secretaries pausing to watch us or turning away, and for the police who arrested us and herded us down to their vans. So many hands — carrying clipboards, thumbing through papers, dialing phones, tamping out cigarettes, rubbing a sore neck, signing off on orders. Hands lifting the chalice, blessing the bread, breaking it: "This is my body broken for you." Hands wielding walkie-talkies, yanking me around, fastening handcuffs. This is what it comes down to: skin that can touch, skin that can bubble and burn — our shared mortality. Hold to that and there is not so much room for fear and loathing.

The civil rights work and these anti-war actions helped me take even more seriously than before the mystical openings I had experienced on the train to Pathankote, and in Dougga and Zembra, and at the Friends Meeting in Lagos. What now seemed most important in social change work was not how brave or brilliant you were, but where you drew the confines of your life. Was it circumscribed by your social role or the color of your skin or your political views? Or was the aliveness, the heartbeat, present everywhere, waiting to link up? For me to understand this, spiritual studies appeared more relevant than ever.

So the intention formed in the Dalhousie hermitage remained strong: I still wanted to do graduate studies in world religions, with a focus on Buddhist philosophy. Maybe I could find a way to translate the Buddha's understanding of self — or non-self — into a Western mode, to help my countrypeople come home to each other and play their part in building a world not based on fear.

I enrolled at George Washington University, where graduate courses guided me through early Asian texts. At forty, my mind was an eager horse.

Research for term papers took me to the Library of Congress, one of my favorite places on Earth. "Now I know what heaven is like," I said to Sally, my old Peace Corps friend and new neighbor. "It's being in a giant brain. That's what the rotunda of the public reading room is like — round and domed and luminous, a sanctuary of the collective mind, timelessly harboring all its thoughts."

This is what I loved: walking in under the high medallioned dome, surveying the concentric rings of reading tables, each numbered station with its own lamp that gleamed on the polished wood. Choosing my place for the day and looking around at my anonymous companions as they turned pages, took notes, scratched, yawned, gazed into space, the buzz of thought like an energy field. Stalking the aisles of the card catalogues with their rows upon rows of exquisite little wooden drawers, uncomputerized then, and riffling through the cards — the older ones with softer edges, a lineny feel. Picking up clues and roaming from reference to reference like a child on a treasure hunt. Noting my desires on the eggshell-thin papers neatly stacked in tiny trays, carrying them to the bigger tray at the main desk, and waiting for the cart to come rumbling up with its cargo, the unpredictable shapes and weights of the titles I had ordered.

In the spring of 1972, we began to pack up again — not for overseas this time but for Syracuse, New York. Fran was invited to create an experimental educational venture for central New York, to help working adults use their experiences and life skills toward high school and college degrees. Over the next five years he would fashion the Regional Learning Service, which was to become a national model of self-help in higher education.

When we weighed the decision to go, I argued at first that any move from Washington should allow me to study at an eminent center for Asian religions, such as Harvard or Columbia or Wisconsin. What did Syracuse have to offer? I went up to look and discovered that the Religion Department at Syracuse University was a pretty lively place. It was noted for pursuing issues of religious meaning in contemporary culture, psychology, and literature. I could feel at home here — these people thought in categories as broad as I did.

When I showed my résumé to Bill Hall, the chair of the department, I felt my usual embarrassment that my life had been such a hodge-podge. No linear progression from an early, clear resolve; no disciplined hewing to a single line of inquiry — just this apparent crazy-quilt of ad hoc jobs and pieces of writing, to say nothing (and on my cv, literally nothing) of raising a family or the many ways I had come to love the world. What scholarly promise could that typed sheet convey? I fidgeted in my chair.

"How wonderful!" said Bill after perusing the résumé. "What a rich life you have made." His smile was glowing. I looked at him incredulously. "But it's such a patchwork!" I exclaimed. "All the better," he said, "it shows the breadth of your interests." Bill said that with a Syracuse University Fellowship, I should have no financial worries — and he was right, I didn't.

Before setting up house in central New York, we spent a month in Maine at the lakeside camp of Fran's colleague in the Syracuse venture. There Fran started drafting plans for the adult education service, while I enjoyed the woods and water with Peggy and Jack — Chris at 17 had headed west the previous fall. Before the month's end, with the children off to their cousins near Boston, I visited Chogyam Trungpa's retreat center at an old farm in northern Vermont.

Trungpa Rinpoche, of whom I had heard so much from Mummy, had arrived in the States and, with his followers, established Tail of the Tiger, a meditation center now known as Karma Choeling. On this, my second week-long visit, I enjoyed the excellent teachings and the company of fellow Dharma practitioners, but I knew that I would not be joining Trungpa's entourage in a formal, ongoing fashion. The whole set-up was quite hierarchical, with a Byzantine flavor. The secrets and gossip and jockeying for rank made me impatient.

I was hoeing in the lower vegetable garden when the news was brought to me. My husband had suffered a heart attack that morning. He had been taken to the hospital in North Conway, New Hampshire.

An older Canadian woman accompanied me on the drive, and her sisterly presence helped, especially when she was good enough to stop talking. I prayed without ceasing. I promised all I was and had if only Fran survived, but the vipassana that Mummy had first taught me six years earlier steadied me the most. It focused everything into sheer attention to the present moment — hands on the wheel, sips from the water bottle, speed limit, exit signs.

I found Fran in the intensive care unit of the small North Conway hospital. He had been stricken with dizziness and nausea while practicing a new tennis serve in the midday sun — buckets and buckets of balls, he told me later. The cardiac infarction did not actually occur until he had been driven to the nearest medical center, across the Maine border. There on the examining table, hooked up to an EKG, an excruciating pain exploded in his chest. Watching the lines on the screen go wild, he called to the nurse who had stepped out. "I think … I am … having a heart attack," he tried to tell her. It was a massive one, the doctor informed me. "He's doing well now, though, and the chances of recovery are fairly good. If all goes well, he needs to stay here for at least a month."

I stood by the bed, putting my hand on his beloved shoulder, his arm, his forehead, telling him, over and over, "I'm here, honey, I'm right here." I watched him breathe through the tubes of oxygen, watched the lines pulse across the monitor. Thin, jagged little lines traced the beat of that big, valiant heart — weak, but still alive. He was groggy when he opened his eyes and looked at me, but I couldn't wait to tell him something. I had an important piece of information to convey. "Fran, don't worry, I'll stay right at your side. I'm not going to graduate school, that's not important. I'm not going to do that, do you hear? I'll stay home and take care of you."

I was eager to deliver that message because I thought it would reassure him. Instead, he grew agitated. Despite the oxygen tubes coming out of his nose, the IV tubes going into his arm, the EKG wires running off his chest, and nurses rushing up to hold him down, he managed with a massive effort to heave himself up to a near sitting position. "Joanna ... you will do no such thing ... you must go to school ... you must...." His eyes, huge with effort, glared at me.

The nurses glared at me, too. "Okay, OKAY, I'll go to school" — and I did. That meant moving on to Syracuse forthwith to put our stuff in the house, Jack and Peg in school, and me in the university.

Fran's month in the North Conway hospital was a chapter in his life that he still treasures. He had never taken time for solitude, never allowed himself the luxury of surrender to stillness. Now he could lie back and watch his meandering thoughts, or not think at all. Something happened to him there that changed his life, and our marriage too. Some knot of ambition, tied by our striving culture, undid itself.

After months of indolence around the house, he began the work he would pioneer in central New York. In another year he was ready for the ski slopes near Syracuse, delighting at the prowess Peg and Jack had acquired. What a joy it was that snowy Christmas of '73 when we sped down the hills together, all in a line, like a family of whizzing ducks. The following summer came the gladness of canoe camping again, in the wild reaches of Ontario. His heart was sturdy enough to venture, for weeks at a time, beyond the reach of the telephone.

"When the heart attack was happening," he recounted, "I kept telling the nurses to get the Tail of the Tiger and find you. They thought I was delirious."

12

Mother of All Buddhas

SYRACUSE UNIVERSITY, a jumble of Victorian brick and modern cement sprawling over a hill near the Erie Canal, became beautiful to my eyes. For five years, from 1972 to 1977, its Religion Department was my intellectual home, giving me free rein to think and good minds to think with.

When the idea of graduate studies in religion dawned on me in India, it had come with a vision of a stone bridge. I assumed that it was a bridge between East and West and that to serve as one stone in it, I should become a scholar of Asian religions, particularly the Buddha Dharma. But then the civil rights and anti-war movements made me look afresh at my own society, with questions that extended beyond interpretations of ancient scriptures.

I came to a good place for such questions. The Syracuse Religion Department pioneered in the exploration of modern society's sense of the sacred since the "death of God." Its most noted professors took Nietzsche's proclamation that God is dead as a fairly accurate description of what had happened to our culture's beliefs in a moral authority. But these thinkers did not stop with the obituary offered by Nietzsche. They did not assume that the sacred had vanished — it had just detached itself from a patriarchal God. Often in the department I would hear Martin Heidegger's dictum that "we are in a time of a double lack and a double Not, the No-more of the gods that have fled and the Not-yet of the god that is coming."

In this "in-between time," as we called it, Syracuse professors of religion looked for intimations of the sacred in culture itself — in poetry and art, in story and depth psychology. This required a wide-angle lens. Specialists, who depended on and took pride in the narrowness of their focus, were seen as comic figures. It was the generalist who could discern the larger, half-hidden patterns and detect what was emerging in the culture as a whole.

One of the patterns *I* soon discovered was a loss of belief in that pillar of Western thought: the autonomy of the individual self. That we are the captains of our fate and the masters of our soul was simply no longer true for the poets and thinkers of my culture whom I now read. Though unacquainted with Buddhism, they saw quite clearly how delusory was the separate, Cartesian ego, and how imprisoning its pretensions. So I began to see my own response to the Buddha Dharma as part of a larger paradigmatic shift in the West, as an urge arising within the Western mind — the urge to reconnect.

I was impressed by the particular courage with which the Western mind faced the bankruptcy of its own self-belief. Two contemporary figures became for me emblematic of that kind of lonely valor: the American poet Theodore Roethke and the Argentinean writer Jorge Luis Borges.

I loved Roethke for his fierce openness to life; he didn't try to make its beauty and its anguish fit any preconceptions about reality. The way he stayed with what presented itself — be it dew on a rosebud or squirming maggots on a dead rat — reminded me of vipassana practice. Unflinchingly, he turned his gaze on his own suffering too — even on the fear and humiliation caused by bouts of mental illness. He said, "I believe my pain." That phrase had such authority for me! As it was for the Buddha, whom he never read, it seemed to be this poet's First Noble Truth. Suffering is. Roethke chose to see it as the darkness from which, ever again, we can take birth.

And when Roethke sought a solid identity in which to ground himself, he bent to find it in connections that wove him further into life and back through time. "I come a dark way; I swim with the newts and the fish." He took heart from sprouting weeds and amphibian ancestors nosing through the slime — "this is a dear world I can touch." His allegiance to the senses invigorated my own; but it wasn't enough, in the long run, to hold his mind against the illness that hounded him.

To Jorge Luis Borges as well, the Western notion of self was a delusion; but instead of passion, the erudite, blind Argentinean used irony. He concocted stories with arcane plots to show how the ego can entrap itself, its ambitions and arguments turning into fun-houses, or Escher-like drawings with stairs and halls that optically reverse themselves, so you can't get out. These eerie tales fascinated me. I was amused when they ridiculed Descartes and the truth claims made by philosophers and scientists; but at times I shuddered. Borges' portrayal of the strange and awful prisons we build for ourselves — labyrinthine libraries, self-sealing pyramids, sands that engulf — made my skin crawl. The Buddha, too, had seen that what incarcerates the mind is its own arrogance, but in the hands of Borges that insight took on a sense of futility.

Ever again Borges' characters are defeated by their own efforts to get free. But in one story the protagonist simply stops trying to escape. An Aztec priest jailed by the Spaniards, he is obsessed with thoughts of revenge, until he has a moment of epiphany. A vision of reality comes upon him, so compelling and sufficient that he needs nothing else. He is on a wheel exceedingly high and extending in all directions. At moments it seems made of water, then of fire. "Interlinked, all things that are, were, and shall be formed it, and I," the priest realizes, "was one of the fibers of that total fabric and Pedro de Alvarado who tortured me was another." The wheel, where lie revealed all causes and effects, opens the mind of the Aztec priest: "I saw the infinite processes that formed one felicity. O bliss of understanding, greater than the bliss of imagining or feeling."

The vision was astonishingly similar to the experience I had known at Jack's birth. The only difference was that the wheel on which I hung then was turning — around me and through me. And also, of course, it reminded me of the Dharma Chakra that I had seen atop Tibetan temples and gates, where the wheel represented the teachings of the Buddha, the Dharma itself.

Now, reading early scriptures, I learned that the wheel figured in metaphysics too — as the circle of causation. It was employed to show the causes of suffering and of liberation from suffering. Studying it would help me grasp ancient wisdom on the arising of the fiction of a separate self.

To study in depth the teaching of no-self, scholars customarily turn to the Abhidharma, a canonical body of literature written three centuries after the Buddha. Here, to demonstrate the illusory nature of the conventional self, scholastic monks employed the tool of analysis: they took ordinary experience and broke it down into tiny, ephemeral psycho-physical events called *dharmas* (with a small *d*). These dharmas with their subtle distinctions were enumerated and listed, categorized and classified, all with mind-boggling diligence and much debate. The entire exercise came to be understood as wisdom (*prajna* in Sanskrit, or *pañña* in Pali).

My head swam. I was confused and bored with all this attention to hypothetical dharmas, and a little irritated, too. To view them as the building blocks of reality struck me as reductionistic — and, aside from that, the scholastic hair-splitting reminded me of the early church fathers.

I didn't stay sullen as a scholar for long, however. The next semester a teaching and a presence broke into my life — as happened for Buddhist India too, back in the first century of the Common Era. I was reading a scripture from the dawn of Mahayana Buddhism, a Perfection of Wisdom *sutra*. That was *her* name too: *Prajna Paramita*, Perfection of Wisdom. She was not a historical figure, but the symbolic embodiment of true insight. As such she was called the Mother of All Buddhas. It was she who brought them forth and nursed them to enlightenment.

As I became familiar with this text of hers, dauntingly entitled *Perfection of Wisdom in 8000 Lines*, I imagined her blowing into the scholastics' debates, scattering their arguments like dry leaves. I could almost hear her impatient, maternal voice: "Just stop it! This analytic exercise is not what it's about. You don't break free of the self by dissecting it into its components. The separate dharmas, with which you busy your minds, are empty! They're as empty of their own reality as the self is, and as all concepts and conjectures are." *Sunya*, empty, became one of her names.

Wisdom is not about bits and pieces, she said, it's about relationship. It's about the compassion that comes when we realize our deep relatedness. In this fashion, she brought forth in new words the Buddha's central teaching: the dependent co-arising of all phenomena. That's why her scriptures became known as the Second Turning of the Wheel.

To unglue the Abhidharmists' logic, she spoke in paradoxes. As you lead all beings to *nirvana*, the ultimate release from suffering, you lead them nowhere. Nirvana is no separate place. All is empty, there is no solid ground to stand on, but you can fly in that emptiness. It can hold you as the sky holds the birds.

Her scripture offered little to let me picture her, no physical descriptions, just attributes like "space" and "depth" and "endlessness." Her lack of features allowed images of my own to surface — images of strong gray arms and a rustling surround of sun-dappled green. With Prajna Paramita, I was back again in the maple tree on Ouie's farm, where changing light played through her leaves, and through me as well.

This text of eight thousand lines had much to say about those who venture into Prajna Paramita, trusting her wisdom of deep relation. These are the *bodhisattvas*. The hero model of the Mahayana is described here fully for the first time — not just as earlier incarnations of the Lord Buddha, but as a reality we each can be. Reading of their insight and compassion, I recognized the bodhisattvas who had graced my life, like Ouie and the Air Force chaplain at Blair, and Freda Bedi, Choegyal Rinpoche, Father Wendt, and Dr. King — even some Peace Corps volunteers I knew and some folks at the Urban League.

We can *all* be bodhisattvas — the Mother of all Buddhas was quite emphatic on this point. That's because we are, by our very nature, interdependent with all life and engendered by relationships. So we are perfectly capable of treating others as ourselves and of opening to the world as to our own hearts.

It can be scary, of course, to discover that there's no separate self and no private salvation. That's why, over and over again, the Mother of All Buddhas says, "Don't be afraid." When, centuries later, images were made of her in the form of Tara, a celestial embodiment of compassion, her hand is raised, palm outward and open, in the gesture that means "Fear Not."

I was glad that the sutra acknowledged this kind of fear, because I soon experienced it at a vipassana meditation retreat. The sitting felt good at first. The mind stilled into concentration as I watched and noted the passing thoughts and sensations. "Itching, itching." "Peaceful feelings happening." "Hey, I'm doing pretty well," I thought at one point, "just watching and letting go." And before I remembered and retrieved my focus, a question burst upon me: "But who is watching? Who is letting go?"

An awful anxiety took hold. I felt cast loose from all my moorings. "Who is watching?"

The question so shattered my attention that it eventually drove me from the meditation room. I stomped through the snow-covered drifts of leaves, muttering and almost crying. Where was the watcher? I was going crazy because I had spent hours and days watching my thoughts and feelings, so there *had* to be a watcher. Yet I couldn't find her anywhere.

Maybe Prajna Paramita was with me that wintry afternoon, for a light snow began to fall, wetting my cheeks and catching on my lashes. I stood stock-still, as if deciphering a message. Would I ask who was snowing? Snowing simply is. Watching doesn't need a watcher any more than snowing needs a snow-er.

My appetite for Perfection of Wisdom scriptures acquainted me with someone else who loved them, a seventh-century Chinese scholar and pilgrim. Huan Tsang especially loved the Heart Sutra and its teaching that there is "no form

without emptiness, no emptiness without form," for it distills, though somewhat elliptically, the essential message of the Mother of All Buddhas. With that
sutra on his lips, Huan Tsang crossed the Gobi desert. He went alone on foot
from China to Kashmir and down into India, to harvest sacred texts and bring
them back to his people. I pictured him walking along with his staff and
satchel, murmuring about form and emptiness. He believed, he wrote later,
that the sutra kept marauding beasts at bay, and the sun from baking his brain,
and the sands from choking him.

By now Huston Smith had joined our Religion Department, and when he
and his wife Kendra threw a party — "Come as your favorite incarnation!" — I
knew immediately who mine would be. My hair was short; I needed only to
spray it black and rub my skin with turmeric and saffron powder. From my
wall I took the Tibetan begging bowl on its cracked leather strap. Old and
odorous, it had been brought out over the Himalayas by one of Khamtrul
Rinpoche's community. Fran helped me fashion a six-foot staff, and I wrapped
myself in an orange sheet. I became Huan Tsang.

I loved the way I looked, and even more the way I felt. A calm determination spread outwards from my heart. I had traveled from afar, I had farther
yet to go. My face went into repose, my usual itch to be the life of the party
fell away. I moved, if only for that evening, with calm, scholarly trust in my
quest and with the dignity of sheer endurance.

In the spring of 1974, Mummy came to visit us in Syracuse. It was her first trip
to America and the first time I had seen her since leaving her in India eight
years earlier. She had received formal ordination as a nun, so her head was
shaved now, a lovely gray stubble she let me run my hands over. Freda Bedi was
now Sister Karma Khechog Palmo, her bearing more gracious than ever.

Mummy came directly from Rumtek Monastery in Sikkim, where she
had taken residence as a disciple and aide to His Holiness Karmapa. The
Karmapa was the supreme head of the Kargyu lineage of Tibetan Buddhism,
to which Khamtrul Rinpoche and his community belonged. I had met him
years back at a large audience he gave in Delhi. To help lay the groundwork for
his first visit to America, Mummy would be meeting with members of Kargyu
centers and supporters across the continent.

While Mummy was with us, my little study became a shrine room.
There with her, on the third of March, I "took the refuge." The ceremony of
taking refuge in the Buddha, the Dharma, and the *Sangha*, which I considered

equivalent to joining the church in Protestant Christianity, marked a deepening of intention. It was a commitment to take seriously my mind's capacity to awaken (the Buddha), the teachings that lead to awakening (the Dharma), and the precious community that preserves and practices these teachings (the Sangha). For years I had assumed I would take this step sooner or later. Now, with the gladness and gratitude I felt for Prajna Paramita, the moment felt right.

Kneeling before Sister Palmo, this woman I had loved since first seeing her in our Delhi doorway, I rejoiced that it was she who invited me now to own — formally, at last — what my heart-mind wanted. From downstairs came the laughter of Peg and Jack as they returned from school, and Fran's call to them as he walked in from the Regional Learning Service. They had been told what would be transpiring in my study-shrine room and figured it was a "neat" and natural thing for me to do. And so did I, as the light — gray from the winter window, amber from the altar candle — outlined Mummy's head and shone in her blue eyes. She seemed in that moment to embrace it all: my love for the Tibetan world she had joined, my gratitude for the Theravadan practice she had taught me, and also my womanhood.

To take the refuge with her was a non-sectarian act, blessedly shorn of subservience, for Mummy never played guru. She offered her love, her wisdom, her quite extraordinary spiritual achievements. But she never exacted obedience — or even, aside from that ritual moment, assumed a prescribed role in relation to me.

At the culmination of the refuge ceremony, Mummy gave me the name of Karma Samten Dolma. Karma means I was initiated into the lineage of His Holiness Karmapa. Samten means meditation. And Dolma is the Tibetan name for Tara, a devotional form of Prajna Paramita, Perfection of Wisdom, symbolizing her compassion. Frankly, I wasn't thrilled with the name. I had trouble with the samten part; I'd fancied something more action-oriented. But even if I had been so presumptuous as to say I wanted a name more suggestive of engagement in the world, I doubted that Mummy would understand. Though she had gone to prison as a Gandhian satyagrahi and then worked for Nehru, she had become increasingly apolitical. The traditional formulae of her adopted tradition seemed sufficient to her, as if we were all back in ancient Tibet and nothing had happened to the world since then. When I invited her to a large Syracuse class on Asian religions, she did not speak to the amphitheater of undergraduates about the relevance of Buddhism to their modern lives.

Instead she got them to chant with her the mantra of Avalokiteshvara: *om mani padme hung.* That was wonderful, of course. She did something I couldn't do; in her robes and manner she was an embodiment of this ancient tradition. I sensed that my role would be different.

Within ten days of taking the refuge I had an unexpected reaction. Self-judgment assailed me. Had I betrayed my root tradition — Protestant Christianity — by turning to a foreign faith? Waves of disorientation broke over me, to the point of nausea. How could I make this alien religion my own? I looked at the old photo of Ouie and Daidee by the farmhouse. The passion and the crucifixion, the bread and the wine, the stubborn, rebellious intellects of the Hebrew prophets and New England pilgrims — that was the ground I had grown from. Turning from that felt like betrayal.

Then, sitting quietly in my study, I looked at the painted scroll of Green Tara. On the day after the refuge ceremony Sister Palmo had initiated me into the visualization and mantra practice of this archetype of compassion in action. I scanned Tara's tranquil, smiling face as if it held a secret. I noted how one leg was not folded but extended downward as if to step out into the world. I looked at her hands, from which rose the stem of the flower bearing the Prajna Paramita scriptures. It was open, palm outward: Do not be afraid.

13

The Blessing

IN THE EARLY FALL OF 1974, His Holiness Karmapa arrived in America for the visit Mummy had helped to prepare. He granted an audience at the Long Island estate of a Chinese magnate, where he and his retinue were resting before their transcontinental tour. I drove down to attend, eager to see him again, now that I had taken the refuge and his lineage had become my own.

On that sunny September afternoon throngs of well-dressed people drifted about the grounds, waiting for the reception hall to open. I brought a roll of maroon cloth for Mummy — she wanted a mixture of dacron and wool — and also a friend, Eliot Roosevelt, who headed the United Nations office on nongovernmental organizations. A monk appeared at my side, inviting us to meet with His Holiness in his private quarters.

There on a chaise lounge in his undershirt sat the Karmapa, flanked by Mummy and Chogyam Trungpa, who, in monk's robes, was soberly and attentively serving as interpreter. His Holiness' laughing eyes — to say nothing of his attire — seemed to mock the formal protocol with which he surrounded himself. Again there was the immediate warmth of contact I'd felt on meeting him in Delhi eight years earlier. Oddly enough, it didn't extend to Eliot, whom he engaged in a mocking manner; he seemed pleased when Eliot soon responded in kind. The two began sparring. Irritated, I let my attention drift. His Holiness' question to me had to be repeated. Yes, I answered, I was studying now; I had decided, for this lifetime, to take the scholar's path. I hoped to make new translations of the Perfection of Wisdom scriptures and to write commentaries on them.

"Since that is the case," I heard myself saying, "I would appreciate it very much if Your Holiness would bless my head."

Taking his smiling silence for consent, I drew near to him and leaned my head over his lap, expecting him to waft his hands above it in a generalized benediction. Instead I felt my head grasped in both his hands, like a football.

Over and around me rolled his deep-chested rumble, which I later assumed was a blessing of Manjushri, the celestial bodhisattva of wisdom. With the strength and warmth of the hands, the vigor of the chant, and whatever else — my own astonishment — it was like having my head in an electric socket. For long moments I felt a charge going through me. That's all — except that I barely slept for the next three weeks.

The wakefulness started that night, after a dinner party in Princeton. I had been talking to a writer, Jerry Goodman, who under the pen-name of Adam Smith was writing a book on the powers of mind. At one point he asked me, bluntly, if I had ever had a mystical experience. "Sure," I answered. "Tell me about it," he said, drawing me aside to a sofa — as if I could give him a numinous sound-bite in the middle of a party. I felt so tongue-tied I had to laugh. "But a mystical experience is hard to describe! By definition it can't be put into words." Jerry, unabashed, kept pressing me, but to no avail.

I slept that night in our host's home. At about three in the morning I found myself sitting straight up in bed, fully alert. Words resounded in my head: "a synapse in the mind of God."

Why, yes, I thought with excitement, that is exactly what a mystical experience is like! I wanted to phone Jerry Goodman immediately and tell him: "It's like being a synapse in the mind of God." But after groping my way downstairs to a phone in the kitchen, I looked at my watch. Better wait until morning. I was too keyed up to go back to bed. Images of neural connections opened before me, as if I were moving through a vast net of nerve cells, a giant brain. I heated and drank some milk to calm me down to sleep, but in vain, so I stalked around in the dark — as I would for many nights to come.

Back in Syracuse the days were normal, but each night was a torrent of revelation. After an hour of sleep, I would snap awake, my eyes popped open, my mind stretched wide like the large end of a funnel. For a while I'd just lie there beside Fran's slumbering body and behold the images and thought forms cascading through me. In shifting patterns of breath-taking elegance all that I had ever learned, from Descartes to Jesus to the Buddha Dharma — all I'd seen and known and been — suddenly fit together.

Though I laughed and wept, it was the mind more than the heart that ignited with knowing. The laws that governed the interplay of forms — bringing forth worlds and dissolving them — were comprehensible to me then, but all that I can now recall are the images. Two visual themes predominated.

One was the tree, with its branching limbs and roots. The other was the neuron in the neural net, with its intricate dendrites and synaptic connections. In their continual self-transformations there wasn't one stable point, nothing to hang on to, but I felt no fear — just wonder and a kind of exultation.

All this incurred some emotional wear and tear. One night I sat in bed crying. Hearing me, Fran struggled awake. "What is it darling?" he murmured, putting an arm around me. I said to him, tearfully, "It's so beautiful, so big; I know just how Einstein felt!" It is a measure of the man that he did not laugh. Respectful and tender, he stroked my back, and muttered, as he lay down again to sleep, "Yeah, there must be a lot to take in."

It was during those sleepless weeks that I walked into a graduate seminar on general systems theory. Offered by the Religion Department, it concerned, I gathered, some new conceptual framework emerging from science. I couldn't imagine it would interest me — yet there I was, taking my seat, notebook in hand. Almost immediately I saw that the systems view of reality fit the patterns that I had been seeing all those wakeful nights since the Karmapa's blessing. I enrolled.

Indian summer 1974 was unseasonably warm. After school we'd drive out to our lake cabin, have a swim and supper, then sit around the table with our homework. Homework for me was my first readings in systems theory. The introductory book by Ervin Laszlo described flows of energy, matter, information — flows that interacted in coherent patterns, patterns that gave rise to cells and galaxies and minds. The first night or two I stopped every few pages and went outside. Walking back and forth, I looked up at the stars and hugged myself and cried. I wept to know that I was alive in a time when concepts like these were being crafted.

I had known this excitement once before. It was when I encountered the Buddha Dharma. Back then, with the Tibetans, I saw the Dharma as a luminous way of being, a selfless ground for serenity and compassion. Later, with Prajna Paramita, I discovered that this way of being grew out of a very distinctive understanding of reality. That the ground of being is fluid. That it is empty of everything but relationships. Now here came general systems theory with a similar vision of reality, and also new resources. It brought language and concepts and empirical data, showing how these relationships constitute our world, and how they work.

Avidly I studied how open systems self-organize in interaction with each other and life around them — through feedback. Soon I could chart the positive and negative feedback loops that generate bodies, societies, selves.

My fellow-students in the seminar — mostly from sociology, biology, engineering — were a bright bunch, keen to grasp the tools that systems theory provides. They seemed less amazed than I. Not coming from Buddhist study and practice, to say nothing of weeks of nocturnal visions, they had little cause to experience such a shock of recognition. They smiled at my enthusiasm when, at my turn to present, I drew for them sweeping diagrams on the board — not only feedback loops but tree forms and neural nets — and showed them how epochal was this turning in Western thought. "See, it's no longer a question of finding the basic building blocks of reality, as classical science tried to do. Instead we're moving to a process view, where everything arises through interaction and nothing depends on a first cause, aloof from change." I even told the seminar that, back in sixth-century India, the Buddha had made the same move.

Was it really true that the Buddha cut loose from any first cause? From *all* hierarchies in the structure of reality? That question drove me back to the earlier texts, which first set forth the doctrine of dependent co-arising. Because available English translations were composed by Victorian scholars imbued with their own assumptions about reality, I learned enough Pali to decipher for myself the original phrasings. I was amazed to find myself doing this. Until now I'd found the Buddha's teaching on causality ultimately boring. In the hands of scholars I'd read, it had struck me as either obvious (everything has a cause) or too arcane to comprehend. Now it gripped me totally. It revealed the Buddha's audacity, given the assumptions of his time, and it also revealed an awesome coherence with everything he taught and did — from mindfulness practice to his rejection of caste and private property in the order he established.

The texts I pored over took me back through time. I could almost smell the dawn-fresh fragrance of that moment in history, as if I were there myself in some ancient Bihari grove, where the Buddha's teachings broke upon my world. I could almost recapture the atmosphere of mental clarity, the freedom from old strictures of caste and class, the sense of self-respect and close-bonded community. I imagined watching with bated breath as learned Brahmins came to argue with the Buddha about the nature of the self and the causes of suffering. How simply and elegantly my beloved teacher sidestepped their traps, revealed their inconsistencies, and let the most subtle, elusive notions of causality — of how things work — appear as clear as day.

That year a Vietnamese monk came to Syracuse. In 1974, the war in Indochina was still grinding on, for despite massive incursions from North Vietnam, the American-supported dictator, President Thieu, refused to negotiate. In the humble garb of a Buddhist monk, Thich Thien Chau came to plead for our removal of President Thieu and our inclusion of democratic elements in the peace process.

Having helped to organize his visit, I escorted the slight, tired, brown-clad figure. On our way to press conferences and classrooms and churches, we took moments to talk together. We talked about the political forces tearing his country apart, about Dharma practice and the scriptures we loved. Thich Thien Chau, I discovered, was not only an activist but a meditator and a schol-ar as well. He was what I had wanted to believe was possible: a blend of schol-ar, contemplative, and warrior.

I watched his self-composure as he moved through altercations and triv-ialities that must have torn his heart. When the *Daily Orange*, the campus newspaper, distorted his words and his mission, I was furious. I tried to excuse my anger in Dharma terms.

"Dukkha!" I exclaimed. "Here comes suffering again."

Thich Thien Chau glanced at me and smiled. "Dukkha doesn't mean that everything is bad, just that everything is not perfect." Then he added, as if to reassure me, "It also doesn't mean that we are too attached; pain comes from the actions of others, too."

Yet he didn't condemn those "others." His mind was schooled. Mine, unschooled, fell into old patterns of resentment. Could I choose not to let this happen?

"My heart is a pop tart," I said to Peggy the next morning. "Wait half a minute, laugh, and it will pop up again out of the toaster — out of the misery and self-pity game. Pop up unhurt. Yep, it'll do that if you just wait and be still for a moment."

My choice of dissertation topic aroused understandable concern. Since no pro-fessor in our Religion Department, or anywhere else for that matter, had mas-tered both Buddhist philosophy and general systems theory, who could judge my work?

Common sense told me this should not be an obstacle because in any endeavor someone, somewhere, sometime, has to begin. The Syracuse department resolved the problem by inviting external scholars onto my dissertation committee: from Colgate University a Pali linguist immersed in early Buddhism, and from the United Nations systems philosopher Ervin Laszlo.

So I went to work — and discovered more and more how these two bodies of thought, one from the ancient East and one from the modern West, illumined each other. In academic terms, this was called a "reciprocal hermeneutic." To me it was a dance and a deep integration.

The endeavor was so new, however, that I often fell prey to fears of failure, fears of looking foolish to the very world I wanted to impress and serve. It helped then to sense others accompanying me. Roethke and Borges were at my shoulder reminding me to venture into the dark, to get lost, so as to be found by that which needs to be known. I fancied, too, that I could hear the reassuring murmur of Prajna Paramita: "Go on. Don't be afraid. The teachings of my Buddha-sons must find words in the science language of your people, just as they will again in the speech of those to come."

There was the smell of apples, that last fall in Syracuse, and skeins of geese honking overhead. In the bracing air, the bright showers of leaves, wild harmonies rang. I sensed them in us as well, in Fran, Chris, Jack, Peg, and me. In our daily doings, we seemed to be moving not around each other so much as through each other — as if we were buzzing fields of vitality, interpenetrating and moving on, enhanced by each encounter.

Though I was mostly at my desk, I felt this exhilaration of community. Along with the excitement erupting inside me then, there was also the sweetness of being held, of being an intrinsic part of something larger. It was like being a synapse. An essential, reverberating piece of nothingness. Just one little, empty gap.

14

Family Journey

OUR YEARS OVERSEAS TOGETHER — nearly ten, counting Germany, India, Tunisia, and Nigeria — shaped the character of our family life. Moving about to unfamiliar places, we became more dependent on each other and more present to each other as well. As Jack had observed, we learned to "make our own good times." Coming to Syracuse in 1972, three years after our return from Nigeria, our family was once again thrown back on itself in a new setting and a culture that seemed strange to us after metropolitan Washington.

In an ill-conceived attempt to make up for having dragged the children around so much, Fran and I opted for a Syracuse suburb with its better-funded public schools, instead of an older in-town neighborhood. Dewitt turned out to be racially and economically so homogeneous that it seemed more alien to us than India or Africa ever had. Instead of the quiet tree-arched streets of our Washington neighborhood, used car lots and fast food chains lined the main artery to our cluster of houses. Across the way in a concrete desert stretched a shopping mall.

This was the Middle America in which Peggy, moving into sixth grade, and Jack, moving into ninth, had to adjust to new schools and make new friends. They also had to get used to living with a convalescent father and a student mother — and an older brother who was away more often than not, for Chris at 18 had abandoned formal schooling and spent many months at a time on the road. Fran's mother, whom they dearly loved, had died that summer, and the loss of her deepened the shadow cast by his illness. While it was pleasant for them to have their father's company over the months of his recovery, it was also unsettling to find him home at all hours, horizontally disposed on bed or sofa. As for their mother — when I wasn't off at the university, I often had my nose in a book or was closeted with my typewriter. There was more discussion than usual about helping with the housework.

As we navigated these changes, I was helped by counseling I'd received back in Washington. It had started when Fran and I sought guidance for Chris and for ourselves, as we tried to motivate him to finish high school and steer him clear of drugs. Consulting with Esther Osterman, the psychiatric social worker, had such value for me personally that I continued on my own account — and Fran came too, from time to time. A canny, motherly woman, she was forever knitting, her feet up on a hassock, and as I walked into her office, she would peer at me over her needles with those sharp eyes that never missed a trick. "So, Joanna. How's it going?" she would say slowly and invest the simple question with such warmth that what I seemed to hear was: "I'm ready to hear anything. Whatever is happening and whatever you're feeling, I know you're doing the best you can."

Esther was a pretty directive therapist, focusing on the current dynamics of my life rather than seeking to unravel psychic knots tied in childhood. I liked her matter-of-fact approach; it conveyed respect for my present experience, and confidence that any sufferings of mine in the past could only enrich, rather than limit, my competence to live well now. She helped me believe in myself at a critical period when I felt both inadequate as a mother and desperate to find my own professional direction, without any models to follow. Gradually she helped me drop — like heavy and useless baggage — the sole blame I had been carrying for Chris's fascination with drugs and his refusal of any formal education. Esther took seriously my appetites for life — the spiritual and intellectual hungers, the passion for justice, the itch for action. She helped me to affirm, rather than decry, my capacity for deep relationships, including those over the years that had become sexual. This was a pretty tall order, since I had habitually chastised myself for not being a perfect wife, any more than I was a perfect mother, and had automatically felt at fault for any lacks and hardships in my marriage and family life.

There was one telling insight which set the seal on Esther's gifts to me. I was packing up for Syracuse, busy with the thousand and one details of a major family move as well as the completion of my courses at George Washington University. In contrast to Fran's apparent calm, I felt anxious and rattled. As usual, I indulged in comparisons and judged myself a lesser being for not possessing my husband's equanimity. One day I recounted to Esther how Fran, in a moment of stress, had coldly admonished me for my volatility, and once again I blamed myself. The wry comment from Esther was not unlike others she had uttered, but this time scales fell from my eyes. I suddenly saw how Fran and I had developed, over the years, a neat little division of roles. Fran would play strong and sane, and I would play crazy. His would be the voice of pure, unassailable reason, while mine trembled on the verge of hysteria. And the more he played his role, the more I played mine. In an off-kilter attempt to compensate, we had developed attitudes and behaviors that were even more polarizing. "He's anxious, too" was the import of Esther's words, "but if he can't admit it, his anxiety gets projected onto you. And you've fallen for it, you've played your part. To a real extent you've been carrying his emotional life as well as your own."

With sudden relief, I recognized that this was true. And almost as quickly I saw that it was also true of most married couples I knew: the wife was carrying the emotional life of the marriage and simultaneously denigrating herself for being "too" emotional. Later, when I began learning and expounding general systems theory, this marital dynamic became one of my favorite examples of a positive, or deviation-amplifying, feedback loop.

Fran's heart attack was a blessing in disguise. For one thing, I discovered the depths of his support for my graduate studies. For another thing, he almost died. As close as he could and still come back, he experienced his dying. In recovery he received anew the preciousness of each moment. The month in the little North Conway hospital provided the spiritual retreat he had never allowed himself — or even wanted. His priorities shifted. To taste the gift of life became more important for him than his professional ambitions.

When Fran was wheeled from the plane at Syracuse airport, and as he continued his convalescence in our newly settled home, he seemed more present to us. He had always cherished his family, but now in his weakened state he positively luxuriated in it, as in some miraculous cocoon. In a state of unaccustomed sloth, he revealed his capacity for sheer attention to whatever the moment brought: leaves blowing against the window, or Peggy's stories, or Jack's homework, or mine.

It was during that period that Fran and I found we could talk about our loving other people in addition to one another. For all the candor we had enjoyed in our twenty years of marriage, this was the one topic we had skirted because we each feared causing the other pain. Now we learned that our mutual trust was solid enough to allow us to be honest on this subject too, and the honesty in turn deepened the trust.

At the outset of my marriage I had assumed it would be monogamous, though I didn't recall that being specified in our nuptial vows. When I discovered I couldn't suppress my love for other people, I tried to stay as conscious in my choices as I could. It was in Munich in the seventh year of our marriage. Avidly I read moral philosophy — especially Schiller on the dialectical interplay between reason and passion, constraint and freedom: passion, breaking up old habits of thought, can give rise to new meta-levels of reason. These philosophic reflections were of considerable import at the time because I wanted to make love with the young doctor who raced me down the slopes over Sankt Anton. The gladness I found in his arms was to me as wholesome as the exuberance of our skiing, and as nonthreatening to my marriage.

A sense of inner abundance rose within me that enhanced my whole family life, like it was a bubbling fountain, spilling over into playful patience with the children and amorousness with Fran. I concluded that the social norm of sexual exclusivity did not conform to the truth of my own experience — nor to my increasingly strong views about the limits of ownership. People cannot own each other any more than they can possess air, sun, or wind. Along with Friedrich Engels, I came to see monogamy as a patriarchal institution whose original motives had to do with economic control.

So Adekimba was not the first man I had loved since marrying Fran, nor was he the last. Just as that cherished Yorubaman had hoped when we said good-bye in Nigeria, there were other loves to come. Each was the ripening of a strong, honest friendship. Each awakened an energy and gratitude that shed grace on my days. Each revealed my fierce joy in life, and taught me equally fierce lessons in letting go. But I never shared with Fran my views about monogamy. I was afraid to, lest he misunderstand and feel deeply wounded, even leave me. And to be honest, I wondered whether my conviction that there was no intellectual or moral basis for sexual exclusivity would be shaken if *he* were the errant one. So I tacitly cast myself as the "heavy," never imagining that my unconventional views might be Fran's as well.

Then one November afternoon, during our second year in Syracuse, Fran came into my study after a lunch he'd had with our friend Tom, a geography professor. There was a twinkle in his eye. Over their shrimp cocktails and pasta Tom had seen fit to divulge the fact that he and I had become lovers. Learning this, I went hot and cold. I wanted to run. Then I saw Fran was grinning. He reached toward me, brushing the side of my face, my hair, to let me know that I was not the only one of us to find pleasure in the arms of another.

It took me some moments to make sense of what I was hearing. When it sank in that Fran had a liaison of his own, with a woman I'd met at the community garden, we started laughing. I laughed so hard I slipped off the side of my desk, scattering my term paper over the floor. As we got down on our knees to pick up the pages, our hilarity brought a tide of relief.

Now there was no more need to hide the joy I found with other people. Never had I loved Fran more than when I looked into his knowing, generous eyes and felt accepted in all my wide-ranging passions. I was even more relieved to discover that I could accept *his*. It didn't seem a loss or violation that another woman knew what it was like to be loved by Fran. Who wants to be the solitary taster of a sweet breed of apple or an exquisite wine? It also struck me that Fran deserved to be well pleasured. Why should that responsibility be mine alone?

Nothing in my culture prepared me for these spontaneous responses, but I liked them.

The nonpossessiveness we then affirmed — privately, lest we offend society and confuse our children — would not always be easy. Feelings of jealousy and insecurity would arise at times, teaching us to express them honestly and to respect each other's vulnerability. If these feelings persisted and became too painful, we changed the relationship that caused them. Neither of us ever seriously considered leaving our marriage. Over the years, far more often than not, monogamy prevailed, but it always felt like a choice — not something we were doing out of inertia or a sense of entrapment. It has seemed, as Fran puts it, that we've appreciated and trusted each other more because of our willingness to love and be loved by others. Maybe that's the true meaning of "open marriage" — a radical openness with each other.

As a family we were discovering the natural beauty of central New York. We explored the rolling farmland that opened up minutes beyond the urban sprawl — picked apples in the fall orchards, found good hills for skiing through the long snowy winters, and discovered in the spring the distinctive character of each of the Finger Lakes. The deepest and purest one, Skaneateles Lake, glowed like a long sapphire set amidst the pastures and woodlands. There, by waters where loons called at night and wild geese stopped over on their long migrations, we found a cabin to buy and painted it red. On the shingled shore we kept a yellow canoe, called the Flying Banana, and a twelve-foot Sunfish called Ishtar that Fran taught each of us to sail. The joy of arrival, whether for a summer month or a late afternoon in the fall, was new each time. Every pitch and turn of the access lane, down along the fields and through the woods, was as familiar as our front door, yet always changing, greeting us with fresh green in the spring and showers of gold as the days grew chill. Before November snows blew in from Canada and blocked the road, we boarded up the windows till warmer days came round again.

Winter offered other pleasures. When the ice was bare of snow, we would lace up our skates on the bank of the Erie Canal and speed for miles into a silence broken only by our shouts and the sound of our blades. And when snow covered the land, we stuck our skis on the car as soon as classes let out. Good slopes were forty minutes away and so well lit that, as evening came on, we were still catching the lift, jumping off at the top, pursuing each other down again. The white wind from Canada pouring across Lake Ontario dwarfed the dirty sprawl of Syracuse, made our city seem intimate and brave in the vastness of winter.

The friends who gathered for evenings of talk and games were, for the most part, shared by us all. Most of my fellow graduate students were in their twenties and early thirties, and Peg, Jack, and Chris spun their own friendships with them, as they had with the Peace Corps volunteers overseas. It was a congenial era in the Religion Department, and a number of its faculty belonged to our extended family. We also grew close to a group of townspeople who formed a network called the New Environment Association. The aim of NEA, as we called it, was to envision ways of organizing our lives that were more in harmony with ecological realities. The thinking was bold, the focus local, practical. Soon NEA meetings and potlucks were regular features of our family life, along with work parties in the collective garden.

The OPEC oil crisis during our first year in Syracuse dramatized the fragility of our fossil fuel-based economy. It lent a sense of urgency to the questions we explored with our NEA colleagues, questions about our American lifestyle that had been nagging us. The war in Vietnam was still dragging on under Nixon, and we asked ourselves, too, how this lifestyle related to the foreign interventions and militarism of our government.

Fran and I decided to attend a weekend workshop on simple living. It was offered by the Movement for a New Society (MNS) in Philadelphia, a network of collectives first organized by Quaker activists early in the Vietnam war. There we could step back and reflect: How is it for us to live in a country that consumes half the world's resources? In the group we looked at the wasteful use of these resources and the kind of bondage we put ourselves in to buy all the clutter that clogs our lives. We considered our truer needs — the need for community and creative work. And we took a fresh look at how we were actually spending our energy, money, and time.

Though shocked by what we had recognized about our country and ourselves, Fran and I felt invigorated. We liked the way these MNS folks walked their talk and the basic workability of their collective living arrangements.

This mattered to me because I wanted to do more than manage our home with greater frugality. It was the nuclear family itself that made no sense to me. Its essential isolation, its wasteful duplication of goods, the exhausting burden it imposed on wife and mother, the loneliness to which it relegated the unmarried — all of this had appalled me in the fifties, when I embarked on marriage and motherhood. In the sixties it impelled me to devote a month of home leave to visit a kibbutz in Israel, where I hoped that the logic and pleasures of collective living would rub off on my children. Now in the seventies in Syracuse, the nuclear family system felt as onerous as ever. We talked a lot about sharing household work "because Mom is going to school now," and Fran and the children did help a lot. The problem was that they performed their chores as a favor to me, as if kindly helping me with what was essentially my job. I didn't know how to escape from this.

Then, in early 1975, Fran, Jack, Peg and I — Chris had left for a year on a communal farm in Tennessee — drove down to Philadelphia for a weekend orientation with the Movement for a New Society. It was a turning point in our lives.

From the start Peg and Jack were treated as competent and interesting people. They were on their own — sitting elsewhere from Fran and me in the large circle meetings, managing their own time and contacts, and having their own things to say. MNS organizers were articulate not only about the racist, sexist, and class oppression that bred injustice, but about "ageism" as well. They consciously tried to correct for the way youth was marginalized in American society and deprived of real responsibility. Peg and Jack, at thirteen and seventeen, found themselves challenged to be as fully present and on-the-ball as anyone else. When discussions turned theoretical, analyzing ways the military-industrial complex wastes our ecological resources and erodes our democracy, they made total sense to this eleventh grader and his eighth-grade sister. "It's not that complicated, Mom," Jack reassured me when I looked at him speechlessly after one of his comments.

"There was some great dancing last night," Peg informed me. "I like being with people older than the kids at school and younger than you guys. I'm treated like a real person here."

We unrolled our sleeping bags in one of the collective houses, signed up for kitchen duty in another or bathroom clean-up in yet a third, studied the bulletin boards, stepped through clusters of conversation, hunkered down in a corner to read a leaflet, or joined the singing by the old piano. I noticed the grime and the peeling paint, but if the other Macys did, that hardly detracted from their fascination with collective living. The main fascination, I think, was its moral coherence: here people were living in accordance with what they believed was true and important in their world. No wonder they were having such a good time.

Driving up the Susquehanna Valley on our way home, the four of us decided together: "Let's do it!" Within two months we put our suburban home up for sale and began to look inside Syracuse for a bigger place to share with others. On a corner lot of Allen Street, not far from the university, we found a large old house. Despite its extreme shabbiness, there was a promise of elegance in its generous proportions; the cobwebbed ceilings were high, and between its broken banisters the stairway curving down into the entry hall looked wide enough for *Gone with the Wind*.

The transformation was swift and high-spirited. For the plumbing, wiring, and carpentry repairs we hired experienced friends, and then, welcoming and feeding all volunteers, we unleashed an orgy of scraping, painting, sanding, varnishing. Those working for pay noted their hours on a pad by the back door, operating by the honor system, and the quality of their work was checked by a hired contractor.

By the start of fall semester, we four Macys were once more rolling out our Tunisian carpets and hanging our Tibetan paintings and African carvings. But this time four others moved in with *their* goods, too — pressure cookers, guitars, pick-up trucks in the driveway — to join us in the creation of a common household. The Allen Street house offered ample room for the eight of us, occasional guests, and Chris, too, when he came through town. And it was beautiful.

Phil, one of our housemates, said, "I'm happier every day I'm here." What was it about this house? Everything flowed and mingled, the living room smelled Tibetan, the garlic-strung kitchen bubbled and chortled. The spaces sang, and I imagined that all who walked in breathed deeper, felt their bodies loosen up.

Just as our move to cooperative living had to be a unanimous decision, so did the selection of those we'd invite to share this venture. Even Peggy at thirteen could exercise a veto — and she did. When another family with two children wanted to join us and Fran and I thought that was a lovely idea, Peg was clear in stating her reasons against it. "It will be too generational," she pointed out — the household could easily fall into a group of adults and a group of children. "And I don't want Jack and me to be lumped with the kids." She was wise. The four who joined us were single people in their twenties and early thirties. This created a continuum of ages, which encouraged Peg and Jack to feel as significant and responsible as anyone else.

In the nuclear family the age gap between parents and children makes it hard for the kids to see the unfolding stages of the life journey. It looks as if the parents have always been grown up and in their present roles. The children don't get to witness many key passages in life, such as finishing school, getting a job, finding a mate. At the Allen Street house, Peg and Jack were able to watch how their friends navigated these waters.

Since household members did not pool income and assets, we did not constitute a collective so much as a cooperative, sharing costs for food as well as all household responsibilities. Rosters were set up for cooking, cleaning, and shopping, including the hours of service we owed to the local food co-op. I bought groceries every month or so, cooked once a week, and enjoyed seeing Peg, Jack, and Fran consult others besides me when it was their turn to make dinner. We kept a big spiral notebook by the telephone. Here, in addition to noting incoming calls, we wrote messages to each other — impromptu appreciations as well as requests and reminders. It was the first thing any of us looked at when we came home.

"Phil, thanks for the popcorn last night. Best ever."

"Hey, Fran, wasn't it your turn to take out the trash?"

"Mima, can you sub for me at the co-op this Thursday?"

"Joanna, you left your ski boots on the cellar stairs and I nearly broke my neck."

"Who can give me a lift to the garden Saturday? I'll love you forever."

"Cook: I'm missing dinner tonight, save me some of your dee-licious fare."

The big open notebook was an amazingly simple tool for communicating without an emotional charge: irritations didn't build up because they could be noted immediately. And I for one could stop carrying household minutiae around in my head. It was a relief to realize I could stop master-minding the universe.

One night a week we reserved for our House Meeting. With our busy lives, we really needed these moments to stop and reflect and plan together. We practiced "rotating facilitatorship," expecting each member in turn to pull the agenda together and chair the meeting. Peg and Jack became as skilled at this as anyone, and I soon didn't blink when either one told me I was getting off track and to please attend to the subject at hand.

No matter how much business we had to deal with, the first agenda item was always "Feeling-Dealing." One at a time around the circle, we had a chance to report to the others how we were feeling at that moment in our lives — what was exciting or troubling us in school or work or home. No comments were allowed in response. One just put it out: "I've been lonely this week", or "I've got this new song going through my head." No need to justify the loneliness or produce the song. Such a simple process, yet it repeatedly amazed me to discover in the speaking how my own life felt, and also to hear those whom I loved and saw every day say things I hadn't suspected. Given the pace of our lives, we don't usually pause on our way out the door and say, "By the way, I'm sad," or "… scared," or "… in love with the cashier at the co-op." It was when we shared our lives with others that I saw my own family in fuller dimension and sharper focus.

Peg and Jack, and Chris when he visited, were a lot more motivated now in carrying out household responsibilities. They were not doing it for Mom any more but for themselves, to be respected housemates of young adults they liked and admired. In matters pertaining to how we all would live together, each of them was given a voice as definitive as any of the adults. Since we decided many issues by consensus, this often amounted to veto power. If Fran or I felt any anxiety about how Peg and Jack would handle their new degree of power, it soon evaporated. They were as committed as we were to making this venture work, and in some areas smarter than we were. When we hit emotional snags, Peg and Jack often had a clearer understanding of what was going on than Fran or I, and wiser suggestions to offer. I learned lessons in humility when the dynamics in question included my own attitudes and behaviors.

Clearly, Fran's and my roles were changing. The two of us talked late into the night, wrestling with how we would define our authority as parents. It wasn't all that difficult. Educational choices were to be made in consultation with us, and we retained authority over issues concerning family finances and our children's health and safety. That meant, among other things, the hours they were to observe and the places they could go in their burgeoning teenage social lives. Since the activities of Peg's and Jack's schoolmates were hard put to compete with the liveliness of our own household, few problems arose in this domain. Earlier efforts to limit use of television were irrelevant now, and for the same reason: canned programs on the screen held little appeal when so much else was going on, from NEA potlucks and song nights to volleyball games in the backyard.

Peggy and I worried about the dolphins, and one day we decided to help boycott the tuna industries. Armed with the posters we had painted on the floor of her room and photocopied sheets of information, we spent some afternoons at local supermarkets. Standing out front — or inside, when we were allowed — we talked to customers as we handed them our leaflets. Peggy's shyness made her more convincing.

Our communal lifestyle freed up time and energy to turn outward in such ways. It was easy to give an hour to leaflet for the dolphins, when others were on duty to cook dinner and clean up. Furthermore, having made the change to cooperative living, we felt somehow more competent to act on larger issues. And there was always some household member willing to join in and lend support. "Anyone want to come along with me?" Jack would call as he headed out to a recycling meeting.

I had not anticipated that communal living would provide me so much privacy and freedom. When I got home, I could head straight up to my desk if I needed to work on my Pali, because there was other companionship for the kids. I would hear Peggy playing the piano with Scott downstairs or Jack's shouts as he tossed the Frisbee with Phil. Without pain I made the sweet discovery that I was dispensable.

I had hoped, as part of my study program, to return to India for a spell. Now, within our first year on Allen Street, I did. I was able to set off on my three-month junket with a lighter heart and clearer mind, knowing that I wouldn't be missed all that much. The way the household was functioning, it was even possible for Fran to take off for several weeks to join me. When I returned from my Asian pilgrimage, the household welcomed me with a festive dinner cooked by Phil and Peggy. What I remember most is a comment of admonishment from Jack. He was sitting at the head of the table, with me on his left. At some point, unthinkingly, I brought up a chore that I saw needed doing. I was automatically reverting to overseer mode, when Jack turned to me in the candlelight and put his hand on mine. Gently, firmly, he reminded me that the appropriate way to handle the concerns I had raised was to put them on the agenda of the next house meeting, to be handled collectively. "Mom, you've been away so long, I think you've forgotten how we do things now."

15

Tashi Jong

THE BUS LET ME OFF AT A ROADSIDE TEA STAND. It was five hours past the turn-off to Dalhousie, and Kangra Valley looked different here — towns farther apart, mountains closer. "Tashi Jong," the driver pointed, before the bus lurched into gear and roared off. Looking at the hillside about a mile away, I made out low buildings half-hidden in the trees, and a glint of gold above them.

It was March 1976, my first return to India since the Peace Corps days ten years before — and the first time I would see my Tibetan friends in their new home. In the late 1960s they had left their rented quarters in Dalhousie and acquired land of their own, which Khamtrul Rinpoche named Tashi Jong — "auspicious valley." Here at last the refugee lamas and lay people could rebuild their lives in exile. I had followed each step of the process through Choegyal Rinpoche's letters.

After the overnight train to Pathankote and eight hours on the bus, it was good to be alone in the ringing mountain air. Dropping my gear at the tea stall, I started up a narrow road. The fields all around were emerald green with new wheat, and the banks between them bobbed with wildflowers of blue, yellow, white. White, too, shone the snows on the Daula Dhar range before they sank from view. Emerging from the trees on the hillside up ahead, the structure with the glinting roof grew clearer now, yellow walls in afternoon sun. The monastery temple of Khampagar, whose ruins lay in far Tibet, had risen again.

On a rise in the path I paused to look at it, and saw, too, in my mind's eye, how Khamtrul Rinpoche used to sit at his table over tea, making the sketches that would serve as blueprints. How he paced out on the leveled dirt the dimensions of the great hall. How the walls took form, and how even the monks and yogis climbed up on the rickety ladders to heft pans of mortar. The scenes were vivid to me from the drawings Choegyal had sent.

I had so often imagined this return to my friends that I felt I was being reeled in by an invisible line attached to the solar plexus. It drew me over the bridge, then through the gate, under strings of prayer flags and up between the rows of lay housing and the lay children's school, and past the carpet center, its doors wide open to the clatter of looms and weavers singing. Two boys shouted greetings, then raced ahead.

I followed them up wide steps toward the temple, and before I reached the terrace stretching in front of it, I heard the drum. Of course! The monks were rehearsing. I'd timed my visit to coincide with the annual lama dances in honor of Padmasambhava; they were the liturgical high point of the year. And there was the dance master himself, Khamtrul Rinpoche, standing off to the side. Now he spoke to the drummer and moved out onto the dancing ground. Arms outstretched, booted feet lifting, swiveling, he demonstrated a sequence for the monks, his great bulk gliding as smooth as a ship in sail.

Later he showed me every room and statue in the temple; on murals by the main altar were scenes of the very earliest forms of Khampagar, when it moved about the hills of Kham in tents. Then Choegyal joined us, gaunt from recent illness, and Dorzong, looking almost fat by contrast, and once again we sat over tea. For a moment nothing seemed changed since those Dalhousie afternoons a decade past.

Coming straight from four years of graduate school, I had much to recount. I was excited by my studies of the Dharma, and since Khamtrul Rinpoche had initially inspired me on the path, I was eager for him to know what a good scholar I was becoming. I told him how I was learning Pali so I could read the ancient scriptures in the original and how I was discovering new depths of meaning in the Buddha's teaching of dependent co-arising. "Oh, Rinpoche, now I am understanding so much!"

"Aahh," he breathed, smiling on me affectionately, with infinite patience. When I paused, after rattling on some more, he simply asked: "Does this help you to increase in compassion?"

He seemed genuinely interested to know, but I was tongue-tied. His great moon of a face had kept beaming at me so I would not feel chastised as he explained: "It does not really matter how many things you know, so long as you fully experience what you do know. It seems you have learned a great deal about the Dharma. Now, if you let it permeate, it can change you totally."

He said, "It is not your getting knowledge or even enlightenment that matters. It is your wanting it for the sake of all beings." And he spoke to me of that rarest and most precious thing of all, motivation — the motivation to relieve the suffering of others, which is called *bodhicitta*. Without it, all striving and all uses of the intellect are not worth much. But with it, aahh, everything self-realizes; you're already home. So compassion is key. "Try to really feel the suffering of another, even an animal. Pull it into yourself, fearlessly."

On an embankment carved by a mountain stream that marked the eastern edge of the land perched a small house. A room was swept for me there, and I unrolled my sleeping bag, strung a line for my washing. In the week before the dances I divided my days between helping in the office and basking in the life of Tashi Jong. Some of the children who used to play with Chris, Jack, and Peggy in Dalhousie were monks now, others apprentice carpet weavers, and a new crop of youngsters raced up the lane when school was out. When I stopped by their classes, they liked showing off the singsong English they were learning.

The blowing of the conch wakes me early; I lie in my bag and listen. I can't hear the chanting, but the drums and horns carry far in the dawn air. The omelet Poonam brings for my breakfast is delicious, and often cold. From its temperature I can judge how many conversations he's had en route from the rinpoches' kitchen.

Little Yeshi Chodon and four of her playmates come to my door, all wet this Sunday morning from bathing in the stream below my house. They are going on a picnic, so I give them my tangerine to share, but instead of running off, they cluster at my elbow watching me write. Five little *dakinis* disguised in dirty clothes and runny noses. Relinquishing my table, I set them to drawing. They're irrepressible; their giggles make the phlegm rattle in their throats and chests. A boy monk comes in to join the drawing party, but I don't detect much reverence on the part of my phlegmy dakinis. To them he's just another playmate.

Choegyal Tulku and I go through his paintings of the last years, choosing the ones to document with photographs, in case he sells them or gives them away. His Buddhas and celestial bodhisattvas, unusual for their grace and delicacy, seem to glow with the same light I see in him. But I most love the scenes he paints from life — quick watercolors and pen-and-ink sketches, so immediate and full of cherishing. Those that rise from his memory seem just as vivid — like the one of the Khampagar he visited as a boy to take teachings from

Khamtrul Rinpoche. A hazy golden splendor of gates and pennants and curving roofs amidst the blue-shadowed green of mountain forest.

Another watercolor, made this week, depicts Choegyal's own monastery of Dugu, but only partially. A speckled wash of soft grays — green-gray, pink-gray — blurs the lines of the amber-colored walls. "This is how I saw it last," he says, "looking back in tears." The foreground is a jumble of figures on horseback, monks' robes and hats, ponies, legs running. The Red Guards plundering the monastery are not visible.

"Now the whole world fills with that kind of suffering." Choegyal knew my grief over our war in Vietnam, and I had written, too, about the assassination of Dr. King, the riots, the crackdown in the name of law and order. To Choegyal the tragedy that befell Tibet was but one aspect of a more widespread disintegration. It challenges us, he said, not only to take the Dharma seriously, but also to adapt it in fresh ways.

He nodded as he listened to my reports; in return, he spoke of the old predictions — semi-secret prophecies attributed to Padmasambhava. Instead of the words we give our twentieth-century technologies, they use vivid images: horses running on wheels, iron birds flying. And for the competing nationalisms of our time, he relayed the phrase "a thousand thorns sprouting, each waving its own flag."

"Tell me, Choegyal Rinpoche, about the coming of the Kingdom of Shambhala."

Among the Tibetans I had been hearing references to this ancient prophecy, and conjectures that, after twelve centuries, it was coming true in our time. "Can you please tell me in your own words?" I asked. And slowly, with pauses to reflect, he did. Watching his face, I listened to every word. I was arrested by his description of the Shambhala warrior, for this was clearly a metaphor for the bodhisattva — the hero figure that had so caught my attention in my studies of Mahayana Buddhism. Later in my room by the gully, I wrote down what he said.

"There comes a time when all life on Earth is in danger. Barbarian powers have arisen. Although they waste their wealth in preparations to annihilate each other, they have much in common: weapons of unfathomable devastation and technologies that lay waste the world. It is now, when the future of all beings hangs by the frailest of threads, that the kingdom of Shambhala emerges.

"You cannot go there, for it is not a place. It exists in the hearts and minds of the Shambhala warriors. But you cannot recognize a Shambhala warrior by sight, for there is no uniform or insignia, there are no banners. And there are no barricades from which to threaten the enemy, for the Shambhala warriors have no land of their own. Always they move on the terrain of the barbarians themselves.

"Now comes the time when great courage is required of the Shambhala warriors, moral and physical courage. For they must go into the very heart of the barbarian power and dismantle the weapons. To remove these weapons, in every sense of the word, they must go into the corridors of power where the decisions are made.

"The Shambhala warriors know they can do this because the weapons are *manomaya*, mind-made. This is very important to remember, Joanna. These weapons are made by the human mind. So they can be *un*made by the human mind! The Shambhala warriors know that the dangers that threaten life on Earth do not come from evil deities or extraterrestrial powers. They arise from our own choices and relationships. So, now, the Shambhala warriors must go into training."

"How do they train?" I asked.

"They train in the use of two weapons." That is the word he used — weapons.

"What are they?" I asked. And he held up his hands the way the lamas hold the ritual objects of *dorje* and bell, as they dance.

"The weapons are compassion and insight. Both are necessary. We need this first one," he said, lifting his right hand, "because it provides us the fuel, it moves us out to act on behalf of other beings. But by itself it can burn us out. So we need the second as well, which is insight into the dependent co-arising of all things. It lets us see that the battle is not between good people and bad people, for the line between good and evil runs through every human heart. We realize that we are interconnected, as in a web, and that each act with pure motivation affects the entire web, bringing consequences we cannot measure or even see.

"But insight alone," he said, "can seem too cool to keep us going. So we need as well the heat of compassion, our openness to the world's pain. Both weapons or tools are necessary to the Shambhala warrior."

I awoke the next day to shouts from the temple terrace. The first day of the dances had dawned. I hurried over to watch lay men attach the ropes and heave on them in unison, slowly raising the great white canopy. It looked heavy till the poles were upright and the breeze billowed it from below. Blue knots of eternity were stitched into the fabric, and through their open centers I could see the blue sky. As the ground beneath was swept with brooms and blessings, it became the sacred mandala of mind. Along its sides, thrones were set in place for the rinpoches, musician monks lined up with their horns and cymbals and drums, and the families congregated, settling down with toddlers, umbrellas, prayer wheels, rosaries, dogs, baskets of pastry, bottles of pop — and among them were Indian hillfolk from nearby villages and the occasional camera-hung Westerner. Poonam had set up a chair for me, but I sat with Yeshi Chodon's family, on a corner of their mat near the rope, where I could see better.

The first day's Black Hat dance was the most beautiful of all to my eyes. Gauzy veils of all colors of the rainbow floated from the wide black brims, and through them I could glimpse the faces of monks I knew. Their features were in the concentrated repose of meditation as they stepped out slowly, majestically, lifting and turning their brocade boots under their brocade skirts. To see them give themselves over to the ancient steps and embody what transcended them moved me as powerfully as when I had first seen it back in Dalhousie. As the dance moved to its climax and the drums and cymbals quickened, the monks began to wheel and leap. My dancing brothers in their heavy robes under their tall, heavy hats with streaming veils twirled and leapt, faster and faster, till two by two they spun up the temple steps to disappear.

On the third day — I could hardly wait — came the Dance for the Dismemberment of the Ego. Once again I would see how the self-preoccupation that blocks our wisdom and corrodes our lives can be consumed. And there it was, in the center of the dance ground, a small clay doll in an open, triangular box. The three sides of the box stood for what holds the ego together: greed, hatred, and delusion.

The horns and cymbals were quiet, no sounds at all except birdcalls of morning, prayer flags flapping, a truck a mile away on the Kangra road. Suddenly a sharp staccato rattling, as four sprightly young skeletons entered with hand drums of human skulls. They wore grinning death's heads and short tattered shrouds, their boys' legs bare for once of monastic robes. Embodying fearlessness, they turned the dance ground into a cemetery, moving around the three-cornered box as if it were an open grave.

Soon, in succession, other forms appeared: damask-clad dakinis with ancient implements — hook, chain, bell — symbolizing the powers of meditation. Their movements and gestures were slow and repetitive, reminding me that to begin again, over and over, could be both tolerable and good. Then came the vigorous figures of Crow and Owl, dancing the energy and emptiness of daytime and nighttime consciousness. And then, at last, the stags. With flags fluttering from their antlers, they represented the enlightened mind. Leaping to ego's box on legs like coiled springs, they reached right in and made their meal. Dismembering the doll, they put pieces of its body to their mouths, cast the crumbling remains over their shoulders. The long horns sounded a victorious blast that the mountains echoed back.

Over the years since then I have returned to Tashi Jong. At different times, I came with Fran, Jack, Peggy, and Chris, and, as often as not, in the spring when the lamas dance. Their dances embody so much that I love in Tashi Jong — the vigor of the community and the wild beauty at its heart, its faithfulness to the Dharma — that they seem like one continuous, flowing tableau. Against that backdrop of moving figures, major changes for Tashi Jong were accepted and folded into the mind. Like the sudden death of Khamtrul Rinpoche.

When Choegyal wrote in January 1980 that his beloved teacher had just died in Bhutan and that his body was being brought back for cremation ceremonies in Tashi Jong, I didn't go right away. I decided to wait two months until the dances, because I thought that occasion might be the saddest of all for my friends there, and I wanted to be with them then. I could hardly imagine the rituals undertaken without the great dance master who had brought them out of Tibet and guided them in every year and every detail.

There was the new *stupa* for Khamtrul Rinpoche's ashes and also the grief that Choegyal shared with me, but once the dances began, little seemed changed. The huge white canopy was erected, the ground beneath it swept, and the horns blew for the Black Hat dancers to enter. The sight of them had always made me want to cry, but now more than ever. For solemnly, with utmost concentration and a strange kind of assurance, they were doing it without him. Without their lama and dance master, they were carrying on.

"There he is again," said the nurse from Holland, who had been serving Tashi Jong for the past year. She pointed to the white eagle we had been noticing on and off throughout the day. It had simply appeared that morning out of the blue, circling high over the dancing ground, then swooping down fearlessly, close over the spectators' heads. It would soar, wheel, and then again fly in, near and low, lower than the edge of the canopy, as if to see under it and bring the dancers into its line of sight. Sometimes, for a breathless moment, it would alight on the ground among us, like a stopped frame in a film, before lifting off again.

I had never seen such a bird, so majestic in its wingspan and gleaming feathers. It was foreign to northwestern India; the Dutch nurse, being an ornithologist of sorts, was quite sure about that. But she *had* seen it before — just once. That was at Khamtrul Rinpoche's cremation ceremony. She described to me how, when the smoke rose from the burning stupa that held the remains, a white eagle appeared, ascending in circles through the cloud of pale, drifting ash. Now here it was again, as everyone could see.

A huge happiness filled me, but none of the Tibetans seemed to share my astonishment. The monks were too focused on the ceremony to be diverted. As for the lay people, they watched the bird from time to time, and when I caught their eyes and gestured my amazement — "There he is!" — they just grinned back at me and nodded.

In the dusty twilight, as the canopy was lowered and folded for the night, the great bird flew off. I thought, how pleased he must be with what he had seen.

On the day of the Dance for the Dismemberment of the Ego, there again, in the center of the ritual ground, was the little open three-sided box with the clay doll. More keenly than ever I watched the powers that assailed it — the skeletons of fearlessness, the dakinis of meditation, the flag-bedecked stags of enlightened mind. That evening I sat talking with Choegyal and Dorzong on the verandah of their hillside house above the temple. Still filled with the excitement I found in the dance, I began telling them how I had shared it with friends in America and even adapted it at a retreat center for social activists.

"We dug clay out of a stream bank and each person made their *own* ego doll." I recalled how absorbed and even tender my companions had been in shaping their ego figure out of clay — and how appropriate that seemed because each, with its different defenses, was the work of a lifetime.

My tulku brothers listened attentively. I went on. "We didn't have skeletons and dakinis and stags, of course. Instead we displayed our egos to each other and paraded them around, because egos love to be admired. That very act seemed to free us. With chanting and drumming we cast them back into the flowing stream and … watched them … dissolve."

My words began to falter. Discomfort overtook me. In the presence of these rinpoches I felt embarrassment, even shame, that I had taken their ancient, sacred ritual and adapted it — with people who were not even Buddhist.

"I'm sorry," I said, "if I was disrespectful."

The two rinpoches listened to me with straight faces, avoiding each other's eyes. No, they saw no problem. After all, I had not claimed to be teaching or reenacting the dance itself. Dorzong excused himself now for his evening meditation, and Choegyal walked me down the path.

We stood at the swinging iron gate, where the path dips down toward the temple precincts. It was almost dark, the first fireflies appearing, dancing, disappearing. Choegyal Rinpoche had an observation to make about the matter I had raised, of disclosing Dharma teachings to people who aren't Buddhist. Leaning toward me, he said, in a stage whisper, "Joanna! The Buddha was not a Buddhist!"

MOVING INTO DEEPER WATERS

16

Bridge Over the Charles

JACK LEFT FOR TUFTS UNIVERSITY in the fall of 1976 to study environmental engineering. When he came home for Christmas at the end of his first semester, he handed me a term paper he had written for one of his freshman courses. "Maybe you'd like to read this." The title was "Thermal Pollution from Nuclear Reactors."

I embarked on it dutifully, wading through statistics and footnotes about the volumes of water being continuously cycled through American nuclear power stations to cool their cores. Soon sheer fascination took over, as Jack's paper reported what the heated water was doing to our rivers and lakes when it was pumped back out. "This can't be true," I protested in disbelief. I could understand how a change in temperature shifted the balance of an ecosystem, but I did not want to believe that the damage, once known, would still be permitted. "Is this common knowledge? How can our government allow this to happen? Why aren't fishermen and biologists raising a furor?"

"And, Mom, those are only the *thermal* effects of nuclear power. I didn't even deal with the radioactive pollution." Neither of us realized it at the time, but over that Christmas holiday, amidst the parties in our cooperative household and ski days on our favorite slopes, Jack was beginning to give me an environmental education that would change my life.

The following spring, in May 1977, Peggy and I drove to Boston for a weekend visit with Jack. He showed us around the Tufts campus, took us to his favorite Indian restaurant, and told us that he had gotten us tickets for a big event the next day. Jacques Yves Cousteau, a family hero, would be speaking at the Boston Coliseum, where the Cousteau Society was staging an all-day symposium on threats to the biosphere.

Gulping down breakfast, the three of us caught the T in Cambridge and crossed the Charles River in time for the morning program at the Coliseum.

John Denver was singing "Rocky Mountain High" when we took our seats. Then we listened to an array of speakers, including the wiry, ageless Frenchman we had come to hear. With bitter passion Cousteau described the condition of the seas he had traveled in all corners of our planet: the drifting garbage, the decimation of marine life through oil spills, sludge, plutonium, and, most ominous of all, the dying of the plankton. It seemed we needed those micro-organisms not only for the nourishment of ocean species but for oxygen — and pollution was killing them off. If current pollution rates continued, we could suffocate. Other voices brought us news about deforestation, soil erosion, famine. In the interludes John Denver's music, reminding us of our love for our Earth, helped us keep on listening and not go numb.

Peggy, Jack, and I spent the afternoon moving from one exhibit to another, from briefings and workshops to panel discussions by scientists and activists. It was an immense bazaar of apocalyptic information, backed up with first-hand reports, film clips, photographs, sheets of data. We listened to a panel on radioactive contamination from nuclear power plants, then another on oil spills. A law requiring double hulls would cut oil spills in half, I learned, but the oil companies were blocking it. I stared at maps of the Adirondack and Ontario lakes — fifty percent already lifeless from acid rain. Scrubbers on smokestacks hundreds of miles to windward would change the picture, but industry resisted the added cost. Another booth showed charts on the worldwide spread of deserts, recalling the changes I had recently encountered in Delhi. Just ten years after we had lived there, the droughts were longer, the temperatures higher, the dust storms from Rajasthan blowing in stronger. Graphs showed how reforestation and permaculture could reverse the trend, if the political will could be found.

The information had a familiar ring. Our New Environment Association meetings in Syracuse had acquainted me with many of the issues, but I had never been subjected to such a broad and unrelenting barrage of bad news. My feet ached.

It is late in the afternoon. Peg and Jack have spun off for a soda in the canteen. Alone, I sink onto a chair in a darkened alcove. Almost no one is there, but the screen in the depths of the alcove is alive with projected images: a film on the fur trade is playing over and over. I watch it dully, wondering how the camera person managed to hide from his subject in such a flat, bare landscape. Surely he stayed out of sight, for who would want to be filmed in such an occupation?

The man in the cowboy hat, who is working on the Arctic ice, could be straight out of a Marlboro ad; he's handsome and rugged-looking and pauses now and then to light up a cigarette. On the ground, wedged tight between his boots, a baby seal is squirming and bobbing. The work is slow and methodical; great care must be taken while clubbing the head, so as not to mar the fur and reduce its commercial value. As well as strength in the legs, it requires skill to strike with precision and just enough force to cause internal bleeding, without breaking open the skull or popping the eyes. But the Marlboro man is clearly experienced; he looks so sure and calm, whacking away like some expert golfer, then straightening up to take a breather and rest his eyes on the horizon, squinting a little against the wind.

That stunned me the most — not the little seal, whose sleek, still perfect-looking head reclined now on the ice, but the utter composure in the face of the man. I leaned forward to try to see the mouth and the eyes under the broad-brimmed hat, peered at the features as if catching my own reflection in some kind of collective mirror. For he was all of us. Weren't we all, in the ways we lived and consumed, wasting our world?

This realization was followed by another. It occurred as I was heading back to Cambridge across the river.

Peggy and Jack stayed on for the rock concert that culminated the symposium, and I headed back on the T to dinner with friends. The benches ran lengthwise; I sat facing the passengers on the opposite bench, looking through the windows behind them as the train emerged into daylight to cross the bridge. It was an idyllic scene, the sunset gleaming on the broad expanse of the Charles, sailboats heeling in the wind and light. At that moment something gave way inside me. I found myself looking at the faces across the aisle through tears that I was powerless to stop or hide. It felt like the collapse of some inner scaffolding that for years had been holding the kind of information I had harvested all day, holding it up and out of the way, on a shelf in my mind. As that scaffolding crumbled, years of stored knowledge about what we were doing to our planet — to ourselves — cascaded into my heart and body, bringing a realization I could no longer keep at bay: yes — we can succeed now in destroying our world.

Hadn't every exhibit of the day demonstrated that? Hadn't that knowledge been lurking all along in every sight of streaming smokestacks, clear-cut forests? That knowledge came out of hiding now.

I had no idea how to live with it. Over the coming days and weeks and months it would return at odd moments, like a blow to the solar plexus. The most ordinary things, the slamming of a screen door, the smell of mown grass, made tears blur my eyes. Simply to hear Peggy laughing with Phil in the kitchen, or Scott at the piano playing a Bach partita, could catch me off-guard, and I would wonder how long before those sounds died out forever in the silences of space.

I could not use reason to snap out of it. It was reason that told me what our chances were. The evidence was in, and mounting. We all knew it, at some level, and still chose not to know; and that was the most telling indictment of all. The willful ignorance that I had hugged around my shoulders — for how long? — had been taken from me. Exposed, I felt chilled to the core of my being, awkward with the grief, baffled that we should be born to it.

I, who had always been open with my family and friends, was strangely reluctant now to reveal my state of mind. In bed at night I sought refuge in Fran's arms, pressed my face into his chest like an animal seeking its burrow; but I didn't talk much, not to my loved ones. There was an instinctive desire to protect them from what I saw. Also, I did not want them to worry about me — which they would if they could guess what I was going through. Furthermore, the matter was too important to be cast in terms of "what's wrong with Joanna?" or in well-meaning conjectures about the stresses of dissertation writing. Words of cheer and comfort would be offered, and I wanted none.

With my colleagues in the Religion Department, my other home, I felt freer to speak. Questions of ultimate meaning were, after all, their stock in trade. Those daring, broad-gauged thinkers who confronted the death of God would surely be able to hear what plagued me now. It was hard, though, to put into words when I grabbed some time alone with Jim, my closest friend on the faculty.

"I'm not saying that the world *will* end; you make me sound like some cartoon figure. I'm only saying it *can* end — now, in our time. That realization in itself, when you let it in, is so staggering...." I had always taken for granted that we would survive, as if we had some God-given right to survive, as if we were immune to the fate of other species who, after flourishing for a while, failed to adapt, went extinct. Now that fatuous assumption had collapsed, and all the systems theory I had studied became hideously relevant.

Mildly, reasonably, Jim pointed out that apocalyptic notions were not new. Consider the First Millennium, or the fourteenth century during the Black Plague, when many believed the world was at its final hour. He seemed to be suggesting that, because people's fears had been wrong then, any present fears were also wrong, old hat, dismissable.

But those situations, I argued, were different from today. Now the warnings of apocalypse came not from those who believe in a God of judgment, but from scientists, soberly interpreting their data. "We may pull through, but the certainty of a future is lost to us now. I don't know how to live with that loss without going numb, or crazy. Jim, the very meaning of your work, like mine, is based on the assumption that generations will come after us."

Jim relit his pipe. "Surely, with all your study of self-organizing systems, you can hardly think that all intelligent life in the universe is concentrated here on this one planet." He understood, he said, that the loss I felt was distressing me, but in the larger view of things it was far from final. We can certainly assume that elsewhere in this vast cosmos consciousness will continue to unfold.

I waited for the wink or laugh that would show that he was kidding, that he was just treating me to a parody of academic detachment. But when he glanced at the clock and said he had to leave soon for his son's basketball game, it sank in that he had been serious. I was too nonplussed to respond; but on my way home from the department, I had plenty to say.

"How fine," I muttered as I drove, "that the premise of consciousness existing somewhere else helps you face so calmly the passing of our own world. Try telling me that as you cheer your son on the basketball court, or behold your lovely daughter figure skating, or sip your cherished Tanqueray gin. Try pretending you're not in love with life on Earth — it's not the center of the universe, but it's all you know and have and are."

That evening after badminton, when it grew too dark to play and the others went inside, I stayed in the back yard, staring into the sky. It was the deep blue of a late northern spring, moonless and strewn with stars. Of course, among those trillions of suns and their planets, there had to be conscious life. I only wished it could see us and learn from us. Then our situation would be easier to bear.

Peering into the Milky Way, I imagined other minds out there capable of connecting with ours. With an urgency of intention, I reached out to them.

"See us," I whispered. "See this beautiful planet of ours, where life has flourished with ferocity and brilliance. And see, above all, how we are stomping it out. See what fear and greed can do."

On many nights that summer, I'd find myself doing it again — stopping in my tracks and staring upwards. The prayers I beamed out, and often wrote later in my journal, were not for rescue, but for attention, that our story here on Earth might serve as a teaching.

"I don't ask that you save us, only that you learn from us. Learn what happens when you fail to love the life you're given, when you turn your world to profit and possession. Please take heed, lest the music of your Mozarts be silenced, the words of your Buddhas and Shakespeares disappear, as if they had never been uttered."

We moved back to Washington D.C. that year, settling once again into the Lowell Street house. Fran was setting up a national program modeled on his adult education service in central New York. Peggy had two more years of high school and I my dissertation to complete. Soon I took a part-time job teaching a world religions course at American University.

All the while, below the surface, a dark, obsessive labor continued to grip me. It seemed to have taken hold of both my mind and my body, emerging as sensations and feeling states that activated intense thought. Since it did not *start* on the cognitive level, as a philosophical problem, I could not say with any precision what this labor was. I only knew it had to do with the meaning of life in a world that humans were destroying.

I kept thinking, we have to find a way to live in this planet-time without closing our eyes to what we're doing. Both systems theory and Buddhist practice helped. I remembered how open systems restructure themselves in response to challenge. In order for new values, new organizing principles to emerge, they undergo "positive disintegration." In our evolution, we have been through this process many times; it is inevitably disorienting. To survive, the system just needs to stay open to feedback.

Vipassana practice seemed designed for that purpose. It had taught me that we're perfectly capable of sustained attention to the flow-through of experience, including the failing condition of our world and the despair that evokes. Vipassana provided me no haven from the world and no protection from my sorrow, but that was why I trusted it and found that it could steady me.

This bare-bones meditation practice was more help to me than conversations with real-live American Buddhists. The Naropa Institute in Boulder had recently been founded by Chogyam Trungpa, and I spent a week there during the summer of 1977 and again in '78, along with Gregory Bateson and other systems thinkers. To some friends there I spoke of my struggle to come to terms with the plight of our world and the collective suffering in store for all beings. I wanted to take action on at least some of the social and environmental issues, I said, and Buddhist equanimity seemed beyond me.

My friends at Naropa let me know that they considered me rather attached to the world of appearances and easily sidetracked from the real aims of Dharma practice. The goal, I was reminded, was to liberate the mind from suffering. "Joanna, how can you be liberated from suffering if you still cling to it like this?" Mitchell asked. There was pity in his question, if not contempt.

Nina detected some self-righteousness in my concerns for the fate of the world. She herself had jettisoned such concerns when she relinquished her activism of the sixties. "Even nonviolent action is laying a trip on somebody, and probably worse for its piety. It is hubris to assume that you know what others need, and useless to try to change society. All you can change is yourself." Fed up, I dropped the subject.

Back in Washington I started showing up at conferences and working groups of Ralph Nader's anti-nuclear organization Critical Mass. It felt good to confront, in immediate, practical ways, the specter that had haunted me since Jack's paper on pollution from reactors — and, for that matter, since August 1945 in the farmhouse kitchen and the CIA screening of the H-bomb blast seven years later. Now there was much to learn and to do. And there were such good folks to do it with that something happened to the lonely despair that had come upon me on the Charles River bridge. It wasn't banished but absorbed, put to use.

I volunteered to help with an understaffed project. Vigorous new friends entered my life; with hard work and laughter, they taught me a lot as we undertook a lawsuit concerning a reactor complex to windward of Washington. Its name was North Anna.

17

North Anna

OUR PROJECT WAS A CITIZENS' LEGAL INTERVENTION against VEPCO, the Virginia Electric Power Company. We sought a court injunction to stop it from overloading the storage pool at its North Anna reactor. The power station was located near the town of Louisa, forty miles to windward of Washington, in the Piedmont area of Virginia where jobs were few, farming poor, and, I now learned, the old rock layers unstable. The reactor had been built astride an earthquake fault.

Its concrete pool, where irradiated fuel rods were suspended to cool once they were removed from the reactor core, was practically full now. VEPCO wanted to solve its waste storage problem by placing the rods closer together than safety regulations permitted. This move increased the risks of contamination, and of an accidental chain reaction.

Since we lacked funds for lawyers to compete with VEPCO's legal squads, four of us prepared the case ourselves. My three colleagues, about twenty years younger than I, were keen and experienced strategists. I loved their quick-wittedness and buoyancy of spirit as they designed our intervention, sorted through the evidence, and told me what to do. My job was fairly straightforward: to collect data on the known health effects of radiation from nuclear power stations. So I spent afternoons poking around the library of the Nuclear Regulatory Commission down on "H" Street, and then late hours at home poring over whatever independent research we could get our hands on.

My brain was painfully slow in grappling with the radiological and medical reports, deciphering their graphs and columns of statistics, but the import of it all, as it gradually dawned on me, was staggering. Proximity to reactors, even those which had reported no accidents, correlated directly with sharp increases in miscarriages, birth defects, stillbirths, leukemia, and other cancers. I was both horrified and triumphant, sure that the court would be swayed by the shocking fruits of my research. My teammates laughed good-naturedly at my naiveté.

One night during that period I had a vivid dream. Before going to bed I had leafed through baby pictures of our three children to find a snapshot for Peggy's high school yearbook. In the dream I behold the three of them as they appear in the old photos and am struck most by the sweet wholesomeness of their flesh. Fran and I are journeying with them across an unfamiliar landscape. The terrain becomes dreary, treeless and strewn with rocks; little Peggy can barely clamber over the boulders in the path. Just as the going is getting very difficult, even frightening, I suddenly realize that, by some thoughtless but unalterable pre-arrangement, Fran and I must leave them. I can see the grimness of the way that lies ahead for them, bleak and craggy as a red moonscape and with a flesh-burning sickness in the air. I am maddened by sorrow that my children must face this without me. I kiss them each and tell them we will meet again, but I know no place to name where we will meet. Perhaps another planet, I say. Innocent of terror, they try to reassure me, ready to be off. Removed, and from a height in the sky, I watch them go — three small solitary figures trudging across that angry wasteland, holding each other by the hand and not stopping to look back. In spite of the widening distance, I see with a surrealist's precision the ulcerating of their flesh. I see how the skin bubbles and curls back to expose raw tissue as they doggedly go forward, the boys helping their little sister over the rocks.

I woke up, brushed my teeth, showered, had an early breakfast meeting on a proposal for research in Sri Lanka. Still the dream did not let me go. As I roused Peggy for school, I sank beside her bed. "Hold me," I said, "I had a bad dream." With my face in her warm nightie, inhaling her fragrance, I found myself sobbing. I sobbed against her body, her seventeen-year-old womb, as the knowledge of all that assailed it surfaced in me. All those studies on the effects of ionizing radiation, with their statistics on genetic damage, turned now into tears, speechless, wracking.

Jack, now in his sophomore year at Tufts, had joined in efforts to stop the construction of a large atomic power plant on the coast of New Hampshire. Seabrook, as the place was named, had become a major focus of the growing anti-nuclear movement. To complement legal challenges with direct action, including civil disobedience, networks of affinity groups, trained in nonviolence, sprang up in New England and the mid-Atlantic states. They were modeled on the mother of them all: Jack's Boston-centered Clamshell Alliance.

An occupation of the Seabrook site was planned for a weekend in June. I decided to join Jack there and signed up for the required training in nonviolence, so that I could hook up with an affinity group of my own. The group I joined was organized by the Movement for a New Society, the Philadelphia-based organization which had inspired our family to shift to a cooperative household. Mixing Gandhian teachings with Yankee ingenuity, it now played a key role in the anti-nuclear movement, sharing its philosophy and decision-making methods with the Clamshell Alliance, and later with the other networks modeled on it. The members of our affinity group were to serve as marshals for the several thousand protesters who, the next day, were to camp on land adjacent to the Seabrook power plant. We were allowed to enter the grounds the night before.

It was dusk on Friday when we parked at the end of a dirt road off Route 107. Scrub woods extended between a swamp and the wire fence enclosing the massive, silent hulks of the almost completed reactor. The bleak area had been used for a now-defunct chemical factory and, more recently, as the town dump. On a mud bank in the mosquito-filled woods, I opened packets of dried soup and stirred up supper for twenty over a single flame while the others raised our tents. Two ran back to find a phone, to check on the toilets and truckloads of wood chips ordered for the next morning. The chips were to cover the nearby mountain of stinking garbage, the only open space large enough for the protesters' meetings and the mammoth public rally planned for Sunday. Meanwhile the area had to be protected from troublemakers. I took the midnight watch with a young physicist from the University of Maryland who had driven up with a demonstration solar heater on his trailer.

Tired, I slept on in the bright morning sun until a rattling roar awakened me. I opened my eyes to see, through the mosquito netting, helicopters hover, pass over, return, as they would throughout our time there. But what kind of war zone was this, with voices laughing, joking, singing around me? Crawling out of my tent, I discovered a giant teepee standing nearby, and beyond it a geodesic dome had appeared overnight. My friend David, a Sanskrit scholar from the University of Pennsylvania, was tooting on a kazoo as he set up a table of leaflets. Amidst his sheets of data on nuclear power, I saw dozens more of the irreverent little mouthpipes. "Here's one for you, Joanna! A revolutionary is unprepared without a kazoo!"

Mid-morning the occupation commenced. Down the wide dirt path from the road off 107, the people of my country came, by the hundreds, walking in affinity groups, pennants fluttering from their backpacks. They had been walking for miles, and here they were at last — gray heads and baby buggies, banners, guitars, jugs on sticks — as if to take possession of their future. The papier-mâché seagulls of the Bread and Puppet Theatre bobbed higher than the scrub trees, undulating wings wider than the road. And then, behind them, I saw Jack with his affinity group from Tufts, bearing its banner, "Genesis." "There's Jack's Mom," I heard one of them shout, but I couldn't shout back, being too choked up with excitement, with pride.

On the chip-covered dump that afternoon a meeting was held, comprising some eighty or so "spokes," or spokespersons, from the affinity groups. Its purpose was to come to agreement on the nature and extent of any civil disobedience — such as actual entry into the power station and a sit-in at the state house in Manchester. Voices argued about whether or not to tape the discussion, but the police helicopters overhead and the screaming of the seagulls made the speakers hard to hear. Some militants from Boston seemed opposed to the idea, but Mark from Harlem, squatting near me, said, "Hey man, what've we got to hide? Aren't we building a world where everything's open?" That preliminary discussion went on for almost an hour. In the hot sun and the stench of garbage, I itched with impatience. I yearned for someone to leap up and take charge, issue a decree.

Yet I felt something else besides exasperation: a fascination with this living experiment in decision-making, everyone listening so carefully to each other, never interrupting. As slow and awkward as it was, it was beyond any kind of democracy *I* had known. I felt grateful for this glimpse of how, in the long run, we might be able to negotiate the big changes ahead that would affect us all.

By the time the "spokes" reached a consensus that they could report back to their groups, others had joined us on the dump. A bare-chested mime in bright suspenders performed Marcel Marceau's butterfly act, and we all did it with him, watching with delight our own dancing hands, our fluttering fingers. The poet Denise Levertov, a member of Jack's affinity group, stood up on the refuse to read to us, her mild voice needing to shout against the din of helicopters and gulls. Her Hiroshima poem articulated the anguish I felt for my people; but I did not see my dread reflected in the young faces around me. They listened with gentle appreciation, as if the apocalypse of our world was a given, and perhaps, for this moment, transcended.

An eddy of wind caught the stacks of informational sheets that David had so carefully arranged on his table, and whirled them skyward. "We're leafleting the helicopters!" laughed a voice at my side.

In this kind of crowd I would expect to catch whiffs of marijuana. I turned to Jack, "I haven't smelled any pot." "That's the agreement," he said. I had neither seen nor heard any announcement to that effect. Whence this agreement and how was this rock-solid discipline enforced?

That night I wandered alone through the protesters' encampment, slowly walking the winding paths they had traced through the woods. Back amidst the trees, the tents — sprung up like multi-colored mushrooms — glowed in the dark from the lantern-lights within. They murmured with voices, shadows of bodies dancing on their walls. In one of them, I didn't know which, Jack's affinity group was holding council on whether to engage in civil disobedience — there was no pressure, he said to me later, just quiet questioning: "What do you each want to do?" "What support do you need?" From an orange-glowing tent under low branches I heard a guitar, from another the humorous hum of a kazoo. The scene seemed ancestral. It both awakened and eased some nostalgia within me, as if I were coming home to something I had not known I yearned for. It reminded me of J. R. Tolkien stories I had read with the children, of his description of the elves' forest where the hobbit warriors, on their valiant, exhausting journey, found refreshment. Even stronger was the sense of being granted, as I wound through the lantern-silhouetted trees, a glimpse of the future.

On Sunday our numbers swelled tenfold, as people from Portsmouth and the surrounding towns poured in for the giant rally the protesters had organized. From a platform of planks, bands played rock and country music and speakers addressed the crowds. Water jugs and sunscreen were passed from hand to hand, and Jack made me a paper hat to shade my face as we listened to the teachers of the day. There was John Gofman, pioneer in isolating plutonium, precisely describing its lethal effects; and Barry Commoner, scientist and organizer, playing on the theme of our meeting on a dump, the refuse of a doomed society; and native Americans from the Longest Walk, who had crossed the country on foot. There was Pete Seeger and Benjamin Spock and Dick Gregory, who thanked the resisters here for showing that the enemy is not the redneck southern cracker but the capitalist system itself. I had some minutes on the platform, too, standing at the mike to lead a litany in praise of the one nuclear reactor we can trust: our sun.

Dirty at day's end and streaked with sweat, Jack hugged me good-bye. I clambered into the pick-up that had brought me; soon the swamp, the woods, the dark shell of the reactor were behind me. Out on 107, the truck picked up speed, taking us back into the world of lawn sprinklers and shopping malls. I hung out the window, letting the wind sting my eyes. The stars were coming out — the same stars I had called to earlier in despair. But now something inside me had lifted.

It was hard to hang on to the optimism I'd felt at Seabrook. A society of university teachers in science and the humanities met in Notre Dame that summer, and I was to chair a week-long working group on "The Prospects for Human Survival." The reports I read in preparation — on what was happening to the oceans, croplands, forests, all of it so out of control — churned up dread. Where, in the face of this knowledge, could we find hope and the courage to act?

Dispassionate professorial papers seemed inappropriate. To set a different tone, I invited the forty-some participants to introduce themselves not by referring to their academic positions, but by sharing a personal experience, or image, of how they'd felt the global crisis in their own lives. Some offered vignettes from their work on world hunger or arms control. A young chemist said simply, "My child was born." A psychologist recalled a day when his small daughter talked about growing up and having babies of her own and he discovered he doubted the world would last that long. Others offered images: dead fish washed up at a summer cottage, strip mines leaching like open wounds. Most encompassing was the image given by a teacher at Yale: the view from space of planet Earth, so small as it glittered there that it could be covered by the astronaut's raised thumb.

That image of our home, so finite that it can be blotted out by a single human gesture, kept re-emerging, cutting through the verbiage and academic one-upmanship to touch some raw nerve connecting us all. The group didn't disband when our sessions were over but reclustered around cafeteria tables at meals and kept reconnecting throughout the day; our talk was laced with laughter and plans for joint projects.

I learned two things that week: that the pain for the world which I carried around inside me was widely and deeply shared; and that something remarkable happened when we expressed it to each other. Instead of miring ourselves in doom and gloom, the opposite had happened. We had turned some key that unlocked our vitality.

What was this key? In the middle of the last night at Notre Dame, I found a canteen in the basement. Getting a coke from the soda machine, I stayed in that cement-block room scribbling notes as fast as my hand could move.

As with the turn of a kaleidoscope, my thoughts and dreams of the past year, since riding the T from the Cousteau symposium, reassembled themselves. A new pattern emerged, and in it I saw the logic of despair work. I named it that — "despair work" — because I knew about grief work and the need to validate anguish over the loss of a loved one. This was different, of course, because the full loss hadn't occurred yet and we hardly wanted to resign ourselves to it. But it was similar in the eneergy released by our willingness to feel inner pain.

The liberation which that willingness brings — the clarity of response as the feedback loops are unblocked — made total sense to me now, in terms of both systems theory and the Dharma. I remembered the first "weapon" of the Shambhala warrior: *karuna,* or compassion. Hadn't I understood, as Choegyal Rinpoche told me the old prophecy, that it meant to be unafraid of the suffering of the world and its beings — even our own?

The lawsuit against VEPCO failed. Despite our efforts, the operators of the North Anna reactor went ahead and crowded the irradiated fuel rods more tightly in the storage pool. Still, I had all this information on the health effects and wanted to share it with those most directly involved: the workers at the plant. I also had the idea of showing them a video, made by students at Hampshire College, dramatizing a meltdown at a nuclear station. With the help of a local activist, a public meeting was arranged to be held in the courthouse of Louisa, the town closest to the North Anna reactor.

In that Piedmont region of Virginia, folks were glad for any jobs that came their way. I didn't expect them to take kindly to criticisms of their nuclear power station — especially after I learned what had happened to the young geology teacher at a local college. While excavations for the reactor core were underway, he took pictures of the exposed layers of rock, which clearly revealed the suspected earthquake fault. He was trying to use them to stop the construction. One Sunday morning when he answered the doorbell, he was shot dead. The sheriff's office never managed to find a suspect.

I wondered if anyone would show up for the meeting besides Fran and Peggy, who accompanied me on the drive to Louisa that late March day in

1979. But should any townspeople or atomic workers attend, I was well-armed, not only with the video but with grim statistics on the dangers of nuclear power. As we drove south, I was rehearsing them in my mind, until we turned on the car radio. Something was happening in Harrisburg, Pennsylvania, at a nuclear power station called Three Mile Island.

Due to human error or technical malfunction, one of its reactors had gone out of control. A meltdown and explosion could occur momentarily. The governor of Pennsylvania was considering the wholesale evacuation of the area. The Atlantic seaboard from Connecticut to Delaware was on alert, as the country faced its first major nuclear accident.

The Louisa courthouse was packed that night. Atomic workers and their families crowded in; even some VEPCO officials were on hand, and the sheriff, too, leaning in the door frame. There was a hush as the meeting began and I stood up to talk. I looked into the faces before me — the mothers, the children, the men who were trying to support them. With sideburns, hair curlers, chewing gum, they were faces I would pass at any supermarket or gas station, but suddenly, somehow, they seemed intimate to me. My plan to show the video dropped away, along with all the arguments I had prepared.

"I've got to hand it to you," I heard myself say. "Here *I've* been worrying about what can happen here at North Anna, while I and my family live a hundred miles away. But *you*, you live and work right here in its shadow."

Babies squirmed and children broke free to run through the courtroom, but the adults were motionless. I was sure they knew of the accident at Three Mile Island; no point in my mentioning it. "I expect you have an evacuation plan," I said and looked at them inquiringly. And they looked at each other, and the VEPCO representatives looked at their hands. "Of course there's an evacuation plan," said one of them finally. "Well, where is it?" barked the sheriff from the doorway. And the people began to query each other. "Does it exist?" "Is it public?" "How would we know what to do?"

From then on I acted only as a kind of referee, helping people confer with each other and take turns to speak. Occasionally I threw in a question: "Are the firefighters and health workers drilled for an accident?" "Have you designated escape routes and communities you can flee to?" "Should those who are contaminated stay here or be removed?" "Should livestock and pets be left behind?"

"I guess you want to form your own committees," I said — somewhat after the fact, for people were already moving into clusters, buttonholing the sheriff, challenging the VEPCO officials, listening to each other. Nothing I could say could match what they were learning now, and preparing to learn together.

18

Sri Lanka

"REAL DEVELOPMENT IS NOT FREE TRADE ZONES and mammoth hydro-electric dams," the young trainer told us. "It's waking up to our own needs and our own power."

It was the summer of 1979. I was sitting in an open-walled classroom with two dozen Sri Lankan village workers, absorbing the principles of a movement that promised to revolutionize Third World development. "This awakening happens on different levels. It's personal and spiritual as well as economic and cultural. These aspects of our lives are all interdependent." I wished planners at the World Bank could hear him.

A Buddhist-inspired people's self-help movement, Sarvodaya Shramadana Sangamaya was the largest nongovernmental organization in Sri Lanka, active in several thousand villages. It modeled a different kind of development than that preached and promoted by the industrialized countries. I had encountered it three years earlier on a trip to South Asia while I was still at Syracuse. Throughout my graduate studies, I had sustained a strong interest in the potential for social change to be found in Asian religions, especially Buddhism. "Go talk to Ari," a community organizer in Bodh Gaya had advised me. He was referring to Sarvodaya's founder and president, A. T. Ariyaratne, a former high school teacher. "Some call him the Gandhi of Sri Lanka."

I did as I was told, and on that same trip in 1976, I flew to Sri Lanka.

When I walked into Ariyaratne's crowded little office in the Sarvodaya complex outside Colombo, it took me no more than two minutes to know that I wanted to stay and learn from his movement. For in this voluble, diminutive dynamo I found a scholar-activist who took the social teachings of the Buddha seriously and dared to believe that they could inspire change in the modern world. He had banked his life on that conviction, drawing from ancient traditions to empower what he called "the poorest of the poor."

From Sanskrit, Gandhi had coined the term *sarvodaya*, meaning the "uplift of all." Ari brought it to Buddhist Sri Lanka and recast it in terms of awakening. That's what the Buddha did under the bodhi tree. He woke up. And that is what we all can do — awaken to our innate wisdom and power to act. Ari added the word *shramadana*, "gift of labor," so the movement's full name means, in effect, "everyone wakes up by working together". I listened with growing excitement. Here was the "liberation Buddhism" that I had imagined might be realized some day, with luck and the blessings of all bodhisattvas.

When I completed my doctoral dissertation two years later in 1978, Ari invited me to come live with Sarvodaya for a year and study how it worked. And so as soon as Peggy graduated from high school in 1979, a couple of months after Three Mile Island, I took off. I finished the teaching job I had at American University, wrapped up the failed lawsuit against VEPCO, helped Fran and the children make their plans for the coming year, and got on the plane for Sri Lanka. I came equipped with a typewriter, a modest grant from the Ford Foundation, and half a year's instruction in Sinhalese from kind monks at the Washington Buddhist Vihara. I had just turned 50.

My new home was a tropical island republic the size of Ireland or West Virginia. Known as Ceylon in its colonial past, it had a population of fifteen million and was considered among the poorest of Third World nations. Yet it presented an intriguing anomaly: its quality of life — measured in literacy, infant mortality, and life expectancy — was higher than that of more moneyed countries like India and Brazil. This might have puzzled development economists, but not Sarvodaya workers, who always remembered that, in its precolonial history, Sri Lanka was called the Isle of Dharma and Granary of the East.

My year's sojourn occurred during an expansive moment in the life of the Sarvodaya movement. Ari's ambitious plans were amply supported by foreign donors, mostly Dutch and German — and still tolerated by the new pro-industrial Colombo government. No one could know that within four short years the sanity and tranquillity of Sri Lanka would be shattered by a bloody civil war which would ravage the country for decades.

As soon as I arrived, I wandered around the expanded Sarvodaya headquarters. Most offices were now housed in a new complex called *Damsak Mandir*, Abode of the Dharma Wheel. A bright, white octagon of two-story buildings surrounded a flowering courtyard, with each of its eight sides representing an aspect of the Eightfold Path. Training offices were lodged in Right View, the library in Right Speech, accounting in Right Mindfulness. Wall maps dotted with pins marked Sarvodaya villages — over four thousand at last count — as well as the dozen district centers, where local projects were launched. Across the road I found a labyrinth of tree-shaded paths that linked assorted bungalows, workshops, and outdoor classrooms, every section teeming with activity. Training facilities for traditional crafts like batik were flanked by models for windmills and biogas generators.

At sunset, I retraced my steps to the eight-sided courtyard where I joined the evening "family gathering." With palms together, I added my voice to the chanting of the precepts, hummed along with a Sarvodaya song, tried to pick out recognizable Sinhalese phrases from the speeches. Alongside the Dharma wheel and the Buddha statue were symbols sacred to Hinduism, Islam, and Christianity. These minority religions, accounting for a quarter of the island's population, were revered along with the faith that so stamped Sarvodayan thought. My mind wandered. I was too fatigued from jet lag not to rest my eyes on my new companions — white shirts and sarongs on brown skin; brown midriffs between tight bodices and long, wrap-around skirts; flowers tucked in gleaming black hair.

I jumped at a familiar sound, a version of my name: *Joanna-akka*. I was introduced and invited to speak, just as I had been on my visit three years earlier. I told them I had come back to learn the lessons of Sarvodaya so that I could help my own country "wake up."

Joanna-akka — "big sister Joanna." I was part of a family now, where family names are used. When you add the suffixes denoting kinship — *nangi* for "little sister," *malli* and *ayya* for "younger" and "older brother" — trust is evoked, and a readiness to share. It cuts across all differences of class and caste. I'd soon hear myself also referred to as *Suddu-akka*, meaning "white big sister," and later on as *Motorcycle-ekeng-akka*, or "motorcycle-going big sister".

I earned this name after I bought a used Honda 90 from a Colombo policeman. I had to get around on my own, and this form of transport not only suited my needs but gratified the part of me that loved whizzing down a ski slope. Swift enough to overtake trucks and tough enough to handle anything this side of a stream bed, it was cut away in front of the saddle, permitting a long skirt. In the villages, no Buddhist woman my age would be seen with bare legs or in slacks. The obliging cop threw in lessons, for I had never driven a motorcycle except in fantasy. He drilled me in a grassy field, where I swooped and swerved between the cows before venturing into the terrifying traffic of Galle Road, the main artery running south through Colombo and down the coast to the port-town of Galle at the island's tip. I would come to know it well. I christened my Honda "Pruey," after a workshop game my family and I liked to play.

I decided to enroll in two Sarvodaya training programs for village workers. Each lasted two weeks. The first laid out the overarching principles, and the second was just for women. Through its preschools, community kitchens, and classes in nutrition, health, and prenatal care, the movement engaged village women from the start. This built the "psychological infrastructure," as Ari called it, which fostered lasting change for a village.

When the other trainees left headquarters to return to their villages, I left, too, for the rural community of Baddegama in the South, which I had chosen as my home for the rest of the year. There, near one of its district centers, I would study Sarvodaya in action.

I opened Baddegama slowly, like an extraordinary, unhoped-for gift. It was a small town, or network of villages, set amidst rice paddies, stands of coconut palms, rubber trees, and occasional low-land tea gardens. Only in dreams do things unfold like this. Only in dreams do I walk the early morning between emerald paddy fields to palm tree islands where hidden dwellings cluster and a man in a white sarong steps off his bike to walk beside me and invite me to breakfast with his family, his stunning, studious son, his books. Only in dreams does the gabled, fretted house on the knoll, with its fanciful staircases curving down toward the road, announce itself as the place where I will live. It wasn't like coming home — the place was too foreign to all past experience — but I felt that some cramp in me would ease. The sunlight and breeze and rain washing across the sea of paddy would, I knew, wash through me, too.

Venerable Saranankara, the seventy-year-old *bhikkhu,* or monk, presiding at the local Buddhist temple, took an immediate interest in my welfare. He swiftly persuaded a Colombo businessman to rent me his ancestral home. Perched on a rise under towering trees, it was halfway between the temple and the Sarvodaya district center. A fluctuating number of the landlord's family servants occupied the rear portions, and now shopped and cooked for me as

well. I usually had more than I could eat, since Ven. Saranankara took to sharing with me the *dana,* or alms, he received from the faithful and sending over
clusters of king coconuts, stalks of sweet ripe bananas, woodapples, mangoes.
It struck me as marvelously appropriate that his name meant "giver-of-
refuge".

The old bhikkhu and I became good friends. I often heard him refer to
me as a "brave and learned lady" — brave, I assumed, because of the motorcycle and learned because of my study of the Buddha's awesome doctrine of
causality. We talked about it some, but mostly we gossiped. Our conversations
skittered from subject to subject. Any topic would do; it was each other's company that mattered. His temple enchanted me. The *vihara,* or monk's residence, the bodhi tree, the preaching hall, and the domed stupa, or *dagoba,* all
were on different levels and angles of a verdant loaf-shaped hill. To climb the
wide stone stairways, mossy with age in the shadows of flowering jacarandas,
to run my hand along the parapet and lean my body against it to look out
across the land, to answer the greetings and grins of the younger monks, gave
me a pleasure indescribably sweet. From the start it felt familiar.

"Bhante, do you think I was a monk here once?" I asked early on. "Of
course not!" Saranankara sounded shocked. "You were my sister." I had no lit-
eral belief in the transmigration of souls, but I enjoyed playing with the notion,
and in these temple precincts the sense of déjà vu was so strong I indulged the
fantasy that I had lived here once, in robes, with him. Perhaps, in a distant
drama, I had chosen to leave, driven by some compulsion, or curiosity, to take
the Dharma beyond the confines of tradition, to test it in the outside world.
But the old bhikkhu was sure that I had never been a monk and soon started
saying with casual certainty, "You were my mother." He gazed with fresh interest on my snapshots of Chris and Jack and Peggy, commenting on the intelligence he detected in their faces, as if sensing a sibling tie to them. When once
more, in an off-hand manner, I raised the possibility of my earlier monkhood,
the old bhikkhu dismissed the idea as absurd, almost as if I were accusing
myself of some crime. I finally realized I was doing just that. A monk reborn
as a woman must have been a very bad monk indeed!

To reach my quiet Baddegama home from Colombo, I would ride south for two
or three hours along Galle Road. One day as I started out, my mind was preoccupied by an article I was finishing. It concerned Buddhist teachings in the light
of general systems theory. The questions I had raised in it still echoed in me.

Since both bodies of thought see change as the prevailing feature of reality, can steadiness be found in change *itself?* Maybe the early Buddhists focused attention on the body's decay because life in those times seemed so steady and *un*changing. Today, battered as we are by shocks and future shocks, we need no reminders of transiency. Instead we need to learn to feel steadiness *in* the beat, constancy *in* the flow, so that change can be ridden smoothly like a wave.

As I maneuvered Pruey through the fumes and chaos of urban Colombo, I began to answer my own questions. Change is only scary when it catches you off balance, when it hits you broadside or socks you from behind. If you go *with* it, there's all the joy and exhilaration of skiing, where you have to keep your weight forward, away from the hill, using the moguls as springboards and not holding back from shifts in the terrain. When you clutch and lean back, that's attachment. It turns to timidity and greed, and makes you more likely to fall.

Could there be an experience of *time*, I wondered, that would allow us to be unafraid of change?

Traffic was easing now as the road ran along Sri Lanka's southwest shore. Then an amazing thing occurred. That whole eighteen-mile stretch from Induruwa to Hikkaduwa turned into a kind of *satori* experience. I began to feel the motion of the motorcycle not as *change*, but as pure unbroken continuity. I was trying to reach for a still point within the movement itself, when all at once, without any transition, I was *in* it. I was suddenly not moving. I could feel the vibration of the motor under my seat and the wind on my face, but I was not moving. I sat there, suspended in the stillness at the center of all phenomena, where there's nowhere else to go. I seemed, incredibly, not even to be driving the bike. It was like the penny arcade game where you steer a car down a road that is coming at you on the screen while you yourself don't move. Yet it was not exactly like that, because I wasn't the one driving the bike, certainly not the only one. The road was driving it, and so were the people and buses and carts, and the crazily leaning palms.

Consciousness was everywhere, no longer contained in my skull, no longer divided up into separate heads and walled in behind separate pairs of eyes. The air was thick with it, mythically dense and spongy, all colors very vivid. The world was coming toward me and greeting me — a steady thrum of greeting, with me not moving and all my senses freshly open to each face as it approached me and moved by me. Each angle of house and tilt of gutter was so perfect, so couldn't-be-otherwise. Everything was orchestrated to permit us,

each and all, to reach this moment with perfect timing and precision — the guy
walking out of the privy, all the eatings and shittings that enabled him to arrive
just so on the scene, exactly on cue. "Oh, here you are again!" I thought — you
bank of purple flowers by the white wall in the wash of afternoon light — "I've
been seeing you always, I've been waiting for you always."

It was that sense of homecoming, in the golden glow on the faces along
the western sea, that made me begin to cry. There I was, going down Galle
Road, through the erratic traffic of a Wednesday afternoon in December, with
tears trickling down behind my sunglasses. As the consciousness-broken-loose
swerved my bike neatly between buses and carts and an occasional tourist lim-
ousine, the thought arose that with this experience of time, you need no haven
or final rest to strive for. You make your home in the very midst of change.

My fascination with the shramadanas was growing. From the start, these village work camps had constituted the movement's central organizing strategy.
When Ari was still teaching high school, he heard about church-sponsored
work camps in postwar Europe. He immediately saw how that practice could
fit with the Buddha Dharma and how it could generate self-reliance and solidarity. But he didn't say, "Here's a great idea from the West, let's adopt it and
imitate it." He said, "Let's draw from our own traditions and our own
strengths." Using the word Gandhi had coined for the maintenance of his
ashram and the cleaning of its latrines — *shramadana*, gift of labor — Ari took
the concept much further.

Sarvodaya's slogan was "We build the road and the road builds us." The
process started early. A movement organizer would invite villagers to gather,
perhaps in their temple's preaching hall, to discuss their needs and to deliber-
ate on the choice of a project. Should they first dig some public latrines, or
clear the weed-choked irrigation canal, or open a short-cut to the nearest bus
route? Then they considered where tools would be found and who would do
what. This process was slow, involving more and more people, from elders to
children. By the time the actual shramadana began, a good part of its purpose
— to get the community working together — had already been achieved.

Teenagers were lugging out car batteries and hanging loud speakers
from the trees when I arrived at my first road-building shramadana. "You
can't work without music!" they informed me. Huge cooking pots appeared
as well, along with baskets of the food that the children had collected from
every household. Older women scolded and laughed as they cleaned the rice,

chopped pumpkin, and scraped coconut for curries. I joined one of the eight work teams, and we counted off to see who would be our leader for the first shift. The lot fell to a thirteen-year-old who made sure we each got a *mamoty* — a heavy Dutch hoe — and led us to our work site.

There we set to, hacking at an embankment above the narrow footpath while another team heaved the dirt away in a bucket brigade. Once the path was widened, it would be flattened to allow passage for carts and cars. I was barefoot like the others, and a little worried about losing a toe to my unwieldy mamoty. So I was awkward at the start, in my long skirt, dancing my feet out of the way, but no one made fun of me.

When the sun was directly overhead, we propped our tools against the bank, walked back to sit on woven mats in the shade, and ate the fine curries the grandmothers had cooked for us. Then we lingered for a midday "family gathering." The bhikkhu led us in chanting the Triple Refuge and the Five Precepts, and Priya from the Baddegama center gave a talk on Sarvodaya philosophy. "It's better," he told me, "to teach ideas *after* people have worked together. That way you give words to what they have already experienced for themselves." Now a local member of Parliament stood to speak — and, inspired by the occasion, broke into song. It was a fairly long song, in the island's ancient mode of spontaneous verse. Next came the traditional oil-lamp dance, which somebody's great-aunt had taught the village children. It always riveted me with concern, for the dancing flames spun around in the children's sweeping gestures. Finally random participants in the shramadana stood up to address the assembly. Some had never spoken before the whole village, where they might have felt resented as an estate owner, or despised as a landless laborer, or ignored as a woman. Yet whoever we were, we had just been toiling side by side, addressing each other in kinship terms, eating from the same pot. It was easier now, and a relief, to break through the old social barriers.

Sitting on the matting in the latticed shade, my dress sweat-glued to my skin, I thought of the work parties at the communal garden back in Syracuse, the potlucks afterwards. As with the folks here, I couldn't imagine us doing it for pay, or without fun. My mind began to travel through time. Was I back with my ancestors in one of the Minnesota barn-raisings Daidee used to describe? Or was I sensing the promise for the future that I had felt at the Seabrook encampment? Were these two visions related somehow?

Much of my "participant observer" research entailed interviewing Sarvodaya monks, for the more progressive ones offered vivid examples of the role that clergy can play in social change. They opened their temple precincts to Sarvodaya preschools and literacy and sewing classes. They drew from old Dharma stories to teach courage and self-respect. They used their status to draw villagers together in "family gatherings," recruited school drop-outs to help organize shramadanas, and encouraged the young women and girls to take part. By their very presence they stilled any disapproving gossip about village daughters mixing with boys. My hunger for these lessons was insatiable.

Many of these monks were accessible within an hour's ride of my village home. I would head off on my motorcycle in the afternoon, notebook in saddlebag and Ramani perched behind me. A bright eighteen-year-old, Ramani served as my local interpreter, for my Sinhalese was inadequate for discussions of philosophy and social change. Ramani was Christian, which accounted for her spunky readiness to straddle the rear seat of my motorcycle as we careened down the packed dirt roads; Buddhist females were conditioned to be more shy about their person and less venturesome. Across the countryside we sped, singing rounds — our favorite of the season was "Happiness runs in a circular motion" — till the gleaming dome of the dagoba that was our destination appeared round a bend. We would park Pruey by the gateway of the temple's compound and cross the broom-swept sand to look for our monk in the open-walled preaching hall, or inquire for him at the door of the vihara.

Ah, there stood our venerable bhikkhu, all smiles. In a swift gesture of reverence that now felt natural to me, even good, I ducked to touch the monk's feet, or the ground before it. Our hands were not to meet, I had learned, for unlike my Tibetan monk friends, bhikkhus of the Theravadan school of Buddhism are not to be touched by a woman. Then I scuffed off my thongs and followed him in to tea and conversation. The seats Ramani and I took were a hair lower than his own chair, but the tea was the same: strong, milky, sweet. I tried reckoning once the quarts of tea an Asian Buddhist monk must drink every day; no wonder so many become diabetic. Over tea, the talk was of my host's work with the villagers, his life in the Dharma. Sometimes the temple was still, suspending us in the fly-buzzing timelessness of mid-afternoon. Sometimes we talked amidst a continual traffic of novice monks, devotees, local teachers and organizers, temple workmen, children, dogs. Whenever I called on my bhikkhu friend Samitha, a Marxist with the build of a rugby player, his pet mongoose would slink between our legs.

What I loved most, as we spoke of village plans and scripture passages, was the scent of courage. I never heard a word of complaint from Sarvodaya monks, but I began to realize the price they paid for engaging in community development work. It was more than the time it took, added on to hours of puja, temple care, and pastoral duties. It was more than the physical exertions involved: leaving the tranquil comforts of the temple for the wattle and daub shacks of the poorest families, or suffering the brain-addling sun of a shramadana, or trying to navigate the daunting bureaucratic labyrinths of government. The harshest cost was in reputation and prestige. One was not applauded by the larger, traditional Sangha, nor by the larger, conservative laity. On the contrary. The forest-dwelling monks in meditative retreat and the scholarly ones in their libraries received the most reverence. *Their* kind of renunciation did not rock the boat. When I had the nerve to raise the topic outright, the Sarvodaya monks responded with a calm yes. "Yes, that is true, by engaging in social change work we lose some measure of respect, we are considered a lesser kind of monk. It doesn't matter. It makes no difference."

The monks who ventured out into social action, I found, were also the least chauvinistic and sexist. Oh, how traditional and narrow were monks I met outside of Sarvodaya! Their misogyny became increasingly hard to take. Women must lodge outside the gate. Women must cover themselves despite the heat. Women must keep their eyes and voices lowered. What the ladies can do is bring the *dana*, hovering over their pots like obsessive mothers as the impassive monks walk in, deigning to be fed.

Sometimes I couldn't keep my mouth shut. I trotted out my arguments that the misogynist passages in scriptures were inserted centuries after the Buddha, but even Nyanaseeha, the most original scholar among Sarvodaya monks, refused to accept this. There was the real rub! So long as those contemptuous words were put in the mouth of the Buddha and believed to have been actually *said* by him, this religion, I realized, would be repressive of women.

Malini, a lay woman some years older than I, became a good friend. One day in the temple she adjusted my white cotton shawl, saying, "We must cover our arms. The monks haven't shed all the fetters yet, and lustful thoughts can be aroused in them." "Well, I haven't shed all those fetters either," I snapped back. "Why don't the monks cover up *their* naked shoulders so I won't have lustful thoughts?"

She looked at me, dumbfounded. She couldn't say the real answer: because we as women don't count, because it is useful to the patriarchy for us to feel ashamed of our bodies. The status of women in Sri Lankan Buddhism was a topic she and I fell into frequently. Malini knew my views. She liked to provoke them because they gave her ammunition when she spoke with her Dharma sisters.

On a meditation retreat — a week at a vipassana center north of Colombo — I was confronted with the prudishness in Buddhism that is linked to its fear of women. A Bengali meditation master, Munindraji, was teaching contemplations on the loathsomeness of the body. He named the thirty-two "impurities": blood, sweat, urine, pus, bile, and so on (he listed them all, except for semen). He said that remembering physical changes and decay helps us check the "hot stream of foolish desire" and despise as a snare that which allures.

"How measly is this rejection of desire!" I thought as he spoke. It's so spoilsport. It's like deciding there's nothing valid to learn in passion's embrace — nothing to eclipse the ego, or to offer wider landscapes of meaning. "Oh, God!" I nearly groaned aloud. And it's not lust and passion that are killing the life of our planet, I reflected, so much as fear and envy of its wild beauty.

"Fresh fruits and curries appear pleasing," Munindraji said, "but consider how repulsive the food looks in your mouth as you masticate, and how yet more disgusting it becomes in the stomach...." He went on in this vein, bringing in digestive and intestinal activities. "There is nothing coming out of the body," he concluded, "that is not disgusting."

I exited at that point. I paced back and forth under the palm trees, muttering. "Oh, Munindra, I'll show you three things that came out of my body that aren't disgusting. As a matter of fact, I'd like to introduce them to you."

Later I talked to Munindra directly. He told me the meditation on the foulness of the body was never meant for universal use, but for special applications, especially for those who are getting high on bliss, enraptured by *samadhi*. For folks like me who are disposed, on the other hand, to anger and hatred, it was not appropriate. Instead we need more *metta,* or loving kindness, practice, where we behold the entire world and all that's in it with fond delight and no sense of separation.

The bhikkhus, I decided as I came to know them more and more, were more winsome than their metaphysics. Their philosophic pronouncements were too pious and pedantic to delight the soul, but *they* — the freshness of their composure, their endless generosity — gladdened me greatly. Though many of their assertions struck me as life-denying, it was the very same bhikkhus who wouldn't sweep ants away, lest they be hurt. Their metta was bone-deep. It struck me as ironic that Western Nietzschean affirmers of life are readier to destroy it than these gentle viewers of its "repulsiveness," who tenderly gather blossoms to make their puja — or lasso intrusive scorpions in order to carry them to safety.

Midway in my Sri Lankan year, I had to make an admission to myself. I had fallen in love with a monk. I had never thought it could happen. Maybe I assumed that celibacy emitted some glandular sedative, or a hormone-killing substance. I was sort of pleased, all the same, because I love surprises. And for all that can be said for loving kindness, there is nothing like *eros* for opening one to the sly, secret pulse of a land.

I loved recalling my first encounters with the Venerable Paññasagara. The name means Ocean of Wisdom.

At Sarvodaya headquarters we passed in the gateway, turned to each other, spoke for about ninety seconds. As I watched him walk on, one of the trainers came up beside me. "That bhikkhu is a very fine organizer, Joanna-akka. You should see what he has done for his people. Though it is far away, you must try to visit his place." "Yes, I will," I said, "he just invited me."

A month later, I took the time to go. It wasn't easy, on that first trip, to find his village center in the remote hills beyond Kurunegala. The setting was spectacular, with huge boulders rising out of the luxuriant flowering jungle. I was looking for him by the vihara when he rode up on the running board of his jeep and jumped down to greet me. And I saw again that quick, radiant grin.

With barely a pause he strode me up the steep hill behind his vihara, a giant domed rock from which we looked out over a sea of green. He explained how there was nothing else there when he first came, not the busy compound below with its schools and workshops — just hamlets of families trapped in sullen, dead-end poverty, who had forgotten how to care for a bhikkhu. So he took up residence on the rock — in that hut right over there — and with his begging bowl went out on *pindapatha,* or alms rounds, every morning, teaching people to share, and began slowly, slowly, to stir things up. Meditation instruction first, then literacy classes. He seemed eager to tell me all this, and kept looking and laughing straight into my eyes.

"When did you become a monk?"

At sixteen, he said. He was in a Colombo prep school when one day he heard a Dharma talk. He decided on the spot. When I said, "Tell me about that talk," he sang me a Sinhalese song. It's about a man being chased through the jungle by a mad elephant, he explained. To save himself, he dives into a well, where, spying a poisonous snake below, he grabs a vine to stop his fall. The prickly vine hurts his hands, but down his forearm trickles nectar from a flower. Hanging there, with the elephant rampaging above and the venomous snake waiting below, he licks the delicious nectar from his arm.

Then the crooked, heart-stopping grin, as if that song were explanation enough for a lifetime of service — or at least the 34 years since he became a monk, for he was just my age.

It wasn't until my next trip north that I realized what was happening to me. I had overnighted at the Kurunegala Rest House before heading out to Ocean of Wisdom's village center — I'd decided I needed more data on his methods of organizing shramadanas.

As I stepped off the verandah from my room, I turned and saw the morning sun flaming on an orange robe. It was actually a golden apricot color, very fresh, and above it that grin. There he was, coming toward me. And that — the sheer, breath-taking fact of his existence — became suddenly all I would ever need to know. Around that fact the universe rearranged itself.

He told me he had appointments in town, and would I mind waiting a day before meeting with him back in his village? I didn't mind at all because that meant I would see him again while we were both still alive.

It became clear the next day that Ocean of Wisdom had been working on his English. He also got a kick out of making me speak Sinhalese. I was so awash with happiness that I was more fluent than usual, but I kept forgetting what my questions were almost as soon as I asked them. I wanted to touch him and knew I could not. I watched the corner of his mouth, his hands. I decided to learn synesthesia and began to discover that vision, with concentration, can produce the sensation of touch.

Once I came to see him unannounced. He was ill, but up and about, suffering from what I took to be bursitis. He was in pain and looked a bit seedy, tired and stubbled, grayer than I'd seen him. I wanted to massage his aching shoulder. Instead I drank in the sight of him, his indomitable flair, that inerasable elegance. I watched him talk with the children, the way they took his hand and the way he looked at them.

His innate authority had something regal about it. I imagined he had been a raja in a former life. But now that he was sick, and a little out of sorts, there was a sternness in his authority. He did not enjoy repeating himself when I was slow on the uptake and asked the same question twice. That happened because I kept getting distracted. I was fantasizing that if only he were bitten by a snake — say, on his ankle — I could touch him. I would put my mouth to the bite to suck out the venom. But no snake came along. And when I passed him my glasses to write something down, he wouldn't use them. Was that because his arm hurt too much for him to write, I wondered, or because my glasses would pollute him?

I asked him: what is the aim of the monk? Some of my bhikkhu friends said it was to minister. Others said it was to win release. Ocean of Wisdom combined both views: nirvana comes when you sacrifice everything, even the robes, your eyes, your life. "It may be quicker," he said, "if you go to the forest to meditate. But if you want to bring everyone with you, ah, that takes a long time." He had no interest in becoming an *arhat*, an enlightened saint, in this life. There was too much to do. He seemed to want a lot of company when he walked through the gates of nirvana.

Before leaving, I walked alone up the great rock behind the vihara, to the little tree-shaded shrine and the hut that were there when he first came. I breathed in the view, as if I could breathe in who he was when he ventured here alone from the big city. I stubbed my toe and it bled. I put a temple flower in my buttonhole and it fell out. Unable to touch him, I tried to touch his past, to imagine how hard and lonely it must have been for him then, my beloved Ocean. Same face, same body, same smile, as he stood here like this, looking out over this sea of palm tops, these jutting promontories of rock, these slivers and rivers of paddy. No temple awaiting him, no devotees, no welcome yet in the hearts of the villagers. Nothing but the courage he chose to find in the Buddha Dharma.

Before I climbed on my motorcycle to leave, he insisted that I eat a mango. He wanted it cut just right, and impatiently took it from the hands of his assistant. At least he touched that. I watched him slowly peel the fruit, down from the tip, and slice around the cuttlefish bone seed with those lovely, elegant fingers of his. Then he smiled into my eyes as I put each section in my mouth.

As I sped on Pruey back to Kurunegala and on south to the coast, I was thinking up new excuses to see Paññasagara. Given all my other plans, including a
trip to the Jaffna peninsula, I'd have to wait a while.

Yet soon I seemed to be catching sight of him everywhere. The first time
it occurred, I had stopped to swim at Unawatuna, a lovely beach beyond Galle,
and saw how the light shone on the topmost branches of a tall palm. That light
on the dancing fronds was so clean, so true, and kind of laughing. When it
caught my eye, I rolled over on my knees in the shallow, crystal water and rose
up on them a little, my head back, looking, looking, as if watching someone —
the universe, perhaps — do a subtle and wonderful trick.

It was a cresting sort of light, like on the helmet of a knight riding into
tournament. It made me think of the song Ocean sang about hanging there in
the well between the elephant and the snake, licking the nectar from his arm.
And I remembered how he laughed. He lived, as we all do, with threats of
destruction, between the jaws of mortality. But for him those looming dangers
just triggered a high-hearted self-offering to life. Simply to know that was a joy
to me — and somehow sufficient.

How odd, I thought as I toweled dry, that I should find this sufficiency
in a relationship that does not exist, or that consists at most of beholding a particular embodiment of beauty and bold compassion. And odd, too, that the
tears I feel now in my throat are not about the distance between us. On the
contrary. They come from the presence I feel all around me — its flaming
emptiness, its freedom.

Back in Baddegama, I beheld the shapes of things, their colors and textures. I
saw how they all fit together, like pieces of a jigsaw puzzle once they find their
place. Everywhere I looked I saw contours meeting, greeting, full of happy
secrets, one about the other.

Now plays of light, color, scent brought little starts of recognition and
pleasure — as if my beloved were continually adorning himself for my delight.
The green hand-woven spread on which I meditated in the morning made me
want to congratulate him for the fine cloak he'd put on for me. The waterbug
in the well, the cow as she lay by the jackfruit tree, the underside of a kitten,
the butterfly in the john, with rust-orange on its lower wing — each fit into
my own being, as astonishing and necessary as that moment when I turned to
a flash of sun on an apricot-colored robe and saw a particular smile.

Sometimes I seemed to sense my own body from the outside, how its form and skin must feel to air, light, cotton dress. I thought, maybe it doesn't matter where you draw the line between in and out, self and other, even weakness and strength. These differences are but touch points in the dance of complementarity; like epidermal surfaces, they allow encounter and caress.

A light rain spattered as I bathed at the well. It mingled with the splashing of the bucket, and I lathered up with oatmeal soap before going in to my oatmeal porridge. In and out, above, below — how odd and intricate this dance. I remembered what the poet M.C. Richards had said once about solitude: "Learn to move in the world as if it were your lover."

19

Persona Non Grata

DURING THE COURSE OF MY YEAR IN SRI LANKA, animosity grew between the two largest segments of the country's population: the Tamils, who are Hindu and live mainly to the North on the Jaffna peninsula, and the Sinhalese majority, which is Buddhist and predominates in the rest of the island. The Sinhalese-dominated government in Colombo responded with stolid intransigence to Tamil agitation for more autonomy, and then even more so to their demands for independence. Outbreaks of violence on both sides, with equally violent retaliations, were making it ever harder to reach a peaceful outcome.

The ethnic conflict seemed distant from the tranquil Buddhist world where I lived in southern Sri Lanka. Its gravity was hard for me to register because within the Sarvodaya movement I was accustomed to seeing collaboration between the Sinhalese and the Tamils. Sarvodaya appeared to be the one country-wide nongovernmental organization where Buddhists worked amicably with Hindus — and, for that matter, with Moslems and Christians as well. Veteran monk organizers described to me with pride their early shramadana work camps in the North, where youth from all ethnic and religious groups pitched in, side by side, learning to trust and respect each other. These bhikkhus knew, as did Ari, Sarvodaya's founder, the importance of building friendships between populations who had been pitted against each other by the colonial powers.

But polarization was setting in. The Colombo government, egged on by chauvinist elements within the conservative Bhikkhu Sangha, the umbrella organization of Buddhist monks, refused to concede an inch to Tamil demands, and Tamil youth grew cynical and defiant. Instead of joining inter-ethnic shramadanas, many were throwing in their lot with the Tamil Tigers, guerrillas fighting for outright secession and a new State of Eelam. And, of course, with each fresh assault and ambush on either side, anti-Tamil sentiment spread throughout the island — even to peaceful Baddegama.

A painter and his apprentices moved into my temple to begin work. A rich doctor in Colombo was donating a series of murals portraying scenes from the life of an ancient Sinhalese ruler. King Duttugemunu was famous for his military campaign against the Tamils; he waged it in the name of the Dharma and once had Buddhist monks march in the vanguard of his troops. As the colorful scenes took form, Duttugemunu appeared in handsome, pale-skinned nobility, while the dark, furious features of his Tamil foes were so distorted they looked demonic, subhuman. My heart sank.

About that time I received an invitation to the Hindu Tamil North. It came from an organization called the Nonviolent Direct Action Group (NVDAG), which had ties to my friends in the Movement for a New Society in Philadelphia. The group had nothing to do with separatist demands but focused rather on issues of social justice internal to the Tamil community — issues like the caste system and the practice of dowry. I was invited to conduct a weekend training in methods of nonviolent change.

Glad for the chance to visit the Jaffna peninsula, I scheduled the event for late April. I figured that Peggy and Jack, whom I expected to visit Sri Lanka then, could join me there. They were familiar with nonviolence trainings, having taken them with the Clamshell Alliance in protests against nuclear power. Jack and Peg came by ferry from India and met me on the train to Jaffna.

I rejoiced to see them and relished the prospect of our working together as a team. Jack had postponed his spring semester at Tufts to travel in South Asia with two of his classmates, John and Peter. Peggy had taken a year off after high school, and spent the fall in France before joining Jack and his friends. The four young people were in high spirits from their travels in India, revisiting places Peg and Jack remembered from their childhood.

The workshop took place in a lush rural setting outside Jaffna town, with about thirty young Tamils, some as young as Jack. It wasn't hard to adapt the methods we had learned in nonviolence trainings, nor to see their relevance to the social campaigns of our new Tamil friends. In the post-colonial era, the rigidities of the caste system and the costly practice of dowry were growing more, not less, entrenched in the Hindu population. To continue to challenge these institutions, our hosts knew they needed as much courage and creativity as they could muster.

They enjoyed most of all the role-plays we helped them stage. These were improvised encounters in which, say, a young man practices telling his fiancée's parents — and his own — that he refuses to accept a dowry. Or someone who is an untouchable (or with an untouchable) seeks to enter a temple and confronts the priests barring the way and the police who are summoned. The players then switched roles, taking the part of the opponents, the better to understand them and to lessen their own fear.

In one session, however, a young player had trouble assuming the role of a policeman. An earnest boy with a quiet, intelligent face, he kept trying but each time walked away in distress. Assuming that he was merely stuck in stereotyped notions about the constabulary, I challenged him to acknowledge the cop's humanity, but finally he just gave up, shaking his head. Only later did I learn that the boy was a former Tamil Tiger. He had been arrested and tortured in jail by the Sinhalese police, beaten as he hung from his wrists, which were pinned behind him. But he did not tell us that. He did not parade those credentials, or scoff at us for our easy, American idealism. Having chosen to leave the Tamil Tigers, he wanted to learn new ways, from whomever could teach him.

After the workshop my young teammates and I walked the northern beaches, where the tops of tall palms tossed in the wind. Boats from India would soon be pulling up on those sands, under cover of darkness, to deliver weapons. But none of us, not even the NVDAG, imagined this possibility back then. That same evening our hosts met us with the proposal that Jack, Peg, Peter, and John stay on for the next two months. They would be provided with housing, meals, bicycles, and interpreters — in exchange for conducting several workshops a week. These workshops, held in schools and community centers throughout the Jaffna peninsula, would address the same issues of dowry and caste.

"But we don't know much about dowry and caste!" Jack protested. "Precisely," said our Tamil friends. "We would not ask you if you thought you were experts on Hindu culture. *We* are the experts. What *you* offer us are methods that help us see our experience and talk about it in fresh ways."

The four hesitated longer than I would have, but they were finally persuaded. "You are being offered the opportunity of a lifetime," I said. I stayed on for a couple of days to give them a "trainer's training" — reviewing the basic principles of leading workshops, mocking up agendas, expanding their repertoire of exercises.

"Have a good time and watch your tongues," I told them before I left. "It's easy to be misquoted and misinterpreted, so steer clear of politics; there are a lot of political undercurrents here. Just stick to what you know and be who you are, and you'll be great."

Then I returned to the Buddhist south and my beloved Baddegama. Two months remained to wrap up research for my book on Sarvodaya, which I decided to call *Dharma and Development*. I listed questions still unanswered, people still to interview: old Sarvodaya hands, local politicians, bhikkhus, including, once more, Ocean of Wisdom. I hoped to have most of it done before my family arrived in early July to join me for my last two weeks.

Peggy and Jack would come from Jaffna, Fran and Chris from the States, and already I was imagining how my village life would appear to them. They would wake in the morning to the same hollow knocking of wooden wagon wheels; they'd lie in my chairs with the slats that pull out to prop up your feet; they'd see the jasmine blossoms floating in the well, and eat my favorite pumpkin curry. Would they also sense the invisible web of relationships that now wove me into the Baddegama world? Would they feel the regard that linked me to postmaster, curdmaker, monks? To share this with my family would make it less painful to leave. Meanwhile, despite the crushing heat of May, I worked steadily and well.

In the early hours of June 12th came a nightmare so vivid I felt it in every muscle. The night before I'd read, till quite late, a political novel set in Argentina, in which a student organizer against government repression is suddenly *desparicido*, disappeared. Now, in the pre-dawn darkness, an intruder entered my room. I didn't know he was there till he covered my mouth, pinned my arms, tried to pull me from my bed. From his featureless face, looking as if he wore a stocking mask, I sensed this was the secret police, coming without warrant to take me from my home, my work, my life — and disappear me.

I struggled awake but waited long minutes before daring to stand upright and visible, lest he be lurking. Finally, in the twilight of dawn I ran down to the well, poured bucket after bucket of water over my head. The panic subsided, but not the knowledge that this horror was really happening — not to me in quiet Baddegama, but to countless others in Argentina, Iran, Haiti, the Soviet Union. Viscerally I felt their plight, their powerlessness at the hands of the KGB, the Savak, the Tonton Macoutes.

That afternoon, when I visited a close bhikkhu friend in his temple in Galle, I found myself speaking of the disappeared. We talked of the hyper-alert kind of compassion one would need in order to stay aware of those who've been silenced.

We talked so long that it was dark when I drove Pruey the ten miles home. I stopped on the little bridge near my house, gazing into the pond at the reflection of my hilltop temple — the devotional oil lamps were like stars. "Joanna-akka!" Priya ran up. He'd been waiting for me: a dispatch from Colombo, brought by courier; he'd put it on my writing table.

There I found it. A terse order from the Sri Lankan government, with no explanations. My visa was canceled, as were those of my children and their two friends. We were required to leave Sri Lanka within 72 hours. By now I had even less time, since I'd been gone all day.

I ran toward the temple, up the long, broad stairways to the vihara, to take my leave of Ven. Saranankara. The old monk, coming from evening prayers with his bhikkhus, could hardly take in the turn of events. *Sabbe anicca*, he murmured. All is impermanent. "But you must go straight away to see the President himself; he will clear up this mistake. He will help you because you love the Dharma, and you are a brave and learned lady."

There was no time to say good-bye to my other friends, but I left notes on the objects I bequeathed them — typewriter to Ramani, Pruey to the Sarvodaya District Center, thermos and electric fan to the household. I packed all night, and before the sun was up on Friday the 13th, the District Center's little car, crammed with bags, papers, books, the District Coordinator, Priya, and me, drove out of Baddegama.

The dream had given me something more than an emotional rehearsal. As I sensed from the moment I read the government order, it set my own loss within a different and larger context. What was befalling me was befalling countless others in my world; and I knew it now, not only with my mind, but also with my breath and body. I could feel, at least a little bit, what it's like for those distant ones to be ripped out of their lives. And when I started to shake with shock and an irrational sense of shame — as if I'd done something unspeakable — I'd think, "I'm not alone, I'm living this with them." Yet, unlike them, I had a home to go to, and loved ones I'd see again. This took care of any self-pity. Meanwhile, straight to the bank and the airlines before they closed for the weekend. Can't obey orders to leave the country without a ticket, without some money. After that, the Embassy.

The Ambassador was waiting with his chief political officer. It seemed I was the first American to be declared *persona non grata* in Sri Lanka. No explanation had been extracted from the Sri Lankan government, but contacts there revealed that the order came directly from "number one," President Jayawardene himself. The only reason for the expulsion that our Embassy could think of had to be the workshops among the Tamils in the North, which I had encouraged my children to lead.

The First Secretary detailed the most plausible scenario: since the Jaffna workshops in nonviolence focused on the caste and dowry systems, they were quite unwelcome to conservative Hindus. But these conservative elements were *also* the only Tamil leaders who worked with the Sinhalese-dominated Colombo government and gave any legitimacy to its claims to represent the whole population. The President would have little choice but to listen when they told him: get these Americans out of here.

"Do you want to fight it?" the Ambassador asked me. He'd back me, if I wanted to. I asked for time to think.

I went to consult with Ari at Sarvodaya headquarters. I worried about the impact my expulsion might have on the movement with which I had been so identified. And I was right to worry: for the first time I experienced Ari's anger. He roasted me, fuming over the damage I was inflicting on Sarvodaya by having become a target of the government. I didn't contradict him when he pretended he knew nothing of the Jaffna workshops.

That night I met the late train from Jaffna, as Jack, Peg, Peter, and John clambered off the coach. They looked dazed; Peggy cried when she saw me. The four came along when I returned the next morning to Sarvodaya. Ari now embraced me, gave Peg a long, quiet back rub. His genius for genuine caring for the individual came through beautifully. We strategized, and I made my decision. Instead of going public with a protest, which might make it harder for President Jayawardene to change his mind, I'd leave forthwith, as ordered. But first I would write the president a letter detailing the legitimate nature of my work in Sri Lanka.

That's what I did for the rest of the weekend: eight tight pages, with carbons, on Ari's office typewriter. Tacitly appealing to Jayawardene's well-publicized Buddhist piety and avoiding sarcasm, I pointed out the obvious: I came to work among Sinhalese Buddhists, not Tamil Hindus; my research and writings could only serve Buddhist Sri Lanka, not Hindu separatism; of my fifty weeks in the country, one — repeat one — had been spent in the Tamil North.

Priya came with us to the airport. When our plane took off, we saw him standing by the runway in his yellow shirt.

Only when we landed in Madras did the grief begin. Now I touched the enormity of the loss. I had the odd sense of having suffered this before, in a time I couldn't recall, as if this were not the first time I'd been banished from what I'd just found again: the world of my Dharma brothers. Its outer form was temple compounds, play of light and palm leaf shadow on swept sand, gesture of wrapping and tucking robe, the measured pace, the smile. Its inner form was an ease and stretch of spirit, a trust in the journey undertaken, a journey made before by so many, and by him, the great Compassionate One.

An official explanation for our expulsion was never offered by the Sri Lankan government. In its absence, the newspapers made up their own, often contradicting each other. The Colombo press — with the banner headline MACY MISSION EXPOSED — suggested that we had been abetting Tamil terrorism. Ironically, papers favorable to the Tamils, like Moscow's *Pravda*, cited the children and me as one more example of American imperialist interventionism.

When I finally arrived home, I found a letter awaiting me from the Sri Lankan president. Acknowledging the long pages I had tapped out to him on Ari's office typewriter, Jayawardene informed me I was free to return to his country "for purposes of legitimate research." It would be a while before I was able to go back.

Open warfare between the Sri Lankan military forces and the Tamil insurgent army exploded three years later in mid-1983. The Tigers' almost suicidal terrorism and the equally violent "pacification" measures by the Sinhalese-dominated government would continue to inflame the conflict and bleed the country through the 1990s.

Each side had its backers. While the Tigers were bolstered by arms suppliers around the world, the government's crackdown was reinforced by right-wing elements within the Bhikkhu Sangha. Powerful monks, claiming that Sri Lanka belonged to the Buddhists, opposed any negotiated settlement and viewed all who called for one as traitors. This put Ari himself in danger, for he and his Sarvodaya movement stepped right in to care for the victims on both sides and to appeal for nonviolence and reconciliation nationwide.

In the fall of 1983, after the civil war had begun, Ari announced he would lead a hundred-day Peace Walk the length of the island, from the Buddhist South to the Tamil North, enlisting members of all communities. Gathering at Kataragama, a pilgrimage site in the far South sacred to both Hindus and Buddhists, thousands headed out in solemn silence; but President Jayawardene intervened. He told Ari to stop, or his safety could not be assured. The procession would have disbanded then and there, had not a Sarvodaya monk moved to the vanguard to lead the march onward. I pictured him doing that, just walking out, calm and reckless in his apricot-orange robe. In my mind's eye, I could see him quite clearly — he was Paññasagara, Ocean of Wisdom.

A year and a half later, Ocean of Wisdom was walking off the plane into San Francisco airport, with barely a phone call to alert me. Hastily I arranged an evening meeting with the Buddhist Peace Fellowship; I wanted my friends to see a real-life bodhisattva and to hear how he used the Dharma. But the monk was uncooperatively modest, the gay confidence I had loved in him was not displayed — perhaps he felt that the Sri Lankan Sangha had little to offer the world right then.

The two of us took a day together before I flew east to a conference. We wandered around the pillared gardens of the Palace of Fine Arts and then drove out to Seal Rock. It was there, as we stood in the salt wind, watching the surf, seals, pelicans, that Paññasagara sang me another old Sinhalese song. Actually he'd been humming it all day, and he wanted to teach it to me now. It was not the song he'd sung me years before, about hanging in the well, but another one about a stream as it wends its way to the sea. The stream, he explained, is confident and joyous, despite all that befalls her in the course of her long journey. That is because she is in love with the ocean — and knows that, whatever happens, she will become one with it.

Three years later, on December 31, 1988, I opened an envelope from the Sri Lankan government. Apparently, instructions had been left that I be notified if anything happened. The official letter regretfully informed me of the death, in a jeep accident in Indonesia, of the Venerable Kirimatawe Paññasagara.

That is all it said — not what he was doing there, or whether he was killed instantly, or if it took him time to die. Now he is one with the world he loved, I thought, as I looked out the window to where the setting sun flashed on San Francisco Bay. And I remembered the high palm leaves over the beach at Unawatuna, the way they took the light.

THE WORK THAT
RECONNECTS

20

Shambhala Warriors

UNDER THE TALL REDWOODS, cars were parking and people were removing bags, bringing them into the lodge — and I wished I were somewhere else. It was late summer 1980, weeks after my expulsion from Sri Lanka, and I was here at a Quaker conference center in California's Santa Cruz mountains because I had been invited to conduct a weekend workshop entitled "From Despair to Empowerment."

When I had left for Sri Lanka, a year and a half earlier, *New Age Journal* published a piece of mine called "How to Deal with Despair." I had written it to distill the discoveries I'd made since that moment on the Charles River bridge when grief for the world overwhelmed me. It described what happened when I didn't turn my back on that grief, how a strong new sense of connection came — with my world and the people in it. And I put forth in the article the notion of despair work that had come to me at Notre Dame.

Letters in response to this article followed me to Sri Lanka, often with requests to bring this despair work in person and to guide groups of interested people. Well, I thought, one or two workshops, perhaps, then back to the Sarvodaya book and applications for a university teaching position. But now that I had actually arrived to lead a weekend, I wanted to run. What did I have to give these people who were now gathering in the lodge for supper and the first evening session? They may have liked my article, but they would soon discover that I had little more to offer. There were several dozen of them, from prosperous-looking professionals to young people in jeans and veteran activists greeting each other. They had cleared a whole weekend to come here and now settled themselves on chairs, sofas, cushions, waiting for things to begin. I sat still for a moment to feel my breathing and let some inner silence happen.

There she was, just as soon as I thought of her: Prajna Paramita, the Mother of All Buddhas. She had inspired me with her bodhisattva teachings ever since I first studied her scriptures. Now she revealed herself as a presence I could lean into — just as she would henceforth, time and time again, whenever I faced a roomful of strangers and felt at a loss. Big and invisible, she held me in her lap, shielding my back. She breathed through me. She was the deep space of our interconnectedness.

The hunger of children, the chainsaws in the forests, the reactors' radioactive emissions, the exquisitely precise construction of warheads to incinerate whole cities: those realities were, like her, beyond the reach of our senses. In most of our lives, as in this lovely lodge, we couldn't see or hear or touch them. Prajna Paramita, our interconnectedness with all beings, was at least as real as the bombs and empty bellies. So I felt her breathing, which coincided with mine, and I settled into the power of her presence. Along with her authority, I now opened to her love for these people, whom she saw as her bodhisattva sons and daughters. And it eclipsed my fear of them.

As I began to speak, I took confidence in memories of Sarvodaya. Priya used to say to the villagers, "The so-called experts in Colombo or the World Bank don't know what you know; you are the authorities on your own lives!" The community workers I admired did not bring preformulated answers or blueprints for action. They held "family gatherings", where the villagers could hear themselves say what they hadn't said before — what their lives were like, right then and there — so they would find in themselves the will to step forward and act.

For that matter, hadn't the Lord Buddha begun the same way? With the fact of our suffering, the First Noble Truth? He didn't start off by saying how all things are perfect to the enlightened mind. Or how, with faith, they can all work out to the ultimate good. He started with the pain that can't be wished away.

So I offered some questions to help people speak the feelings they carried for what was happening to their world. Almost immediately, something seemed to break open in these men and women who had earlier so daunted me. Some spoke in a rush, their words fast and forceful, as if they had waited a long time for just this chance. Some spoke gropingly. But their hesitancy came not from embarrassment so much as from the awkwardness of saying what they had not before put into words, at least not for others to hear. They spoke of the arms race, the famines, the extinction of species not with statistics or analyses, but with heartbreak and dread. I ached with respect for them.

Bill, a businessman in his fifties, found the tenor of the talk hard to take. At his turn to speak, he admonished the others for indulging in negative thinking. He was sorry to hear how bad people felt, but he simply had to say that all this indulgence in doom and gloom was weakening. It only sapped our energy and optimism. It was essential to look on the bright side of things.

I wished I could shut him up before he shamed the group into silence, but I had set the rules myself: no cross-talk. As it happened, the others were not deterred. The next speaker wept as she confessed her desire for a child and the feelings of responsibility that restrained her from bringing new life into the world now. The man beside her told of returning to a bay up the coast where all his life he'd fished for salmon, and now it was polluted from a paper mill, the salmon gone.

Before we went to bed, I told them the prophecy Choegyal Rinpoche had given me about the Shambhala warriors. As I did, I saw more clearly what we had come together to do. The first weapon of the Shambhala warrior — compassion — would teach us not to be afraid of our pain for the world. With the second weapon — insight — we would see our interconnectedness with all life, and the power to act that arises from our mutual belonging.

The next morning interactive exercises and rituals took us further in exploring the inner depths of our responses to the condition of our world. The information we shared was hardly new to us, but now it was expressed with raw language and intense emotion as we let its reality sink in. This felt so strong and right that I shuddered at the ferocity of life in us.

Later, we walked quietly among the redwoods, fingering the ridges and crevices of the shaggy bark. We played, too — quick, silly games I'd learned in nonviolence trainings. Laughing and teasing, these men and women seemed to be coming home to each other.

How could I help them trust this sense of homecoming and know that it links them not just with each other, but with all life? I wanted them to understand that this work we were doing was more than emotional catharsis, that it was about opening to the web of life and its self-healing power. Time to turn to the second weapon of the Shambhala warrior.

I was hardly inclined to deliver a lecture on general systems theory; instead, I started drawing on sheets of newsprint to illustrate the meaning and role of our pain for the world. I sketched whirlpools and flames and nerve cells as I spoke — the same images early systems thinkers used to convey their vision of reality. In patterns like these, the universe self-organizes, and so do we.

At another point in the weekend all the others were drawing, too. They took crayons and paper to portray their relationship to what was going on in the world. The lodge was quiet as people reached for colors, gazed into space, bent again to their sketches.

I glanced at Bill, remembering his early objections to "negative thinking." He stared a long time at the blank sheet in front of him. Only in the last minute did he pick up a crayon and draw. When we gathered in clusters to look at each other's work, he displayed his own. It was all in blue and very simple: a circle with a few longitudinal and latitudinal lines, and more blue scrawled around it. Suspended in that circle was a large human tear.

"That's the sadness," he explained. "The sadness I go to bed with every night and wake up with every morning. The sadness that we're wrecking our world and that my kids are just out to make money and don't seem to give a damn."

Next to him, a woman, a local peace worker, explained her picture of a nuclear power plant. Stick figures encircling the cooling tower showed how protesters could close it down, and off to the side a group of kneeling figures showed, she explained, the spiritual strength needed for that to happen.

Bill studied her drawing, then said quietly, "Prayers and protests aren't enough. Not enough to keep us going. To clean up the mess, we need this too. We need our sorrow." He placed his paper beside hers, to complete it.

It was the fall of 1980 when I returned to Washington. Ronald Reagan had just won by a landslide, vowing to protect us against the "evil empire" of the USSR, and the military hawks were having a field day with intercontinental ballistic missiles, Launch-on-Warning systems, and other mammoth new weapons programs. The peace movement was gaining ground and momentum. Reprints and photocopies of my despair article published a year and a half earlier still circulated widely, and invitations to lead workshops poured in.

The name for the work presented a challenge. After the first workshop, "From Despair to Empowerment," I dropped the prepositions, substituting "and." This was not about shedding our pain for the world, but about learning to use it as proof of connection and source of strength. I was tempted to abandon the word "despair" as well, because it connoted loss of hope. In describing the work, a French writer used the term *angoisse planétaire*, planetary anguish, which seemed more apt. Increasingly I referred to it as our "pain for the world". For workshop titles I used a variety of phrases, like "Awakening in the Nuclear Age" and "Taking Heart" and even, on occasion, "Being Bodhisattvas." But by now "Despair and Empowerment" had become the generic term, especially as many others began leading these workshops.

Colleagues appeared from all sides. Organizers, therapists, poets, and artists, each bringing their own wisdom and skills. They helped me to respect this work. We met to hammer out a definition of its purpose: "to acknowledge and explore our deepest responses to threats to life on Earth, in ways that overcome numbness and paralysis and open us to the power of our interconnectedness in the web of life."

A network sprang up, which we called Interhelp. We refined our theory and pooled our methods, disseminating them in the journal we published and a book I wrote two years after the first workshop, *Despair and Personal Power in the Nuclear Age.*

Soon my own children took part, despite my best efforts to dissuade them. Peg was visiting Jack at Tufts on the same weekend that I was to lead a Saturday workshop in Boston. I proposed we meet for supper that night; we could talk late, maybe go skating on Sunday. When I learned that the two of them were planning to attend the Despair and Empowerment workshop, my heart sank. "Please don't feel you have to come. With a whole day in Boston together, think of all the great things you could do."

But they were determined. I wondered why I was trying to talk them out of it. Was it the same dread I felt at the outset of every workshop? There was always that initial fear that people would not take part, that they would just look at me incredulously, as if I were a madwoman, and sit in stony silence, even jeer at me, before walking out. It made no difference that this had never happened; I still carried that fear. So, naturally, I preferred that my children not be on hand: I didn't want them to see me fail and to feel humiliated for me.

But there was another concern: that my children and I would inhibit each other. As I thought about that, it dawned on me that I was probably more concerned that we would *not* inhibit each other. Did I want them to see the extent of my despair for their future? Or me to see theirs? Of course not. I'd rather fall off a cliff.

The next day at a cavernous old loft overlooking Copley Square, all my attention was on the process of the workshop, with no room for maternal self-consciousness. In the despair ritual I witnessed the raw depths of Jack's grief over the poisoning of the natural world; diving into the pillows in the Circle of Sorrow, he sobbed over toxic wastes and the disappearing of animal species. I heard Peg's fury over the violations of women, as she screamed in the Circle of Anger and Fear: "There's a woman raped every nine minutes!" And both of them heard what I had thought I did not want them to hear — the depths of my dread of the dangers in store for them.

One night that week I spoke at the Brattle Street Church on Harvard Square. The audience was with me as I focused on the horrors of the arms race, the massive overkill of the warheads on hair-trigger alert, the shrinking time for human intervention. And they still listened attentively when I talked about the psychological dynamics of repression and explained that overwhelming people with terrifying information can be counterproductive. But I ran into trouble when I told them the prophecy about the Shambhala warriors, and especially when I described the second weapon: insight into our interconnectedness.

When I spoke of recognizing that "the line between good and evil runs through the landscape of every human heart," some of the older organizers in the hall took issue. They stood up and challenged me. Did I really fail to see a "clear line" between the people in the Pentagon and those of us fighting for peace? To draw the line clearly and to close ranks with those on our side was precisely what was called for now; it was both deluded and dangerous to obscure the differences that divided us from our opponents. They seemed to feel I was undermining our resolve to stop nuclear war. On my way out, I overheard someone call me a "passive mystic."

I was in no hurry to offer a despair workshop in my own home town. I knew from experience how thoroughly people in government became identified with the responsibilities and power placed in their hands. Through continual evaluations and jockeying for position, consciousness of their image was so ingrained that it grew almost inseparable from the psyche. And, as I had learned in CIA training, it was easy to take pride in being "tough-minded" and handling alarming, even horrific information with cool. So, when a friend organized a despair workshop for me to lead in the center of Washington D.C., I didn't expect that it would draw any government officials, or that it would be any good if it did.

It was the Saturday before Palm Sunday, in the upstairs drawing room of the Florida Avenue Friends Meeting. Claire, an administrator with the National Institutes of Health, helped Fran and me push back the overstuffed chairs; some twenty others walked in, and to make one large circle we all took cushions and sat on the floor. Introducing ourselves, we each shared a recent incident which had triggered anxiety over our world. The experience recounted by a good-looking, gravel-voiced man part-way round the circle involved a notice that had recently come across his desk. It described a radio transmission, beamed into outer space, which aimed to provide to any intelligence in the galaxy key particulars about life on Earth.

I too had seen a report about this project designed by astronomer Carl Sagan. Its graphics were striking for their ingenuity and elegance. I wondered why Chet, as he'd introduced himself, found it so ominous.

"It's the message in the bottle, don't you see? The bottle thrown overboard when the ship is sinking." He turned to the man beside him. "Remember, Dale, what I said that day in the office when I showed you the memo?" And the man named Dale nodded, recalling the analogy they had both found so apt. Like the crew of a doomed ship, we were tossing a letter on the waves in the meager hope that somewhere, sometime, someone might know that we had been here, on a planet that once bore life.

As Dale took his turn to speak, it began to dawn on me that those two men in sports shirts, sitting on the floor between a white-haired old Quaker and an unkempt young peace activist, came from the Pentagon and that the office they were referring to was the Office of the Secretary of the Navy. Chet, a Marine captain, had been assigned there upon his return from Vietnam; Dale had arrived more recently after an extended tour of duty as a commander of a Polaris nuclear submarine.

The group broke into pairs for a simple exercise that made it easy to speak one's concerns for the world. Tall, lanky Dale was hunkered over, head to head with Claire. When finally they finished and she looked around, her lovely face was puffy and streaming with mascara. I had to check my sisterly instinct to rush over and wipe her clean; but then, no matter, Dale was seeing to that himself.

At one point Chet turned on the dreadlocked peace activist, who was detailing the likelihood of nuclear war. "You don't know the half of it!" he exploded. "It's a lot closer than you think, and a hell of a lot worse than you can imagine!"

In the afternoon, I talked about open systems a bit longer than usual, because I'd learned over lunch that Chet had studied systems theory at the Wharton School. Toward the end of the day, as the group focused on actions they wanted to take for the sake of our future, Chet sat apart, staring at his hands. Then he said to me quietly, "I know how to stop nuclear war. I know what would do it, but I can't tell you."

He spoke with such sad conviction that my curiosity got the better of me. "Tell me," I pressed him; and he did.

"All it would take to bring us to our senses would be to drop a medium-size nuclear bomb on a medium-size American city. Accidentally, of course. I know how it could be done." He squinted with pain. "Problem is, I'll never do it. I don't have the courage."

The sadness and madness of what our country was doing to itself and to those who were pledged to defend it walked with me through the week. It was Passion Week, appropriately enough. On Good Friday at the National Cathedral, the massed choirs evoked the crucifixion as they sang Heinrich Schütz' *Seven Last Words*. In the silence that followed I watched the black-shrouded cross as it was borne slowly through the congregation. It seemed like a solemn last rite on the world, and I imagined for a moment that all were present, inclining their heads as it moved by — Shakespeare and Ashoka and Eleanor of Aquitaine, all the players in the show on this planet called Earth, all gathered now to bow at the final curtain.

And what is Easter? I asked myself. Could it be the discovery that love lies deeper within us than fear? Is it the knowledge that we are woven into each other, as one fabric, even in our dying?

We miss the point all along, I thought, when we take the resurrection as a contradiction of death. It *includes* death. Easter is the fact that we are not separate or separable, that we belong to each other. Each time that staggering fact dawns upon us, it's bigger, wilder — *more*, not less, amazing. No wonder the disciples were stunned with joy.

On the day after Easter Dale phoned: could I meet him for dinner? We set it for Thursday at a Vietnamese restaurant on M Street. Chet joined us, too, but it was clearly Dale's turn to talk. The naval commander wanted to tell me what had happened to him since the workshop; but first, he said, he needed to describe what had come before, on the nuclear submarine.

His spiritual journey had become conscious for him in the course of his duty on the Polaris, he said — three months at a time without surfacing. His bunk lay ten feet from a missile with 180 kilotons in its warheads; his desk was wedged even closer. He knew the names of the cities his missiles were targeted to destroy. No one else on board knew but him. He began to see in his mind a particular city in northern Russia, with its civilian life. Clear images came to him of a family with two children, just the ages of his own; he saw them around the supper table after work and school. The scenes grew more vivid, and there was no place to escape from them nor anyone he could talk to. The submarine became a crucible, forcing him into his own anguish.

Now, during the week since the workshop, the Polaris experience resurfaced with full intensity. Unable to sleep more than an hour or two a night, he started sitting in meditation. Then came the experiences he wanted me to know. The first, at three in the morning, began with an acute sensation of pressure, as if he were being pushed into and through a black hole. In utter darkness, he felt the extreme condensation of mass, extinction to zero. Then everything shattered into shards of light, exploding in glory. It was a letting go, he said, of his final fears, including his fear of loving.

He stared into the candle on our table as he said those words, "my final fears, my fear of loving," and "now I feel beyond all fear." Then he glanced at us and laughed, as if to mock himself for such a claim; but Chet didn't laugh.

"The second experience," Dale continued, "happened two days later. I saw my death." He described the scene: he is being cremated, Indian-style; Chet is piling up the wood, Claire igniting it. He feels utter acceptance and peace, the rightness of it. His words, the way he said them, reminded me of my experience in the Cathedral on Good Friday. When I watched the black-draped cross move through the congregation and I imagined all who joined us in that throng, there had been a similar calm sense of completion.

Dale mentioned in passing that he was thinking of resigning from the Navy. Maybe that new fearlessness would let him quit. As for Chet, it looked like he would stay on for a while in the Pentagon; and toward the end of that long evening, he explained to me why. Giving an immediate example from work, he showed how, if you're placed right, you can sabotage a new weapons training program by simply blocking the feedback. "See," he said, eyes twinkling as he assumed the role of systems teacher, "you just obstruct the channels for self-regulation so the system cannot meet its goals." Then he leaned back, with a wicked grin, and said, "Some Shambhala warriors need to stay on the inside, right?"

Two months later, when we met for coffee on Connecticut Avenue, Dale showed up in his Navy whites. He was gorgeous. The confident, gracious smile he gave me belonged with the uniform; I sensed the authority and pride he had worn for fifteen years. As he leaned across the plastic-topped table that morning and told me his plans — he would resign his commission, leave the Navy, marry Claire — the smile relaxed into simple happiness.

Dale and Claire had four years together before he died. When word of his cancer reached me, I thought instantly of the warheads by his bunk and the death he had steadily taken into his body those long months in the submerged Polaris. I thought of his crucible in the depths of the sea, and in the depths of our nation's soul, and how he let it break him open into wider reaches of his own being.

Wild Goose

ONE OF THE BOOKS WE ENJOYED together as a family was *The Once and Future King* by T. H. White, a recent retelling of the legend of King Arthur. We loved reading about Arthur's boyhood and the sort of education he received at the hands of Merlin. Knowing that great responsibilities were in store for the boy, the wizard changed him, for short periods of time, into various creatures — a falcon, to start with, then an ant, a badger, a wild goose, a carp in the castle moat. Each episode stretched *our* view of things, too, opened us to new perceptions and perspectives beyond those we were accustomed to as humans.

One evening in Tunis, when Chris was sick in bed, the rest of us gathered in his room and read those passages aloud once again. That was because a real live falcon perched on the bed post. Chris, who was twelve then, had found him on the ground with a sprained wing, at a falconers' meet out on the uplands of Cap Bon, and brought him home to mend. The fierce eyes stared back at us as we listened to how Arthur — without a word of forewarning from Merlin — suddenly found himself all feathered in the falcon-keep, then hooded on the falconer's wrist and released to soar into the high day to hunt. He discovered in himself many powers — speed, courage, keen concentration.

My own favorite passage was the one where young Arthur becomes a wild goose, and as usual I insisted on reading that part. I could practically feel in my armpits the cold lifting air as I ran into the wind and opened my wings. The huge sky was calling me, and so were my brothers and sisters as they honked in excitement all around me and the icebound shores fell away and we headed out on our long migration south. I loved the stretch of my neck in the sharp air, the power in my shoulders as they found their rhythm, and the wild, free song we sang together.

"One of the reasons I really trust the Buddha," I said as I handed Peggy her pajamas, "is that he was an animal so many times." When we lived in India we had read from the popular old Jataka tales, or "birth stories," adapted from folklore to describe Gautama Sakyamuni's earlier incarnations. It took many lifetimes of noble generosity to prepare him for full Buddhahood. While many of these lives were in human form, in others he embodied compassion while living as a monkey, a rabbit, an elephant. It occurred to me now, as I put it to the family, that "he got the same kind of education that Merlin gave Arthur."

"Maybe we all did, and we just need to remember it," said Fran. Theories of evolution interested him. We talked for a while about forms of life we had passed through. Memories of being fish and lizard must still reside in us, if we could only unlock them.

Our favorite part of the story was how Arthur pulled the sword from the stone. The children wanted to hear it again before going to sleep, so we jumped ahead in the book — to the great gathering in Londontown that would determine the new king of all England. It was foretold that the king would be the one who could draw the sword from the stone. We loved picturing in our minds how the knights of the land crowded into the churchyard where the stone mysteriously stood, grasped the hilt protruding from it, yanked with all their might. Even the brawniest one failed, as we knew they would; and Arthur, who was only a teenager then, failed too — at first. When he relied on his own strength, as the others had, he couldn't budge the sword. With glad suspense we followed the familiar denouement: how, after straining and sweating, the boy paused and looked around; how he saw, peering at him from the edges of the churchyard, the friends who had been his teachers — badger, falcon, goose, and the others. They were watching and cheering for him. Letting himself hear their voices, Arthur recalled the powers he had known in each of them — the industry, the cunning, a certain kind of balance, a particular gift of patience and timing. Then, turning back to the sword, he grasped its handle and drew it straight out of the stone, as easy as a knife from butter.

That story stayed with me over the years, teasing my mind as if it held some wonderful secret. Grace was a concept I had loved as a Christian. The church presented it as the action of God, enabling us to do more than our own individual powers allowed. When I gave up belief in a Big Daddy God, I didn't stop believing in grace. Sometimes I seemed to feel it coming through great beings like Gandhi or Rosa Luxemburg, sometimes through nonhumans, too. The maple tree on Ouie's farm still filled me at moments with her shimmering, whispering wisdom. And I had only to think of Spotty for that noble old horse to steady my heart, as if his patient valor were always there, ready to fuel me up.

Decades later, in Australia, Arthur's story returned. It was early 1985, and I was offering workshops to Australian activists who were resisting nuclear testing, uranium mining, and the logging of their last old forests. They found that the despair and empowerment work freed them from burnout and kindled their love for each other. What I was offering seemed the best I could do, until I met forest activist John Seed.

He was born Janos Kaempfner in Budapest at the end of the Second World War and had grown up in Australia, trying out a variety of occupations before he co-founded a Buddhist-based community — Bodhi Farm. Three years before we met, his life was seized by a larger purpose when he found himself defending the Nightcap Range, a vestige of the great primordial rainforests of Gondwanaland, Australia's mother continent.

"I'll show it to you," he said at the end of my weekend workshop in New South Wales.

We spent the next day together. Walking into the green-lit stillness of that rainforest, with only bird calls and water splashes breaking the silence, I tried to picture the life-altering confrontation that had taken place there — the screaming chainsaws, the crashing of the trees as they fell, the police megaphones, the songs and shouts of the protesters. The activists had been fighting for time — and they halted the logging long enough for their demand for an environmental impact statement to wend its way through the courts and government offices down in Sydney. That's when Janos discovered what he was.

Standing there facing the bulldozers, what he sensed above all was the forest rising behind him. As he described it to me, he felt himself rooted again in that which had brought him forth. That primordial cradle of life now claimed him. Whatever he had been until then — IBM systems analyst, sculptor, hippie farmer — was subsumed in a vaster and truer identity.

As we followed the winding, spongy path back out to the road, I said, "You're talking about the ecological self."

The term came from a school of thought called Deep Ecology and its chief proponent, the Norwegian philosopher Arne Naess. His writings were familiar to us both. Naess had coined the term "deep ecology" to denote the radical interrelatedness of all life-forms and to summon the environmental movement beyond human-centered goals. When I encountered the term, I was delighted to find a secular analogy for the Buddha's teaching of dependent co-arising and began using it in my work. But until I met John Seed, deep ecology had been just that — a useful concept. Now it assumed a different reality.

John, I was soon to realize, took the human-centeredness, or anthropocentrism, of our culture more seriously than I had; and he let me see the clarity and vitality that arise when we consciously shake loose from it.

Now John was taking me onto the land of Bodhi Farm. He wanted to show me the Rainforest Information Center that he had launched after his experience in the Nightcap Range. An old, vine-draped double-decker bus, it was almost invisible among the trees, but there he kept his finger on the pulse of efforts to defend forests around the Pacific Rim. He described new forms of nonviolent resistance and new economic alternatives. Small, sustainable logging ventures, like the "walkabout saw-mill," gave people an alternative to selling off their ancestral lands to multinational corporations.

But there was no way, John said, that these efforts could save the situation, even if they were multiplied tenfold, a hundredfold. Look at the world demand for lumber and the collusion of local politicians with foreign industries. Look at the accelerating pace of deforestation. Even if activists won every battle they waged, it would hardly make a dent. John saw this with total realism, yet kept on giving his life to this work. I looked at him wonderingly. "What do you do with the despair?" I asked him.

"When I feel despair," he said, "I try to remember that it's not me, John Seed, who's protecting the rainforest. The rainforest is protecting itself, through me and my mates, through this small part of it that's recently emerged into human thinking."

Ah, of course, that changes everything. You would know you were supported by a power greater than your own, you'd feel *graced*.

"How can we adapt despair and empowerment work to free us from the notion that we humans are the crown of creation, that we have claims on the rest of life?" John challenged me. We were squatting on the bank of a forest pond a short distance from the bus, absently watching the waterbugs and considering a swim.

"The work we did on the weekend was powerful," he told me. "It blasted away our numbness, uncovered our passion for life. But it's missing a piece. We're still prey to the anthropocentrism that's destroying our world."

So what would it take, we wondered, as we stripped and dove into the pond. What kind of group work could move us beyond our shrunken human self-interest? The question turned in my mind as I swam down into the brown water, like the carp that Arthur became in the castle moat.

The answer that emerged was the Council of All Beings. By the time we dried off and dressed, it was taking shape in our minds: a simply structured ritual, in circular form, where people would step aside from their human identities and speak on behalf of other life-forms. We planned it with growing enthusiasm but had little idea what it would become in reality, in interaction with others.

"I'll do it during the week-long near Sydney," I said, referring to the final training workshop scheduled for the eve of my departure to the States, "but you've got to promise to be there."

It was easier than I expected. On a midweek afternoon, I simply invited the forty trainees to let themselves be chosen by another life-form. From cardboard, colored markers, paste, leaves, we made masks. To drumbeat, we moved in procession to a wide gorge and gathered in a circle on flat boulders, downstream from a waterfall. We identified ourselves, one by one.

"I am Wild Goose," I said, "I speak for migratory birds."

"I am Wheat, and I speak for all cultivated grains," said the next.

"I am Red Kangaroo, I speak for the large marsupials."

"I am Mycorrhyzae, the fungal network interconnecting the roots of trees in the forest." That was John.

We began to speak of what we saw happening to our world, our lives. Laughter bubbled up at the implausibility of what we were attempting, and tears came, too, for the losses we were allowing ourselves to feel. The depth of feeling and the playfulness mixed well, as they do with children.

"I speak for Weeds — weeds, a name humans give to plants they do not use. I am vigorous and strong. I love to thrust and seed — even through concrete. Pushing through paving, I bring moisture and life. I heal the burned and wounded Earth. Yet I am doused with poison now, as are the creatures living in me, through me."

"I am Woompoo Pigeon. I live in the last pockets of rainforest. I call my song through the giant trees and the cool green light. But I no longer get a reply. Where are my kind? Where have they gone? I hear only the echo of my own call."

"I am Mountain. I am ancient, strong, and solid, built to endure. But now I am being dynamited and mined, my forest skin is ripped off me, my topsoil washed away, my streams and rivers choked."

One upstart species was at the root of all this trouble — its representatives had better come and hear this council. So we took turns, a few at a time, putting down our masks and moving to the center of the circle, as humans. There we sat facing outwards, forced to listen only. No chance to divert ourselves with explanations or excuses or analyses of economic necessities.

When I sat for a spell in the center, a human in the presence of other life-forms, I felt stripped. I wanted to protest. "I'm different from the loggers and miners, the multinational CEOs and the consumers they fatten on," I wanted to say. "I am a sensitive, caring human; I meditate and lead workshops and recycle."

But because I was not permitted to speak and defend myself, the words I would have filled the air with began to evaporate in my mind. I saw them for what they were — essentially irrelevant. The deep ecology that had so lured me with its affirmation of my interconnectedness with other species now forced me to acknowledge my embeddedness in my own. If I was linked to the wild goose and the mycorrhyzae, I was far more linked to the investment speculators and compulsive shoppers. Shared accountability sank in, leaching away any sense of moral immunity.

But by the very plans I had devised with John, I wasn't allowed to stay sitting there as a human, marooned in human culpability. As the others had, I moved back from the center to the periphery, to see and speak from that wider context. From here we could see more clearly the isolation in which the humans imagine themselves to exist, and the fear that seizes them — a fear that generates greed and panic. For our own survival we — all beings — must help them. Could we help these twentieth-century humans, the way we helped Arthur pull the sword from the stone?

"As Weeds I offer you humans some tenacity. However hard the ground, we don't give up! We know how to keep at it, resting when needed, keeping on, until suddenly — crack! we're in the sunlight again. That is what we give you — our persistence."

"I offer you peace and stability," said Mountain. "Come to me at any time to rest, to dream. Without dreams you lose vision and hope. Come, too, for my solid strength."

Each being spoke, often more than once, and what a harvest it was! Much of the gladness in the giving came from the fact that the powers we named were already within us, and were now being brought to consciousness. Could we even speak them, were that not so? I was reminded of the Tibetan visualization practice, in which you offer your body for the nourishment of the Buddhas. As the practice unfolds, you realize that you are, in essence, all three parties to that act: the giver, the receiver, and the gift itself. In the conscious act of giving, they merge into one.

Two years later, John Seed and I, along with our colleague Pat Fleming in Britain, wrote *Thinking Like a Mountain*, a book about the Council of All Beings. The practice spread; John and I found ourselves leading councils around the world. At the outset I was often Wild Goose. She helped me be brave in flying beyond borders over new terrain, into new ideas and experiences. She also knew I needed to cultivate endurance so that I could keep on going for the long haul.

Other people, too, found a gradual disclosure of meaning from the beings that had chosen them in the council. Sometimes their import was symbolic, as in the case of an Ohio woman who was disgusted to be chosen by snake; she hated snakes. Months afterwards she wrote how it helped her to see that her well-paid, high-status job didn't fit her any longer; she had sloughed it off and gone forward in her gleaming new skin.

Sometimes the being that chose a person led to action on its behalf, as Fran discovered when he spoke for Lake Baikal in Siberia. He had always known that this fresh-water sea was sacred to the Russian soul, but now he began to immerse himself in reports about its current condition. Soon he was raising money to take leading environmentalists, like David Brower, out to Siberia to confer with Russian authorities. Baikal Watch was born — and from it came topographical and biological studies, a development plan with controls on the paper mills, and a park for ecotourism. It all unfolded within a few years, as if that mysteriously beautiful sea herself were taking part in her own protection.

Often, in the Councils, I thought of Indra's Net. In that vision of reality from the Hua Yen scriptures of Buddhism, the jewel at each node of the net reflects all the others — *sarvasattva*, all beings — and catches its own reflections in them, too, back and forth in an ongoing display of our interconnectedness. The scripture says there's a way into that epiphany of knowing oneself in all beings. It is the way of *maha-karuna*, the great compassion. You may have been orbiting far out, in isolated pursuit of whatever you thought you wanted for yourself, but when you feel the pain of your brothers and sisters and let them know yours, the door opens. Welcome home. Then not just their suffering but their joys and strengths are yours as well.

The Empress of China, in the late seventh century, was so fascinated by the Hua Yen scriptures that she ordered all eighty volumes translated from the Sanskrit. She often came in person to the monastery to offer food to the scholars. To celebrate the completion of the project, she invited Master Fa Tsang to the palace to preach about Indra's Net and the interexistence and interpenetration of all phenomena. He was brilliant, and she thanked him, and asked for something more.

"You have explained the teaching to me with great clarity," she said. "Sometimes I can almost see the vast truth of it in my mind's eye. But all this, I realize, is still conjecture." She reminded Fa Tsang of the Buddha's insistence that direct experience was more reliable than inference, and she asked him for an experiential teaching. "Can you give me a demonstration that will reveal the great truth of all-in-one and one-in-all?"

A few days later Fa Tsang escorted the Empress to the demonstration he had prepared for her in one of the palace rooms. On its four walls and four corners, its ceiling and floor, mirrors were affixed. Then the scholar placed in the center a small statue of the Buddha with a candle beside it.

"Oh, how marvelous!" cried the Empress, beholding in awe the panorama of infinite interreflections. And she thanked Fa Tsang for helping her to know the great teachings not only with her intellect, but with her senses.

To me the Council of All Beings was that kind of demonstration. Here the concepts harvested over the years from Buddhist teachings and general systems theory, arguments for the intrinsic reciprocity among all things, distilled themselves in tangible, playful form. Each time I was surprised by the spontaneous accuracy, the authenticity of feeling, that arose from those who took part.

In June 1989 John Seed and I met on a Munich railway platform and boarded the Orient Express to Budapest. This was John's first return to his native city since the age of four. And it was my first time ever in the country made real to me by Pal, the long-ago gypsy lover who unlocked the laughter in a disaffected young Presbyterian. So, though I had never set foot in the land of the Magyars, I felt I had roots there, and maybe a favor to return.

John and I were booked for two weekends featuring the Council of All Beings. These workshops were new to Eastern Europe, so some Poles and

Czechs, getting wind of them through John's rainforest network, arrived to take part as well. But nothing was as I wanted it. Our well-meaning Budapest sponsors, too burdened with their own work to have publicized our event, had to dragoon their overworked volunteers to take part. The organizer of the second event, held in a southern town with the unpronounceable name of Kiskunsfelegshazs, was out of reach. John, who had the enviable and maddening capacity to hunker down over his laptop and tune out his surroundings while he communicated with the rest of the world, was unaffected by my anxiety. I was tired and aching from six weeks of workshops in England, Scotland, and Germany.

So, when we arrived in Kiskunsfelegshazs in a cold rain and no one there seemed to know who was coming to our workshop and my raw throat made it harder by the minute to speak, all I wanted was bed.

"You're not going to try masks, are you?" I grumbled at John. He was calmly disassembling some cardboard boxes he had waded out to find. The thought of inducing a handful of strangers, whose language we couldn't speak, to take on nonhuman identities wearied me beyond words. I just wanted to retreat to the room where I'd stuck my bag and crawl under that eiderdown quilt.

Eighteen people were in the gray, bare meeting room — teachers, social workers, an engineer, an architect, our doctor host. It was slow going, with pauses for translation and latecomers opening and closing the door, seeking hooks for their dripping raincoats. I told the people of Kiskunsfelegshazs the prophecy about them, in which they're called Shambhala warriors. They practiced then the first weapon of the Shambhala warrior, the compassion that makes them unafraid of the world's pain. They described the suffering that hid beneath the busyness of their days. Some of their faces as wet as the rain-streaked windows, they spoke of what was happening to their land and their children's bodies under the onslaught of Chernobyl, the chemical plants, the reckless pace of the new capitalism.

People still kept coming and going. I worried for those who left the workshop early, without resolution for the grief they had uncovered, and for those who arrived hours late, without preparation for the Council of All Beings that was soon to unfold. Our key teaching points went unheard by many, and I wondered what they could possibly get out of the workshop.

John's pieces of cardboard boxes were dragged in, along with scissors, paints, glue, yarn, scraps of cloth, and colored paper, and the people of

Kiskunsfelegshazs set to work. There was none of the silent absorption I preferred for the making of masks. Chatter prevailed, and speed too. Before I had
finished my vulture's beak, there was a sudden hush and, looking up, I saw the
floor was cleared of scraps and paints — the other life-forms were ready, posi-
tioned in a circle.

They were awesome. Never had I seen full-body masks in a Council.
Birds bore not only beaks but wings; trees had trunks and branches; the
Danube undulated waves from every limb. And how they moved, these beings!
Even in the initial round of self-introductions, Cloud drifted weightlessly,
Birch tossed in the breeze. Only their voices seemed human — and I needed
no Hungarian to get the sense of what they said.

When time came for humans to sit bare-faced in the center, the other
life-forms were not content to address them from the periphery. One after
another, they moved in close, leaping and slithering around the speechless
humans, thrusting their beaks, shaking their branches. And with all that vivid,
even riotous display, there was total seriousness. The Danube was mesmeriz-
ing. I think he was the engineer, but now he had become pure river, an ancient,
majestic presence, flowing in streaming blue-greens and grays around the
island of humans. In word and sound and movement, he evoked his noble history — source of fertility, artery of commerce and culture. He uttered his
shame for the poisons he carried now and his fear of yet greater harm from the
dams and reactors on the Czech border. And he offered promise.

"Beauty and abundance can come again," the Danube said, "if you
humans would do as your ancestors did — and take joy in me."

The next day when John and I climbed in the car to return to Budapest, several participants in the workshop stood talking by the curbside. They wanted
us to understand what they were saying, so one of them fetched the interpreter.

"These years, we wonder, do we belong to the East or the West? Do we
want to be socialist or capitalist? These confusions divide us from each other.
Now we see what we really are. We are the living Earth."

22

Tibet

I HAD THOUGHT THAT TASHI JONG was as close as I would ever get to Tibet. Ever since their escape from the Chinese occupation in 1959, the high homeland of my refugee friends had been sealed off from the outside world. But in 1981 Beijing sent a new governor to Lhasa, whose milder policies loosened the borders, allowing lamas to return from exile. In that change of political climate, Choegyal Rinpoche and Dorzong Rinpoche were able to visit Kham, their native region of eastern Tibet, for the first time in twenty-five years.

"Next time I want *you* to come too," Choegyal said after his return to Tashi Jong. He was aflame with plans to rebuild his monastic center from the ruins left by the Cultural Revolution. He would apply all he had learned helping Khamtrul Rinpoche build a self-sustaining Tibetan community and a new Khampagar monastery on foreign soil in India. For his homeplace of Dugu in Kham, Choegyal foresaw a school, a craft center, and the democratic participation of the laypeople there. He liked Sarvodaya's use of the word "self-help," so his plans took the name Eastern Tibet Self-Help Project. "When I go back" he repeated, "you'll come too, because you are my family."

I could think of nothing I desired more than to set my feet on the homeland of my friends and teachers and to behold the scenes I'd come to love through the paintings of my Dharma brother. Before I died I wanted to walk with him in the high wild places from which the teachings of wisdom came that had blessed my life. I could hardly believe it might be possible.

A letter from Choegyal in early 1987: "I will be in Kham for the summer months. Meet me there." He hoped that Fran and I would bring Peggy, for the woman he had first known as a four-year-old was training in social work now and that would be useful; also he loved her.

"We'll be there in August," I wrote back from the house in Berkeley we were just moving into. I was 58 years old then, and our daughter would be turning 26 on the trip.

Taking over the dining room, Peggy and I assembled oxygen tablets, water filters, rolls of film, vitamins, band-aids, belly medicines, trail mix, high altitude lip gels, sun glasses, and gifts for our Tibetan hosts. We each bought light-weight mountain boots — in beige and navy for Peg and Fran, aqua for me; they would alternate with our thick-soled thongs.

I hunted for a map of Tibet. The only one I found with details of Kham unfolded awkwardly to a good three feet wide. On it, the region of Kham, about the size of Switzerland, was no bigger than my palm. It showed the route we planned to take, approaching Tibet from the east through Sechuan.

We secured our Chinese visas, but papers allowing us to enter the Autonomous Region of Tibet were unavailable in San Francisco. The agent assured us that we could obtain these Alien Travel Permits after we landed in Beijing. We banked on this hope as the three of us checked our bulging back-packs and sleeping bags and settled into our seats on the Air China plane. Fortunately, we had no idea then just how hard it would be to get into Tibet.

At each successive stop — Beijing, Chengdu, then the towns farther west, where we pressed on for days by bus and hired car — we beseeched every Chinese authority we could find to issue the permits for travel in Tibet. Our last hope was Derge, the town closest to the Yangtse River, which marked the border itself. But there, the police not only refused us the permits, but ordered us to leave the entire area within two days.

A high lama, well known in the West, was overnighting in Derge on his way out of Tibet. He was Akong Rinpoche, who had established the Samye teaching center in Scotland with Chogyam Trungpa. When we called on him in his lodgings, he received us graciously and wanted to help; he had good relations with Chinese border officials. Two of them actually dropped by for tea while we were there, coming straight from their day's duties at the Yangtse checkpoint. But when the rinpoche, in courteous, fluent Chinese, sounded them out on our behalf, their answer was curt and final.

Someone else, however, was in the room, quietly listening to the inter-weaving multilingual conversations. He was Tenzin, a young Tibetan from Derge about to return to his studies in Europe. When we described our now desperate hopes of joining Choegyal Rinpoche in Kham, he overheard me say at one point, "I will do anything to get in. Anything."

Tenzin repeated those words when he tracked us down that night. "If that is so," he said, "you must love your lama very much. I have a plan to propose, if you are willing to try it."

Early the next morning, leaving half of our gear behind so our packs would be light enough to carry long distances, we followed Tenzin to the town's large open market place. There we were delivered into the hands of a local Tibetan who was hitching a long, narrow wagon to his tractor. That's what Fran, Peg, and I came to call him among ourselves — "Tractor." It was best not to know his real name; and having no common language, we communicated only by gestures anyway. We had met him the night before, when Tenzin, on his second nocturnal visit, brought him to us to confirm the plans and look at the map we spread out on the floor. Now, by daylight, Tractor simply nodded, barely glancing at our faces. His was rough and impassive, business-like. Soon some eight other locals, including a couple of monks, climbed onto the wagon, pulled us aboard to sit beside them on the narrow side planks, and off we slowly rumbled, westward out of Derge.

The morning was beautiful: fields of barley stubble shone golden under a spanking blue sky. Our wagonmates' smiles and chatter made it seem as if we were all heading off on a picnic. Even Peggy relaxed now; the night before, as we sorted our gear, it was she who had hesitated the longest, enumerating the risks we were running — like never being seen again.

At the farm vehicle's speed and with frequent stops, it took three hours to cover the thirty kilometers to the Yangtse. By the time we pulled up on a ridge to look down at the glinting river, all but one of our traveling companions had jumped off to proceed on foot across the fields, turning to wave to us. In their place were large, heavy bags of barley, which had been heaved aboard at recent stops. The view was magnificent. Peering down to the left from the riverside shoulder of the road, we could see the far end of the bridge, sentry boxes, figures moving. Tractor yanked us back and sprang into action: swiftly he gestured us onto the wagon's narrow floor, hushing us into silence. No sooner did we lie down — we could only manage it on our sides, spoon-fashion, with Fran curled around my back and me around Peggy's — than the heavy sacks of barley landed on top of us, weighing us down in airless darkness. I had only time to cup my hand above Peggy's face, to try to make room for her to breathe; and Fran did the same for me, but it didn't seem to help much. I learned later that Tractor's companion was sitting on us, atop the bags.

The struggle to breathe — the fear of suffocation — was the hardest thing. As we jolted down the road headfirst, my chest heaved and hammered for air. I prayed to my lungs: be still. I prayed to pass out before exploding in panic. I prayed that Peggy not be smothered. We stopped, started, stopped again. The shrill shouts in Chinese sounded very close, within arm's reach, if I *could* reach. Surely the border guards could hear the thunder of my laboring lungs. Over and over in my mind I repeated the Green Tara mantra for protection, *Om Tare Tutt' Tare Ture Svaha* — as Peggy was doing too, she told me later.

At last the wagon moved again, rumbled forward, made a turn and then another, and now sheer gratitude eased the breathing. "Tibet?" I said thankfully when at last we were uncovered. No, not Tibet. We were back in Sechuan. In pantomime Tractor explained what had happened: the rifles aimed at his head; the sacks at the end of the wagon pulled away; then — Tractor pointed at our feet — the three pairs of American-made mountain boots, in beige and navy and aqua, that had given us away. Why, once detected, had we not been hauled out and arrested on the spot, thrown in some local jail? For that providence we could probably thank the two border officials who took tea with Akong Rinpoche and knew that three American friends of his were attempting to cross the border.

After such a close call, teetering on the likelihood of imprisonment or worse, Tractor could well have abandoned us right there on the road. Instead, he doggedly persisted in trying to get us across the Yangtse. Now he drove southward on the high road above the river's eastern bank, stopping once to buy tins of processed meat that he opened for us, insisting, quite firmly, that we eat it. We shared with him our granola. Fifteen kilometers downriver from the bridge he turned down a dirt track, switched off the motor, walked us with our gear to a glade where a rowboat was hidden. As daylight began to dim, he ferried us across.

The skiff was shallow, the current strong and swift. It took two hair-raising trips to get our bodies and packs to the farther shore — all the while in full view of the high Sechuan road we had just been driving. On the rocks below a steep wooded bank, we turned to say good-bye to Tractor. He was coatless now and shivering. He knew, as we did, that we had to move fast if we were to find our way north to where the road came off the bridge, and then head on inland before dawn. He pointed to the river, the sky. Yes, we understood, keep the river on our right, follow the stars. I touched his arm, trying uselessly to thank him, trying to memorize the face of this man, whose name we didn't even know. I wanted to be able to recognize that face someday, on a street, in a crowd.

Atop the embankment, a thin path through the trees led us northward. Before dark we came upon the camp fire of a Khampa man whose long hair was tied up with red tassels. With him were his son and two horses. Drawing numbers in the dirt, we agreed on a price and set off together, putting our packs on his mounts and our bodies too, trading off to ride, two at a time. Up ahead to the east, beyond the river, we beheld the snow peaks of the High Corrugations — they had been too close to see when we drove beneath them on the way to Derge. Now they spread out before our eyes, glowing salmon-pink, then lavender against the turquoise sky in such sweet majesty that I began to sing. Behind me on foot, Fran joined in — which always helps me stay on key. Soon the stars poured out in brilliance because it was, providentially, the dark of the moon.

For a good hour, the path cut along the rock face of cliffs we could not see, though we could hear the river roaring far below.

"Back, let's go back!" I cried. "In daylight we'll find a better route."

But there was no way to turn around. Only the ponies were skittish; the Khampa father and son, sure-footed as cats, hardly slowed their pace. The tiny ledge sloped outwards, loose with pebbles and shale, no wider than the man who led his pony with me astride it, shining my flashlight over his shoulder to help him see the way. Each time the pony slipped and scrambled, I breathed a prayer; I repeatedly prepared to die. Although I blamed myself for the extreme danger I had brought us into, the terror was different than that under the suffocating barley sacks. This was huge, like the vast bowl of stars; and my prayers for not falling were also prayers of thanks for having lived.

By midnight we reached the spot where the road came off the bridge near the sentry points. Speaking in whispers, we shouldered our packs and headed into Kham. The way was black — for miles it seemed to be a gorge, lying directly below a river of stars. The Milky Way, filling the narrow band of sky, led us westward. That's all there was — steep hillside to the right, fall-off on the left to a rushing tributary of the Yangtse, and above it this avenue of galactic rejoicing. Weak with gratitude that we had made it this far, I meandered a bit on the incline of the road. Now Peggy moved into the lead, striding out steadily, as if she had actually slept in the last forty-eight hours. As a teenager, she had not shown as much physical endurance as her brothers, but now, with two tired parents in tow — parents no longer young, trudging uphill in the pitch dark — she came into her own. Her will summoned mine. I let her energy carry me forward. Her jokes shook the aching from my limbs. Yes, of course we would reach the village we had seen on the map; together we would make it.

But what to do should a jeep or truck come down the road? Word was surely out that three Westerners were trying to enter Tibet illegally. Where could we hide, with a slope to our right and a river to our left and bushes too low to scramble under? This concerned me greatly. I came up with a plan. We would pull out one of our olive-colored ponchos and squat under it; we would look, in the night, like a large rock. I persuaded Fran and Peggy to agree to this procedure, and soon, sure enough, the hillside up ahead danced in the beams of an approaching truck. Hastily we scurried to the side, pulled out a poncho, cowered under it. With a mounting roar the truck drew nearer and nearer, came abreast of us, continued on. But why were its headlights red? As we stood up with immense relief, we shone a flashlight on our camouflage. We had grabbed Peggy's red poncho; we had been a bright red rock. We could hardly walk for laughing, but we made it to Jomdu by sunrise.

There our exhilaration petered out. The villagers seemed fearful of any contact with foreigners. Perhaps that was because the Chinese were more repressive near the border. We walked on beyond the little town, planning to wave down a truck heading westward from the transport yard. In that long, hot, hungry day by the side of the road, one old woman appeared, hobbling toward us with a tea kettle. She was Tara, we decided, as we opened a packet of instant miso soup and put warmth in our stomachs for the first time in two days. When by evening dark clouds rolled in and opened, we turned back to the town and took refuge in the transport yard — a combination of pit stop and pig sty, offering barracks rooms and an equally filthy canteen.

There we were marooned for day after desperate day — three, to be exact, but time passes slowly when you're swatting fleas at night and wading by day through mud, oil, and excrement to try to finagle a way out. Without the Chinese dictionary I stupidly had left in Derge, it took us a while to learn that trucks were forbidden to take hitchhikers, especially round-eyed ones. Now my spirits and Peggy's failed. The vision of meeting Choegyal Rinpoche in his beautiful Tibetan uplands — a hope that had been so compelling till now — drowned in this filth and noise and nauseating food. The two of us talked of finding a way back, since we couldn't go forward.

Fran was unswayed by our complaints and arguments, and in the face of all futility, he kept venturing out, talking with truckers and villagers as best he could. Eventually, he returned with a Tibetan whom he had managed to persuade to drive us in his open truck some thirty miles west to the next town. Everyone was nervous about Chinese soldiers, and we were told to lie down in the back of the truck whenever vehicles approached us.

From that town, the next day, we followed a stream and found a spot to wash our mud-caked clothes. We spread them on the grassy bank to dry, lounged against rocks in the sun, and dipped into our remaining trail mix. That was when we were found. A handsome, well-dressed Tibetan, hard to recognize from the young monk we had known in Tashi Jong, strode up and greeted us without a trace of surprise: "I am Kunga. Choegyal Tulku told me to find you here; I will bring you to him. Would you like to come now? Everything is ready."

Within a matter of minutes, we were ensconced in his jeep with thermoses of hot milk tea, riding off on fleece-covered seats into a mountain land so green it dazzled. To my eyes now everything dazzled — the rooftop racks of golden barley straw, the white sheep and black yaks on emerald inclines, the turquoise pendant on Kunga's silk shirt. The boy monk had become a trader, moving between Tibet, Nepal, India, Hong Kong; but he was still devoted to the Dharma and to his lama, Choegyal Rinpoche. And now, as he had been commissioned to do, he brought us by sunset to a large encampment above the tree line.

On a broad, gently sloping expanse of turf, scores of white tents, bright in the sun's last rays, looked as jaunty as medieval pavilions. Among them moved figures in Khampa dress — on the men fedoras and long-sleeved coats tied at the waist, and on the women and in their hair hunks of amber and turquoise that looked as big as your fist. Through the open sides of a large central tent horns glinted, and brass objects on altars, and the dark red robes of monks. Around the encampment's periphery a line of riders trotted, some lapsing into a canter; "they're circumambulating," said Peggy. One particular tent, on the uphill side, was festooned with a yellow roof. There we were received at last on his native soil by Choegyal Rinpoche. He stood quite still in the doorway of his tent and smiled as we approached.

Peg and Fran and I mused about the change we sensed in Choegyal, as we blew out our candles and nestled down in our own capacious tent that night. The immediacy of contact was the same as ever, but the tulku's features looked stronger here, less vulnerable. The new authority in his bearing was surely in response to the avid devotion of his people — and they were his people, having awaited him for so long.

Choegyal was so busy that for the first week our private visits happened at night. If he saw light still glowing through the walls of our tent, he would lift the door flap and slip in alone to perch on one of our cots and chat. Kham was the Wild West (or East) of Tibet, notorious for its irrepressible, semi-nomadic peoples with their rough and forthright ways. Choegyal enjoyed seeing it through our eyes, as if our presence integrated his two worlds. And his old Tibet was more evident now under the current occupation policy. The Khampas felt free once more to gather; prayer beads, glossy with use, were brought out in the open, and prayer wheels spun in full view to the muttering drone of mantras. Now the men, too, could revert to their native clothing and let their hair grow long. An air of rambunctious festivity reigned, with games and pony races, interrupted only for crowded pujas in and around the ceremonial tent.

One night Choegyal brought a watercolor sketch — a new one, clearly, because it showed uniformed figures pointing rifles at a wagon heaped with bags, from which a number of feet protruded. Below Choegyal had written the caption: "O, very bad! Six foreigner boots!"

After a week in the encampment, Fran, Peg and I were given horses for the full day's ride to Khampagar, the once-great monastic complex of Khamtrul Rinpoche. We headed out in the company of ten lamas. Above their maroon robes, the monks wore jaunty, brimmed riding hats, the likes of which I had only seen in old paintings: white ones for the monks and yellow ones distinguishing the three tulkus or rinpoches in our midst. Among our companions was the familiar figure of Bonpa Tulku, whom we knew from Tashi Jong. The rest had never left Tibet; some, like the current abbot of Khampagar, had spent years in prison camps; others were younger and more recently ordained. One, bright-eyed under a yellow brimmed hat, his horse on a lead, was seven-year-old Dergen Rinpoche.

Settling into a steady pace, we wound our way single-file across the green highlands. Up we rode across slides of shale and hillsides of thick turf, down rocky gullies and up again — most of the journey far above the tree line. Majestic expanses spread before our eyes, flickering in the light show made by sun and scudding clouds. Three hours brought us into a wide grassy bowl, where from black yak-hair tents Khampa herders strode out to meet us and help us dismount. Fresh-churned yak butter tea was ready, and crocks of thick, creamy yak curd, and carpets to sit on.

Blocks of cut turf a foot high made seats and tables to honor our rinpoches, and we drank from bowls of fine china. When a sudden massing of clouds unleashed a downpour, our nomad hosts brought out Tibetan raincoats for us. Large white disks of heavy felt with openings for our heads, they were awkward to manage when walking, but once we were hoisted back in the saddle, they covered most of the horse as well as the rider, and the effect was stunning.

When the clouds dispersed and high rocky peaks appeared above us, Bonpa Tulku had us dismount to walk up to the edge of a gorge. It was a dizzying, exquisite scene, with cliffs as fanciful as on a painted scroll plunging down into half-hidden groves of trees. There, he gestured, hidden in caves and crannies, were ancient treasures of Khampagar monastery. During the Cultural Revolution faithful laypeople had carried them there by night, to save them from the Red Guards. "Do you know where the treasures are?" I asked. "Not exactly. You see, those who saved them died. But some day we will find them."

On we went, down a broad grassy incline strewn with red and purple wildflowers and thick silvery patches of edelweiss. Rivulets sparkled down it to feed into a rushing stream, and where it widened we crossed. Our ponies' hooves slipped on the rocks, splashing and jerking us about; then we followed the waterway westward toward a horizon dominated by a bare rock peak. "The mountain over Khampagar," said Bonpa Tulku, pointing. I looked back to see how little Dergen Rinpoche had fared in the fording. His horse was riderless. But behind it rode a strapping monk who cradled in his arms a small boy sound asleep, yellow hat slipping over one eye.

I stood in my stirrups to tug at the woven saddle carpet, pulling it back again between me and the wooden frame. I thought, "This is the happiest day in my life." To ride along hour after hour in the file of mounted lamas — the steady pace of the ponies, the jingling of their bells, the murmured mantras — stirred something in me that felt like memory.

Images of Khampagar came to my mind as we journeyed toward it. I had harvested them over the years at Tashi Jong from the refugees' stories and paintings. The happy magnificence of that fabled center of the Drukpa Kargyu lineage had become part of my own interior world, like some Shangri-La I too had known: the painted gateways fluttering with prayer flags, the curving roofs shining golden through the treetops; libraries and artists' workshops; ranks of dwellings for the monks, each row with its garden and stable; and higher up the hillside, beyond the outer walls, the hermitages of the yogis.

The rain had let up. A monk, leaning over from his horse, helped me extricate myself from my circular rug. As our ponies edged around a turn in the river, a thin white column of smoke rose from a ridge above us. Then the next hilltop emitted a similar smoke signal, and on a farther height I glimpsed a spurt of flame as yet another was ignited. "They are greeting us," said Bonpa Tulku, turning in his saddle to explain. "It is the custom; the fragrance is to please." Monks of Khampagar, their figures indiscernible, had climbed to watch for their rinpoches and to burn juniper branches in welcome.

As we approached a low bridge in the deepening dusk, all we could see of the monks standing on it were the white scarves of greeting. They took our reins to lead our horses across and the valley filled with sound — the long horns of Khampagar.

At first it seemed that nothing was there beyond the robed figures standing by broken walls and ropes sagging with wet prayer flags. But hands reached to help us dismount and unstrap our gear; others grasped our arms to lead us through an opening into a yard of liquid mud and to guide us across it on teetering planks. On the far side, we entered the low-ceilinged, candle-lit room that had been prepared for our family — the first Westerners to come to Khampagar. Store-bought fabric of gaudy red roses covered the earthen walls; carpets had been laid on the narrow beds, and on the floor waited basins of hot water.

Left alone, we peeled off damp clothes, examined bruises inflicted by the wooden saddles, and relished — sparingly — the warm water. We barely had our clothes back on when we heard a knock on the door. An official visit was announced. In walked Bonpa Tulku with the abbot, the one who had been in the prison camp, followed by monks bearing tea. Formally they offered more white scarves and bade us welcome. As we were confused by fatigue, it took us a moment to register the fact that these two companions of our journey were appearing now in another role, as presiding officials of the establishment, receiving us into their domain. We had come to a great monastery, and if it was to live again, it had to be treated as such. The exquisite etiquette of the rinpoches was not a denial of the muddy shambles of the place, it was a statement of its enduring purpose.

When we expressed appreciation for our room, they told us its history. After successive waves of the Chinese Army and the Red Guards, this store-room of the old kitchens was the only chamber left intact. It served then as a detention cell for the monks before they were driven on foot to distant jails and labor camps. Later it functioned as an office for the Chinese government's attempt to organize a collective farm. The attempt was short-lived because many of the local herders disappeared, either dying of starvation when their goods and flocks were expropriated, or leaving to join forces with the Khampa resistance fighters. Now, as the new occupation policy permitted some monas-teries to be rebuilt and some lamas to return from exile, the room was to serve as the establishment's guest quarters.

When we inquired further about the sufferings inflicted on local Tibetans, Bonpa Tulku turned our questions aside. He had little inclination to dwell on past actions of the Chinese and was evidently reluctant to express any blame, or to arouse it in us.

Sleep came slowly that night, and only in snatches. I reckoned it was the alti-tude. I stared into the dark, listening to the wind and the rain and the barking of dogs. I thought of the monks imprisoned and tortured in this room and wondered if any were still alive. I wondered if I could find my way to the privy, if I had to go again during the night. I turned gingerly in my sleeping bag and imagined ways to fasten a pillow on my saddle for the onward journey.

Loud rhythmic chanting, from directly overhead, awakened us early. Climbing the ladder near our door, Fran and I peered into a newly construct-ed second story resounding with vigorous voices. There was our friend from Tashi Jong with thirty young monks of Khampagar. Precisely enunciating the words of the prayers, his baritone was a steady bass note beneath the general exuberance. He was teaching, in the place where he had learned them, the sacred chants he had helped preserve in exile.

Later that morning Bonpa Tulku gave us a tour of the monastery com-plex. Because he had grown up here with Khamtrul Rinpoche, his memories of twenty-six years of Khampagar life now served as blueprint for its recon-struction. "Here was the library, here the monastic college, there the dancing ground," he pointed out as we skirted piles of ancient masonry and stacks of fresh-cut lumber. The place was a combination of archeological dig and con-struction yard. In the dun rubble it all looked depressingly the same; my pow-ers of imagination deserted me.

In a scaffolded edifice we beheld quadruple rows of high pillars, rising to catch the light from windows off upper loggias. This was the main Khampagar temple. I could see, when Bonpa Tulku pointed them out, the spaces created for altars and banks of butter lamps, the high moldings to hold the banners of brocade. Little Dergen Rinpoche, shyly accompanying us all morning, saw that we were impressed with his playground. Scooping up wood shavings, he tossed them in the air.

As we followed Bonpa Tulku about, we expressed admiration for the work accomplished and the plans under way. But the scale of these plans daunted my heart. With pathetically meager resources, he was acting as if he could restore Khampagar. I was tempted to caution him. I wanted to remind him that his efforts could come to naught, that a change in Chinese policy could reduce his plans to empty dreams. But, of course, he knew that already. He knew it better than I.

Climbing a stairway to the loggia and from there a ladder up to a roof terrace, he showed us upper chambers designated for special ritual uses. On that story only a single wall was in place. Looking through its windows, I saw the green hills of Kham. I turned my gaze to Bonpa Tulku.

He always looked taller than he actually was. His features and unflappable composure had changed little since I first met him at Khamtrul Rinpoche's side twenty-two years earlier. There in India he had helped to build another Khampagar, and there he could be living now in comfort, enjoying the library and ceremonial functions and services of a hundred monks. After the losses and hardships he had known in his flight from Tibet, he deserved that ease and security. But now, unquestioningly, as if it were the most natural, logical thing in the world, he was here — in the ruins of his original monastery. With quiet single-mindedness, he was undertaking an endeavor that, given the political context, seemed impossible, or foolhardy at best. But perhaps, I reflected, it was no more impossible or foolhardy than the building of Tashi Jong, that island of Tibetan culture on Indian soil. Perhaps, for that matter, it was no more unlikely than the arising of the first Khampagar itself, a wonder of art and learning amidst a rough, nomadic people.

As we stood on the outer wall, I watched Bonpa Tulku smile calmly while Fran queried him about Chinese policies and the prospects of another period of repression. I saw that such calculations were conjectural to him, as were any guarantees of success. Who knows? And since you cannot know, you simply proceed. You know what you have to do. You put one stone on another and another on top of that. If the stones are knocked down, you begin again, because if you don't, nothing will get built. Through the vagaries of government policies you persist, because in the long run it is persistence that shapes the future.

Two days later, when we left for Dugu to join Choegyal Rinpoche, Bonpa Tulku loaned Fran his own white mare — the finest and gentlest of all the horses. Kunga had arrived the night before to accompany us onward. He wore a cream-colored cowboy hat — had he bought it in Hong Kong? It suited him marvelously. He liked to wave it when he galloped, and he taught us the Khampa yell — a high, rousing holler that made our ponies go like the wind. At a walk, Kunga fell into a more meditative mood, intoning prayers from his boyhood as a monk. When it rained hard, he ushered us inside the nearest yak-hide tent for lunch — he seemed to know every nomad family on the way. As we were plied with food, we watched the laughing, bold-eyed women grow yet bolder and sassier in Kunga's presence. Peggy and I could understand; we too were enamored of Kunga. Then, descending from high green moors, we met the main road again and crossed it to a dirt track along a swollen stream leading southward between an old stupa and a half-constructed power dam. "Dugu," said Kunga, pointing south. Someone gave a khampa yell — maybe it was I, but the others joined in — and we raced the last mile at a dead run.

His duties at the encampment completed, Choegyal had arrived in time to welcome us to his own monastery. Under peaks too high to see, grassy mountainsides descended to a forking valley; at its center lay a vast expanse of rubble, like a bombed city. Just beyond the ruins we came to a large house in traditional style, made of finished logs atop amber-painted stonework. Kunga had recently built it for Choegyal, and we were to stay there too.

Now we worked and played together in a luxuriance of time. No weather stayed our daily picnics on horseback into mountain landscapes I recognized from Choegyal's paintings. His people always knew where he was taking us, and sometimes a yellow canopy awaited, with carpets and a noonday fire. Kunga, waving his cowboy hat, galloped up with the day's dessert, the large tin of Nescafé he had acquired in Hong Kong; with yak curd and condensed milk, it was excellent.

One day we rode far enough to find some of Dugu's nomad families, who were in high summer pastures with their flocks of sheep and herds of yak.

They took us into their tents, fed us endlessly, and talked of their rinpoche's plans to rebuild his monastic center. Choegyal wanted to create schools and jobs in ways that preserved Tibetan culture. To foster local leadership, he had instigated the formation of councils among the nomadic groups; representatives from the nearest ones now formed a Committee of Seven.

Back at the ruins, members of the committee showed us that the Eastern Tibet Self-Help Project was already underway. We clambered over the foundations for the Tibetan language school and the craft center, permits for which had already been secured from the provincial authorities. We sat up late discussing the needed personnel: teachers in Tibetan and mathematics for the school, trainers in the crafts preserved in exile. Choegyal drew on his knowledge accrued in the creation of Tashi Jong, Fran on lessons he'd learned in the Peace Corps, and I on Sarvodaya experience. We filled pages of notes figuring out a budget — costs for roofing materials and bags of cement, for teachers' and trainers' living needs, for dyes and wool and looms. Since stones and mortar and manual labor were offered free, the monetary costs were modest, but we computed them carefully because I hoped to raise funds in the West. We realized that Choegyal's plan — to reconstruct a hallowed past on a new democratic basis — had no pre-existing model.

At times we wondered: Could this project continue to unfold if Chinese policies changed? What if Choegyal Rinpoche were blocked again in coming back? Ah, but that was why he was giving so much responsibility to the local people.

Fran and Peggy and I felt so at home in Dugu, and so excited about Choegyal's plans, that we imagined we would surely be back again. So our leave-taking felt temporary as hundreds gathered with white scarves of farewell. Kunga loaned us his jeep and driver to take us back — all the way across Sechuan to the airport in Chengdu. We rolled with ease over the miles we had trudged, exhausted and frightened, just a month earlier, but I worried about what would happen at the fateful Yangtse bridge. We still had no travel permits. But Kunga had said we needn't worry — we were on our way *out*, not in. His luck stayed with us; the border guards waved us through with barely a glance.

Within days of our arrival home in Berkeley, the news came through. Chinese authorities had executed a massive crackdown in Lhasa and central Tibet. All Tibetans suspected of deviationist thinking and links with foreigners were subject to arrest, imprisonment, and torture. The liberal Chinese governor was denounced and replaced.

In the months and years that followed, reports trickled out. In central Tibet, especially near Lhasa, monasteries were suppressed as centers of teaching, surviving only as show places for tourists, and the activities of monks were severely restricted. All independent travel was curtailed for both tourists and Tibetans from abroad. The detention of dissidents without trial continued, as did the massive influx of Han Chinese, rendering Tibetans a despised minority in their own land. Wholesale deforestation continued as well, along with the dumping of nuclear wastes and the construction of huge hydroelectric dams on sacred rivers.

And the lid was being lowered on China itself. In Budapest, returning from a Council of All Beings, John Seed and I were pulled to a television set to watch the tragedy of Tiananmen Square.

I knew no way to receive this information without grief and horror, without imagining that once again all was lost. From a foundation I secured some funds for the Eastern Tibet Self-Help Project and sent them on through Choegyal, but my heart was heavy. I walked the Berkeley hills and cried.

Our Tibetan friends, however, seemed untouched by despair. Through Tashi Jong's reliable grapevine, I learned that Bonpa Tulku stayed on in Khampagar for three more years. By the time he left for rest in Nepal, the temple was finished. As for Choegyal Rinpoche, who left through Lhasa on the eve of the crackdown, he seemed, each time I saw him, immune from discouragement. Each time he showed me new photos he had received of the construction and then the completion of the craft center, the school. One featured an exquisite tiger carpet woven there.

I began to wonder if Bonpa Tulku and Choegyal Rinpoche were operating on a time scale larger than ours. Did they draw from deeper wells of commitment? I thought of the difference between their ongoing venture and my one-shot heroics of being smuggled into Tibet. How exciting that had been — hiding under barley bags, fighting the current in a shallow skiff, inching along a cliff-face in the dark. To close friends I loved to recount that story; it let me enjoy the daring for which I pride myself. But Bonpa Tulku's and Choegyal Rinpoche's ongoing efforts define adventure in more enduring terms.

23

The Poison Fire

THE LESSONS FROM THE TIBETANS about faithfulness through time had a particular meaning for me in relation to the care of nuclear wastes. This issue — how to deal with the radioactive materials generated by our nuclear industry and weapons programs — had been nagging at me long before our trip into Tibet. I could not forget what I had learned during our failed battle against the North Anna atomic power station. It was as if the radioactivity, seeping into bodies around our nuclear facilities, worked now in the depths of my mind. Even so, I thought about it mainly as a problem facing those living now. I didn't use my systems training to consider how the radioactivity compounds through time, and what it means inevitably for future generations.

In the spring of 1983, after a workshop tour in Britain, I took off for a week by myself. I rented a car in London and drove out with a map to visit some of the peace camps I'd heard about. They were citizen encampments around missile bases where the United States had deployed nuclear weapons to be launched against the Soviet Union. These camps moved me deeply. Instead of engaging in sporadic demonstrations, instead of coming out for a day's rally and returning to the comforts of home when it was over, people from all walks of life just settled in before the gates and along the barbed wire fences. Hundreds, sometimes thousands at a time, were choosing to sleep on the ground under plastic "benders," relieve themselves in mud holes, cook in the rain — in order to say no to preparations for nuclear war.

Often a camp began with a peace walk of many days and miles, like the women's walk from Cardiff to Greenham Common. People just dropped business-as-usual and headed out together on foot. Along the way they held meetings in towns, and their numbers swelled. They shared their food, their songs and stories, as they moved on to surround a place of nuclear danger. When I joined them around the shifting smoke of a cooking fire, I felt as if I were on some kind of pilgrimage. It mattered to me hugely that people were capable of so totally disrupting their lives for the sake of distant others they would never know.

At Greenham Common, an air base where first strike missiles were being installed, I arrived in time to witness the eviction of the women from their camp near the main gate. To please the military, the town council had just transferred that portion of the commons to private hands. In a steady rain, bailiffs were dragging off the protesters still sitting in the entry road. I watched as the booted and uniformed men trod on hands and breasts, set fire to the tents and gear. I watched a child's gas-soaked doll explode into flames.

"How much longer do you count on staying?" I asked a punk-haired woman rocking her baby as we hunched under my umbrella. She had been an office worker in London. With her free hand she fingered the wet strands of her spikey hairdo. My question puzzled her. "Well, I can't say; I don't know how long it will take." "Take for what?" "To close the base. I'll stay till then, of course." It took thirteen more years.

Making my way from camp to camp — Porton Down, Molesworth, Upper Heyford — I was haunted by a sense of déjà vu. Names like Canterbury and Santiago de Compostella surfaced in my mind. Avignon, Iona, and other pilgrimage sites of medieval Europe. I thought of the monasteries that had kept the flame of learning alive after the breakdown of the Roman Empire, in the long centuries we call the Dark Ages. They too had been training grounds in nonviolent community. There too had been this devotion to an austere and long-term task for the sake of those who come after.

But watching in the rain at Greenham Common I suddenly realized that this déjà vu was not about the past so much as about the future. Of course! For life to go on, this was what would have to happen around the nuclear power and weapons stations. Even after nuclear disarmament, even after the closing of the last reactor, something like these citizen encampments would be necessary to ensure that the radioactivity was contained. For every site and every implement — from uranium mine tailings to reactor cores to warheads and their machineries — will remain both contaminated and contaminating for millennia to come.

The notion of nuclear guardianship first came as a spontaneous vision. In my mind's eye a full-blown, panoramic scene suddenly appeared, in shades of gray, a bit grainy like an old newspaper photo. It recalled to me the woman's drawing in the inaugural despair workshop near Santa Cruz, of stick figures encircling a reactor; for in the middle distance I saw many human forms, sil-houetted against cranes and cooling towers. I couldn't make out what they were doing, as they came and went, forming and reforming in groups. I saw them through a haze, like the damp wood smoke billowing around the Greenham women at their cooking fire.

Throughout that spring week, as I traveled across the lush English coun-tryside, peering through chain link and barbed wire fences at Cruise missile bunkers and rows of F-111s with their ugly pointed snouts, this idea took over my mind. Each day it grew more convincing.

In my mind's eye, I saw surveillance communities forming at today's nuclear facilities. These Guardian Sites would be centers of pilgrimage and reflection, where the cemented cores and waste containments would be reli-giously monitored and repaired. For this ongoing task, the wisdom traditions of our planet would provide contexts of meaning and disciplines of vigilance. Here people, volunteering for varying lengths of time, would take part in an ongoing learning community. Here they would be trained to "remember" — both the story of these radioactive remains and the continual faithfulness they require. As the uranium and plutonium were guarded from negligence and ter-rorists, they would remind us — and continue to remind us for generations to come — of the potential for disaster and the responsibility for care that our nuclear technology has brought upon us. For this technology, which enables us to commit collective suicide, can be dismantled but never uninvented.

Back in the States I started asking scientists, engineers, activists what they thought could be done with our nuclear facilities and materials, once they were no longer in use. At a trial of anti-nuclear activists, I talked with physicist Michio Kaku, who was serving as an expert witness for the defense. He is a brilliant scientist, generous with his knowledge. I asked him what plans exist-ed for decommissioned reactors. We had well over a hundred, and since they were built with a projected lifespan of thirty years, I hoped that government and industry had some idea of what to do with them after that.

The methods that Michio Kaku listed for me boiled down to two options. One was entombment or "mothballing" in concrete. The problem with that option is that the heat of the radioactivity eventually causes the cement to grow brittle and crack.

The alternative was dismantlement and removal. If the reactor is very small, it can be taken away whole — like the Shippingport reactor in

Pennsylvania, the first in the country to be decommissioned. As we spoke, it was being transported by rail and ship through the Panama Canal, to be towed along the Pacific coast to Washington State and barged up the Columbia River for eventual disposal in the Hanford nuclear reservation. The expense was colossal. Most reactors are far larger than Shippingport's and must be sawn into pieces first; that process throws a lot of radioactivity into the air, endangering the workers and the local citizens.

"And what does all that risk and cost accomplish?" I asked. "It just hands the problem to another community, contaminates another part of the country." I didn't know whether to laugh or cry.

"The best we can hope for is some new technology around the corner," Michio Kaku shrugged.

"And while we're waiting for that new technology, wouldn't it suffice just to guard the site, to monitor and repair the containments?" I tried out the idea of Guardian Sites on him. "Could it work?"

"Oh, technically, it would be fairly simple. But the time span is so long, who would bear the cost? How would people be paid? Economically, that wouldn't work." Kaku was called then to the witness stand, leaving me on the courthouse steps where I continued our conversation in my mind.

That's true enough — guardianship of a nuclear reactor would not "work" economically, at least not in terms of our present monetary economy. Other motivations would be necessary, and other kinds of rewards. Would the women at Greenham Common do what they did for pay? Do we, for that matter, require wages to care for our children?

If the disposal of reactors was a serious problem, a more immediate dilemma, I learned, was posed by the used, irradiated fuel rods that were piling up. The solution my government offered was deep geological burial. Chambers were being excavated half a mile below Carlsbad, New Mexico, where a small portion of our military nuclear waste would be hauled by truck across the country and hidden out of sight and out of mind. The place was called WIPP, Waste Isolation Pilot Project, eventually to cost the taxpayers 29 billion dollars. I went to take a look and talk to the manager.

He was a competent man, proud of his work. I liked him, even though he refused to acknowledge that the waste containers would corrode and leak. Independent studies showed the radioactivity would migrate into the Pecos River and the Gulf of Mexico. The WIPP manager and his staff preferred to talk about how safe these wastes would be from human intruders — at least in the short term. High-tech barriers, signs, and alarms would keep away miners and terrorists for a hundred years.

"And after that?" I asked, thinking of the quarter million years the radioactivity endures. I had to repeat the question. "After that? After a hundred years?" My hosts looked at me with incomprehension, as if I had started speaking Sinhalese. Larger time spans were not within their frame of reference.

The best hope is transmutation, said some of my New Age friends. With our technological prowess, this alchemy is just around the corner. It sounded like wishful thinking to me, until I learned that my government was actually funding such a project at Los Alamos Nuclear Lab. Through a friend I managed to get in and talk with one of the scientists involved.

Young, blond, and very smart, he reminded me of Flash Gordon, the space hero from my childhood's Sunday comics. He told me that "transmutation" actually means turning a radioactive isotope with a long half-life into one with a shorter half-life — which you can do by adding a proton or neutron to its nucleus. In order to do *that*, you need this quarter-mile long accelerator to bombard the nucleus. Theoretically, it's a sure thing — computer simulations show it.

"Yes, you're right," he said at one point, "the amount of waste material treated in this fashion will be necessarily small. It's a highly focused, high-energy operation — to say nothing of the tremendous costs involved. If you're talking about *all* our radioactive wastes" — and he laughed at the very idea — "no, transmutation would hardly be applicable."

I sought his views about guardianship, or rather, as I put it, on-site, ground-level, long-term retrievable storage.

"To just monitor and repair the containments in an ongoing fashion, wouldn't that be a feasible low-tech solution?" But Flash Gordon glanced at his watch; the time he had taken to talk with me was over. Only high-tech challenges seemed to interest him.

Another solution I learned about was vitrification, or melting the waste into blocks of glass. At an abandoned nuclear reprocessing plant near West Valley, New York, to the south of my grandfather's old farm, such experiments were under way. One day the authorities offered the public a tour of the premises and a glimpse of this new technology. The small piece of glass they let me hold in my hands was dark green, beautiful — and very expensive. The complex process that produced it was too costly to handle more than a tiny fraction of our country's nuclear waste. U.S. vitrification efforts were soon abandoned.

Although scientists and site managers were not impressed with the idea of Guardian Sites, they were certainly not dissuading me from it. So I began to float the proposal with my fellow anti-nuclear activists. For the first time I encountered outright opposition. It was emotionally charged, as if the notion was not only naive, but treacherous. To many of them — people I admired for their knowledge and tenacity — it seemed treasonable to suggest that anything could be done about radioactive wastes, least of all by local citizens. I realized that they believed they had a strategic stake in the insolubility of the waste problem. The very lack of any viable plan for it was a chief weapon against the nuclear industry.

Their approach to the nuclear makers went something like this: "Look, *you're* producing the stuff, so you must deal with it. Even though you don't know *how* to deal with it, it's your problem, your responsibility, not ours." Though it had not been particularly effective, this position seemed reasonable and occupied a certain moral high ground.

These activists were concerned that if citizens started taking responsibility for the nuclear wastes produced in their name, industry and the military would feel even freer to continue making more. To me the contrary seemed more likely. I believed that when citizens realized the immense, prolonged care required to protect their progeny from radioactive contamination, they would refuse to *tolerate* any more being made. This made a lot of sense to me, but it flew in the face of a standard organizing tactic: "Not in My Backyard." Appealing to people's immediate self-interest, it had proven successful in rallying the public to oppose highway construction and toxic dumps in their neighborhoods. The NIMBY syndrome, as it was called, was fairly compelling.

It seemed to me that people on both sides of the issue were marooned in the present, reluctant or unable to look at it from the perspective of future generations — it would take ten thousand generations, I figured, to exhaust the hazardous life of plutonium. This blindness to the passage of time made it hard for them to consider the fact that no container lasts as long as its radioactive contents, not even fifty years. To keep the contamination out of the biosphere for longer than that, human attention would be required. But *that* seemed the one thing we didn't want to do: to pay attention, to sustain the gaze.

This was understandable. To really face the poisonous legacy we have created — the amounts of it, the longevity of it — dwarfed the mind, threatened to engulf the heart with guilt. We preferred to spend billions on the deepest excavations and the most advanced technologies simply to make the damn stuff disappear from view. I sensed we would do almost anything, anything at all, except look at what we had done.

Yet to the future ones, this legacy would be the hallmark of my generation. How we chose to handle it would matter more to them than any cultural monument or political achievement. They wouldn't care whether an individual had anti-nuclear or pro-nuclear views, but only that he or she belonged to the generation which produced this stuff. I imagined that the future ones would have but one overriding question of me, of us all: "What did you do with the poison fire?"

That's what I now imagined they would call it. The poison fire.

"Did you hide it, out of laziness and shame? Dump it in the ocean, toss it in landfills, bury it in the ground? Abandon it where we, who come after you, cannot locate the source of the contamination that eats our bones, deforms our bodies, stunts our minds? Did you ever think of *caring* for the poison fire? Of passing on to us the knowledge of what it is and how to guard it?"

These questions preoccupied me throughout a solo fortnight at our old lake cottage outside Syracuse. One morning I stuck an overnight bag in the car and drove down to Harrisburg, Pennsylvania. It was August 6, 1984, the anniversary of Hiroshima, and also the trial date for anti-nuclear protesters who had blockaded the reopening of the undamaged reactor at Three Mile Island. It seemed as good an occasion as any to make another pilgrimage — and see a future Guardian Site.

Stopping on the crest of a hill, I stared across at the four cooling towers rising through the mists of the riverbed. Yes, this is how they would appear to future generations. Awe-inspiring. The huge structures swept up in smooth, sweet curves against the sky, like stupendous vases left by some primordial race of giants. They were surely as majestically distinctive as the cathedrals of Chartres and Salisbury must have appeared to the eyes of medieval pilgrims.

In Middletown, the community closest to the power plant, I located the house of a woman I had met by phone and sat down with her at her kitchen table. It was stacked with leaflets, mailing lists, maps, radiation reports. She and two colleagues, whom she'd called in, had a lot to show me. For five years now, ever since the biggest nuclear accident in U.S. history, a handful of Middletown women had been trying to close Three Mile Island. It was hard work, and getting harder.

"There are only four of us now. When we opposed the re-start, people called us hysterical." "You see," said another, "people want to forget."

I called Metropolitan Edison for permission to visit the reactor. "Send us a letter stating your purpose," said a male voice from the Public Relations office. I explained that I was leaving in another day and needed to see the plant because I was writing a story. I was, actually. For my great- great-grandchildren I had begun a tale of how their ancestors developed nuclear guardianship to protect them from harm.

"Are you with a newspaper? What kind of story?"

"It's a story about the monastery at Three Mile Island." Silence at the other end. "The monastery that will be there in the future," I added.

"Oh, it's fiction! Well, I don't see why you need to come in person, if you're making it up."

It's not fiction, I wanted to say, it just hasn't happened yet. But I took another tack, told him I had already talked with citizen groups like Three Mile Alert and wanted to get a balanced picture.

The next morning at nine a company car drove me across the bridge and through the security gates. In one of the squat office buildings beyond the cooling towers, I spent three hours with a public relations man and a couple of engineers. They were preoccupied with the clean-up efforts. Only weeks before, crews with high cranes had removed the top of the containment vessel where the accident had occurred and lowered a remote-control camera to survey the internal damage.

"Would you like to see the video?" they offered hospitably.

On the screen a blurred moonscape appeared. The camera's eye moved across a gray, blocky terrain and down steep escarpments to valleys of twisted, darker debris.

"Those are the burned fuel rods," one of the engineers explained, pointing to the truncated parts of the cliff and the jumbled mass below. "That's how we know that a meltdown occurred."

I wanted to hug him for his honesty — this was what activists had suspected and the utility company had consistently denied. Showing only a mild interest, I learned a lot more before the public relations director remembered his official role and said, "Nothing to worry about now, of course." He reiterated his earlier denials that radioactive water was still leaking into the Susquahanna River and that radioactive gasses still vented into the air, as the Middletown women had told me. They had shown me the measurements.

"This clean-up you're doing is a huge job. No one has tried anything like it before," I said with sincere appreciation. "The experience you are accumulating in dealing with this accident is invaluable — not only for those of us living now, but for the generations to come. I hope you know that and will share it as widely as you can."

The men with whom I'd spent the morning now looked at me with keener attention, as if they were seeing their own grim work from a new perspective.

Between the door of the offices and the waiting car, I dallied. I looked around at the structures housing the reactor cores, the buildings for the storage pool, the soaring towers anchored in their low, accordion-pleated rings. Yes, these would stay as is, and the office buildings would probably serve as dormitories for the guardians and pilgrims. I squinted my eyes to age the scene, blur it with time.

When I returned from Tibet with renewed commitment to long-term nuclear guardianship, the next logical step was to educate myself more. In 1988 I invited a dozen friends to join me in a study group on radioactive wastes. The Fire Group, as we came to call it, included a fine diversity of folks — an anthropologist, a nuclear engineer, a dancer, an environmental lawyer, a wilderness guide, a school teacher, a potter, a writer, an astrophysicist. Soon Fran joined us, too, bringing his clear mind and his enjoyment of group learning. The initial ignorance and curiosity that most of us brought to the subject was more important than any expertise. Many kinds of knowledge would be needed in order for humanity to comprehend and respond to the challenge of the poison fire.

We began to realize that we were giving ourselves the kind of training that our nuclear wastes require of the public at large. It wasn't fair to the future to leave the choices — and the knowledge these choices demand — on the shoulders of bureaucrats and company engineers, whose decisions are inevitably distorted by short-term interests. This stuff was made in our name; attending to it is a civic responsibility, undertaken for our own and our descendants' well-being.

The training we gave ourselves was woven of three strands. We called them the three S's: study, strategy, and spiritual practice. In the first strand we taught ourselves some of the science and technology of the nuclear fuel cycle: the physics of radiation, its biological effects, the known methods of containment, the risks of transportation. To help us digest the cold facts, we invented experiential processes — a square dance for how the nucleus of the uranium atom starts a chain reaction; games on a giant canvas floor map of the continental United States with marks for every nuclear site and dump, and a spaghetti of dotted lines for current transport routes. On this, in our stockinged feet, we enacted scenarios, tracing the effects of leakage, airborne emissions, highway accidents.

The second strand — strategy — was political in nature. We learned about the corporations and government agencies, the laws and regulations, that determine the fate of nuclear waste. Who's deciding what, and where and when? How do citizens intervene? The lawyer in our group read stacks of fineprint late into the night in order to help us grasp some of the legal thickets, and the gaps in them. We showed up at public hearings, offered testimony, and learned a lot there, too.

The third strand — the spiritual — became ever more important to us. How do we stay motivated to look at this toxic quagmire fenced in red tape? It's so easy to turn away and leave it to the bureaucrats and the Mafia, which was already heavily involved. Where do we find enough strength and love for life, even self-respect, to look at what has been made in our name? Slowly, thoughtfully, we worked out a twelve-point Guardianship Ethic, spelling out the moral common sense of public care for the wastes.

These strands were tightly braided; one involved the other. It was hard really to absorb some of this information — be it about corroding tanks leaking plutonium into the Columbia and Savannah Rivers or about pieces of reactor cores to be dumped in shallow desert trenches near the Colorado. We needed tears and prayers, even drumming and dancing, if we were to go forward with any faith in our own hearts.

One November day it was my turn to take the teaching role. The session was to focus on current U.S. containment practices. The information, which I had researched at length and prepared on sheets of newsprint, was fairly technical; it was also so horrific that I worried about my colleagues' ability to sustain their attention and motivation. We needed some help.

On the front door I stuck a sign reading "CHERNOBYL TIME LAB: 2088" and put on some of Fran's Russian liturgical music. As people came in,

I said, "Welcome! Our work here at the time laboratory of this Guardian Site is based on the importance of being able to journey backward through time. This is because the decisions made by people in the late twentieth century on how to deal with the poison fire have such long-term effects. We must help them make the right decisions. So you have been selected to go back in time to a particular group in Berkeley, California, that has come to our attention. They are meeting exactly one hundred years ago today to try to understand, with their limited mentality, the ways their 'experts' are containing the poison fire. It is easy for this group to feel ignorant and discouraged. Therefore, we will go backward in time to enter their bodies as they proceed with their study so that they will not become disheartened."

"Our research reveals," I said, "that in time travel an essential factor is intention — strong, unwavering belief in the purposes the heart has chosen. If our intention is clear, we can travel back a century to embody ourselves in this very group. It will take about thirty seconds." I turned up the music for a bit, then, switching it off, simply proceeded with the day's topic. In the course of the session, no comments were made about its odd beginning. Everyone was too keenly focused on the material itself. But each of us, I think, sensed a heightened caring, like an internal presence that wanted us to understand about the poison fire and not underestimate our own intelligence.

In another few months, when it was the anthropologist's turn to prepare the teaching, we were again taken imaginatively into the future. To portray the perspective of future generations on how their late twentieth-century ancestors came to the notion of guarding the poison fire, she made a slide show. The visual alternation of nuclear facilities with ancient shrines had a timeless, mythic quality — and an undeniable moral logic. Later, along with an evocative musical background, we added images of "guardian" faces carved by ancient cultures and crafted ritual words that the future ones would speak as they remembered what happened in our time.

Soon we were taking the Guardian Site slide show to schools and churches and organizations. The presentation entailed a dramatic displacement in time, as members of the audience were addressed as future pilgrims and guardians of the poison fire. Each time we presented the slide show in the U.S., Germany, the U.K., Russia, Japan, we were grateful for its beauty, its excitement — and the way it invoked human faithfulness across the ages.

By this time the Fire Group had transmogrified into a public education-al effort called the Nuclear Guardianship Project, which in turn gave birth to a tabloid-size publication, the *Nuclear Guardianship Forum*. For three years and three gorgeous issues, we disseminated technical and moral arguments for on-site retrievable storage. We offered the kind of training we had given our-selves in the Fire Group and also put key articles on the Web (at www.nonukes.org).

After six years of monthly meetings, our Fire Group disbanded, its mem-bers moving out like seeds in the wind. Wendy Oser coordinated the writing and publication of the *Safe Energy Handbook* and its translation into Turkish, Chinese, Japanese, Korean, Russian, Ukrainian, Slovenian, French, and Spanish. Susan Griffin completed *A Chorus of Stones*, and was a finalist for the Pulitzer Prize for this book on the human stories and habits of mind behind nuclear weapons. Pamela Dake, our former high-school teacher, crafted a pow-erful video for the successful citizen battle against the Ward Valley nuclear waste dump in the California desert. Ed Fuller, our engineer, left his position with a nuclear industry institute to become a private consultant on reactor safety; he commits a good measure of his time now to Buddhist practice and the care of a Tibetan retreat center. Brian Swimme wrote *The Hidden Heart of the Cosmos* and founded the Epic of Evolution Society, both of which are devoted to helping people understand their intimate relationship with the far past and the far future of life on Earth.

Charlotte Cooke moved to New Mexico to join the citizens' struggle to stop the burial of radioactive wastes at WIPP, and to work with the Los Alamos Study Group. Molly Young Brown, who grew up at the Los Alamos Nuclear Lab, has also returned to the Southwest to teach and organize, but not before she co-authored *Coming Back to Life* with me, a book describing the group practices we developed in the Fire Group and, more broadly, in our deep ecol-ogy work. Kathleen Sullivan, after working to close the Rocky Flats nuclear weapons production site near Boulder, Colorado, went to live in England, where she assisted the campaign against the notorious Sellafield complex for reprocessing and storing nuclear wastes; the guardianship concept was central to her doctoral dissertation and the Ph.D. it won for her at Lancaster University.

The German Fire Group, or *Feuergruppe*, which emerged from my week-long workshop near Frankfurt in 1990, continues to gather for two or three weekends a year. I admire its creativity in devising new experiential methods to explore the psychological and moral challenges of the poison fire. Its members have testified at government hearings on waste policy and participated in successful citizen actions to stop the burial of nuclear waste in the salt caverns of Gorleben. In 1994, five years before Switzerland announced its phase-out of nuclear energy production, I joined a group of them in Bern to present the guardianship concept — called *das Hüterkonzept* — to the Swiss government body in charge of nuclear waste disposal. In 1999 several friends from the Feuergruppe organized a five-week pilgrimage to nuclear sites across Germany, from a uranium mine to power plants to NATO weapons depots. By train and bike and on foot, thirty people took part in what they called "a journey across our irradiated republic, to awaken us, bond us, and commit us to life in the future."

In the course of the Nuclear Guardianship Project, Fran and I began working together quite intensively — compiling data for the meetings, visiting power plants, writing articles, giving testimony, presenting the slide show. In 1991 I joined his delegation to Kiev for the Fifth Anniversary of Chernobyl; there we conceived, for the following year, a series of workshops for people in contaminated areas. Fran found his Fire Group experience very useful as he started working with anti-nuclear activists in Russia and Ukraine. They responded to the learning methods and moral concerns he brought, and they translated the twelve-point Guardianship Ethic for their own education campaigns. Soon Fran's collaboration with these new friends became more systematic and ambitious, involving local scientists and government authorities as well: in Krasnoyarsk, a major waste site in Siberia; in Zaparozha, the Ukrainian city containing the world's largest nuclear power station; in Chelyabinsk, the weapons production complex in the Urals and the most radioactively contaminated place on Earth. To support the activists, Fran, with a growing team of American colleagues and funds from several foundations, created the Center for Safe Energy. I love meeting these men and women from the former Soviet Union, whom the Center for Safe Energy brings through my home. The stories they tell and their quiet determination give me lessons in courage.

My own life continues to be enriched by the challenges that the poison fire presents, and particularly by its summons to experience our living connection with the generations to come. Now the Buddha's teaching of dependent co-arising takes on a new dimension, extends in time as well as in space.

When the seventh-century scholar Fa Tsang used light and mirrors to demonstrate the interpenetration of all phenomena, the Chinese Empress asked him if he could show in a similar physical fashion the interplay between past, present, and future. Fa Tsang said that such a demonstration might be possible to contrive, but that it would be much more difficult and that he didn't have the means at hand.

I want to tell Fa Tsang that we have managed to achieve it. In the radioactive legacy we have created, we have found a way to apprehend our immediate, unseverable connections through time. This legacy has prompted Sister Rosalie Bertell, a radiologist studying the genetic effects of nuclear contamination, to state that all beings who will ever live on Earth are here now. Where? In our ovaries and gonads, in our DNA — and the choices we make now with our radioactive materials will determine whether the future ones will be born sound of mind and body.

To feel the presence of future generations and to be inspired to act on their behalf, the Fire Group invented imaginative games, such as the Chernobyl Time Lab of a century hence, or enacted encounters with those who will live where the poison fire is burned. Now I take these and similar exercises into my classes and workshops — I call them Deep Time work.

Just as the nuclear waste summoned my attention to future generations, so does the whole environmental movement with its proliferating battles to save forests and seas and soil. As I watch these struggles, joining in when I can, the beings of the future become ever more real to me. Sometimes I feel them at my side, urging me on when I'm tired and discouraged. Sometimes I find myself praying, not only *for* the future ones, but also *to* them. I ask them to help us be faithful in the work that we, their ancestors, have been given to do. For a book called *Prayers for a Thousand Years*, I wrote:

> You live inside us, beings of the future.
> In the spiral ribbons of our cells, you are here. In our rage
> for the burning forests, the poisoned fields, the oil-drowned
> seals, you are here. You beat in our hearts through late-
> night meetings. You accompany us to clearcuts and toxic
> dumps and the halls of the lawmakers. It is you who drive
> our dogged labors to save what is left.
> O you who will walk this Earth when we are gone, stir us
> awake. Behold through our eyes the beauty of this world.
> Let us feel your breath in our lungs, your cry in our throat.

Let us see you in the poor, the homeless, the sick.
Haunt us with your hunger, hound us with your claims,
that we may honor the life that links us.
You have as yet no faces we can see, no names we can say.
But we need only hold you in our mind, and you teach us
patience. You attune us to measures of time where healing
can happen, where soil and souls can mend.
You reveal courage within us we had not suspected,
love we had not owned.
O you who come after, help us remember:
we are your ancestors. Fill us with gladness for the
work that must be done.

WIDENING CIRCLES

24

The Elm Dance

THERE IS A CIRCLE DANCE WE DO in every workshop and class of mine, whether it's on systems theory, Buddhism, or deep ecology. We do it to open our minds to the wider world we live in and to strengthen our intention to take part in its healing. Each time we put on the music and link hands, I think of Novozybkov in the fall of 1992.

Our team of four — Fran and I and two Russians — had been traveling from one town to another in Belarus and Ukraine, offering workshops to people living in areas contaminated by the Chernobyl disaster. Now we had come to our final stop: the town of Novozybkov, an agricultural and light industrial city of 50,000 a hundred miles east of Chernobyl, in the Bryansk region of Russia.

Drawing on what we learned from years of leading despair work, we came to offer, as we put it to the authorities, "psychological tools for coping with the effects of massive, collective trauma." We had entitled the workshops "Building a Strong Post-Chernobyl Culture." The name had a nice Soviet ring to it, but I soon realized that the word "post" was wrong. "It suggests that the disaster is over," I said to Fran, "but it's obvious that it isn't over." The radioactivity was still spreading silently through wind, water, fodder, and food, creating new toxins as it mixed with industrial pollution, and sickening bodies already weakened from previous exposures. Our workshops, we soon realized, were not so much to help people recover from a catastrophe as live with an ongoing one.

It was Harasch who insisted that we come to Novozybkov. A Russian psychologist practicing in Moscow, he had flown to Chernobyl within hours of the accident to give support to the operators of the doomed reactor. In the six years that followed, he traveled to towns throughout the region to help the survivors, but no place had touched his heart more deeply than this city and its fate.

On the train, as we headed east from Minsk toward the Russian border, he pulled out the map and told us the story once more. The burning reactor was a volcano of radioactivity when the winds shifted to the northeast, carrying the clouds of poisoned smoke in the direction of Moscow. To save the millions in the metropolitan area, a fast decision was taken to seed the clouds and cause them to precipitate. An unusually heavy late April rain, bearing intense concentrations of radioactive iodine, strontium, cesium, and particles of plutonium, drenched the towns and fields and forests of the Bryansk region, just across the Russian border from Chernobyl. The highest Geiger counter readings were measured, as they still are, in and around the city of Novozybkov. "The people there were not informed of their government's choice — who wants to tell people they're disposable? By now it's common knowledge that the clouds were seeded, but it is rarely mentioned," said Harasch, "and that silence, too, is part of the tragedy for the people of Novozybkov."

In a big open room of a school for special education, fifty people of Novozybkov, mostly teachers and parents, women predominating, were seated in a large circle. Carefully, almost formally dressed, they sat upright, eyes riveted on the speaker, and stood up when they spoke, the way their children stand in school when called to recite.

As I explained the nature and purpose of the work we came to do, I was glad for Yuri's swift and cogent translations. A young physician and social activist, he had used my books extensively in Moscow and had his own things to say about how people can overcome feelings of isolation and powerlessness and reconnect to take charge of their lives. To interpret from Russian to English for me, without delaying things, Fran murmured in my ear. By midmorning there had been so many words, I was glad for a respite from them when I put on the tape of the Elm Dance and showed the simple steps. Then we all just joined hands and moved together to the music.

The fifty-four of us in the room were too many to dance in one circle, so we formed concentric rings. The movements are easy to learn, and soon the rings were slowly orbiting to the music; each time we stepped toward the middle, raising our linked hands high, it was like a giant sunflower or a many-petaled lotus.

As we danced I wondered what the mayor of Novozybkov would think to see us. Our team had called on him upon our arrival the previous day to explain what we'd come to do. The handsome, heavyset man of about forty listened guardedly. "It is good of you to come to undertake psychological rehabilitation," he said.

That was the term now in vogue: "psychological rehabilitation". I was glad that the emotional toll of the disaster was at last acknowledged by the authorities, especially since, in the three years following the accident, doctors were ordered by the Ministry of Health to dismiss its effects. When people insisted that their sickness and exhaustion, their cancers, miscarriages, and deformed babies, had something to do with Chernobyl, they were diagnosed as afflicted with "radiophobia," an irrational fear of radiation. Still the phrase "psychological rehabilitation" irked me; I considered it an affront to the victims of Chernobyl. It reduced their suffering to a pathology, as if it were something to be corrected.

How could we convey to the mayor the basic difference in our assumptions? "Mr. Mayor, we do not imagine that we can take away the suffering of your people," I said. "That would be presumptuous on our part. But what we can do is look together at the two main ways we respond to collective suffering. The suffering of a people can bring forth from them new strengths and solidarity. Or it can breed isolation and conflict, turning them against each other. There is always a choice."

At that the mayor's demeanor totally changed. Leaning back in his chair, he spread his hands on the table and said, "There is not a single day, nor a single encounter in this office, that does not show the anger stirring just under the surface. Whatever the matter at hand, there is this anger that is barely contained, ready to explode." Then, after a pause, "What can I do to support your work here?"

It became clear, however, on that first day of the workshop, that these people had no desire to talk about Chernobyl and its ongoing presence in their lives. They referred to it in passing as "the event" and went on to speak of other things. People in less contaminated towns than this had told us in detail of the exhaustion, the chronic infections, the emerging patterns of cancers and birth defects. Now I'd come to this most toxic place, to be with these people in their suffering, and they didn't want to talk about it. Even when a married couple took turns leaving in morning and afternoon, they said no word about their little girl in the hospital, to whose bedside they hurried.

The group's silence seemed to say, "This we don't need to talk about. We have to deal with this nightmare all the rest of our time. Here, at last, we can think about something else. We can look together at how we can achieve some sanity and harmony in family life." On that last point, they were explicit. They wanted to know how to deal with defiant children, sullen, depressed spouses, backbiting neighbors.

Harasch leaned over to me. "It's all the same thing," he whispered. "Chernobyl. On the conscious level, Chernobyl becomes tension and strife in family relations."

Okay, we'll focus on family life. It was lively, as people took partners to enact encounters between parents and children, switching roles, practicing how to listen to each other. This led them to remember their own childhoods — not only the adolescent frustrations that could help them empathize with their own offspring, but the good times, too. They shared reminiscences of harvest seasons with the grandparents, and sleigh parties, and fishing outings to the Dnieper. It all felt so restorative — as if we were partaking together of an excellent and wholesome meal — that Fran set up more exercises where people could remember together the old sources of joy.

Why did this suddenly feel so important? "We're strengthening our cultural immune system," I thought to myself, then said aloud. Just as radiation attacks the integrity of the body, breaking down its capacity for resilience and self-healing, so does it assault our society. Through physical exhaustion and moral despair, it erodes a community's sense of wholeness and continuity. To bolster our cultural immune system, we need to recall who we are and what we love; memories help us do that.

Evening now, and before disbanding to go home, we are circling once more to the music. A guitar is playing and a woman singing. She sings in Latvian in honor of the elm and in hope of its healing, for that tree ails in the Baltics as in my own country. Her words, I'm told, disguise other meanings as well — a call for freedom from Soviet occupation and for the will to endure and resist. It doesn't matter that we don't know Latvian; it's the lilt of her voice that we dance to and the haunting melody, stately and filled with yearning.

By now the simple steps are so familiar that some people are dancing with eyes closed. Their faces grow still, as if they're listening for something almost out of reach. Once they had their own folk dances. When did those old traditions die away, relegated to a useless past? Was it under Lenin? Stalin?

Our hosts, Fran's and mine, live in a fourth-floor apartment in a cement hous-ing block. Covering one wall of their parlor is a beautiful woodland scene: sun-light flickers through birch trees into a grassy glade. In the room crowded with overstuffed furniture, that wallpaper vista provides a refreshing sense of space and natural beauty. I commented on it that evening as I took tea with Vladimir Ilyich, our host's father and the Novozybkov school superintendent. Sitting there with his ten-year-old grandson, he was showing me the large Geiger counter he carries in his car; it shows him where the poison has newly appeared, and where to tell the children not to play.

Following my eyes, Vladimir Ilyich said, "That is where the children may not go — or any of us, for that matter. You see, the trees hold the radioactivi-ty a long time. And that is very hard for us because, you see, our ancestors were of the forest, our old stories are of the forest. During the Nazi occupation, our partisans fought from the forest. Even in the hardest times under Stalin, we went into the woodlands every holiday, every weekend — walking, picnicking, mushrooming. Yes, we were always people of the forest." Quietly he repeated, "people of the forest."

"Vladimir Ilyich," I asked him, "when will you be able to go back into the forest?" With a tired little smile he shrugged. "Not in my lifetime," he said and, looking at his grandson, he added, "and not in his lifetime either." Then he gestured to the wallpaper: "This is our forest now."

It is the second morning of our three days together, and the people entering the school assembly room take each other's hands and, before any words are spoken, move into the Elm Dance. Every fourth measure, between moving right or left, forwards or backwards, we pause for four beats, gently swaying. To my eyes this morning, we could be trees, slender trunks swaying from firm roots, our arms, as we raise them, looking like branches meeting, interlacing. Do we dance for the forests we can no longer enter?

As I circle in step with all the others, I recall the connections that brought me this dance — how it came to me from Hannelore, my friend in Germany, who had received it from Anastasia, *her* German friend, who had created it from the Latvian song. The dance is not only for the healing of the elm, said Anastasia to Hannelore to me. It is for intention. It is to strengthen our capacity to choose a purpose, and to follow through on the resolve our hearts have made.

I hear again in my mind Khamtrul Rinpoche's teaching about the supreme importance of motivation, bodhicitta. I remember Ocean of

Wisdom, too — the blazing intention that he embodied as he walked out smiling into poverty and danger. And I think: this is a bodhisattva dance.

That afternoon the grief broke open.

It happened unexpectedly, at the close of a guided meditation in which I invited these people of Novozybkov to connect with their ancestors and harvest their strengths. Moving through the room, as on a vast wheel turning, they went backwards in time through all preceding generations, with Yuri's voice guiding them. Then they stopped and moved forward, retracing their steps through time, in order to gather the gifts of the ancestors. But when we came up to the year 1986, they balked. They did not want to come any further into the present. They refused to accept the horror of what happened to them then — and that very refusal compelled them to speak of it.

Talk exploded, releasing memories of that unacceptable spring: the searing hot wind from the southwest, the white ash that fell from a clear sky, the children running and playing in it, the drenching rain that followed, the rumors, the fear. Remember how it was? Remember, remember? Our team had laid out paper and colored pencils for people to draw the gifts they'd harvested from the ancestors, but now there was one theme only. A number of the drawings featured trees, and a road to the trees, and across the road a barrier, or large X, blocking the way.

When we finally reassembled in one large circle, the good feelings that had grown during the workshop shattered now in anger, directed at me. "Why have you done this to us?" a woman cried out. "What good does it do? I would be willing to feel the sorrow — all the sorrow in the world — if it could save my two little daughters from cancer. Each time I look at them I wonder about tumors growing inside them. Can my tears protect them? What good are my tears if they can't?"

Angry, puzzled statements came from others as well. Our time together had been so good until now, so welcome a respite from what their lives had become — why had I spoiled it?

Listening to them all, I felt deeply chastened and silently blamed myself for my insensitivity. What, now, could I possibly say? To discourse on the value of despair work would be obscene. When I finally broke the silence that followed the long outburst, I was surprised that the words that came were not about them or their suffering under Chernobyl, but about the people of Hannelore and Anastasia.

"I have no wisdom with which to meet your grief. But I can share this with you: after the war which almost destroyed their country, the German people determined they would do anything to spare their children the suffering they had known. They worked hard to provide them a safe, rich life. They created an economic miracle. They gave their children everything — except for one thing. They did not give them their broken hearts. And their children have never forgiven them."

The next morning, as we took our seats after the Elm Dance, I was relieved to see that all fifty had returned. Behind us, still taped to the walls, hung the drawings of the previous afternoon, the sketches of the trees and the slashing X's that barred the way to the trees. "It was hard yesterday," I said. "How is it with you now?"

The first to rise was the woman who had expressed the greatest anger, the mother of the two daughters. "I hardly slept. It feels like my heart is breaking open. Maybe it will keep breaking again and again, I don't know. But somehow — I can't explain — it feels right. It connects me to everything and everyone, as if we were all branches of the same tree."

Of the others who spoke after her that last morning, one was the man who regularly stepped out to visit his little girl in the hospital. This was the first time he had addressed the whole group, and his bearing was as stolid, his face as expressionless, as ever. "Yes, it was hard yesterday," he said. "Hard to look at the pain, hard to feel it, hard to speak it. But the way it feels today — it is like being clean, for the first time in a long time." *Chisti*, the word he used for "clean," also means "uncontaminated".

At my turn, I spoke of the meeting I would attend the following week in Salzburg, Austria, the World Uranium Hearing, where native peoples from around the world would testify to their experiences of nuclear contamination. Navajo and Namibian miners would come, Marshall Islanders, Kazakhs, Western Shoshone downwinders from testing sites, and many others — to speak out about the disease and death that follow in the wake of nuclear power and weapons production. I wanted these men and women of Novozybkov to know that they are not alone in their suffering, but part of a vast web of brothers and sisters who are determined to use their painful experience to help restore the health of our world. "At the hearing, I will speak of you, and I will tell your story to my own people back home. I promise you."

I made that vow because I loved them now, and because I knew they felt forgotten by the outside world, which prefers to think that the disaster of Chernobyl is over. As the years pass since that fateful April of 1986, the catastrophe can be wiped from our consciousness as easily as the bulldozers razed the old wooden houses of Novozybkov because, as Vladimir Ilyich said, "wood holds the radioactivity." And now, as their own government proceeds to build more reactors, it can seem to these families that nothing has been learned from all the suffering. That may be the hardest thing to bear.

I have kept the promise I made to my friends in Novozybkov. I spoke of them at the World Uranium Hearing, and then to every group I met, every class I taught. I found it easier to share their story when I shared the Elm Dance they loved. In Boston and London, in Bonn and Vancouver, in Tokyo and Sydney and everywhere else I led workshops, I asked people to imagine they are dancing with the men and women of Novozybkov, holding the hands of Vladimir, Elena, Olga, Igor, Misha. I have wanted them to feel, more strongly than they can through words alone, how their lives are interlaced with the people of Chernobyl.

Now, strikingly, the truth is this: the Elm Dance has become both the medium and the message. Because people do it with their bodies and with each other, the dance has acquired its own reality — its own life momentum, spreading from group to group, city to city, country to country. It has become a teacher in its own right. Being a dance of intention, it helps us strengthen our resolve, not only for the well-being of those around Chernobyl, but for wider healings as well. The custom has arisen, in the last half of the dance, to call out spontaneously the names of those whose healing we desire: salmon, redwoods, topsoil, the schools, the prisons, Bosnia, Kosovo, the Amazon. Entering the dance then is like entering a sort of neural web in which we can experience our interconnectedness with all beings. Or it's like a sonic Indra's Net, letting us feel our mutual belonging and the ways it can sustain us.

We do not say this, though. The dance says it for us as we stop talking and circle up, moving in steps that seem to remember themselves. Afterwards, more copies of the tape are made and taken out to other people, other places — classrooms, churches, meeting halls. Even to beaches, to be boomed out from pick-up trucks.

"The police don't arrest us while we're dancing," say our friends in Australia, who have incorporated the Elm Dance into their direct actions to protect the last stands of old growth forest and to try to block construction of more uranium mines. They dance, they say, to stay connected with each other and steady in their intention: "It helps us remember why we're doing what we're doing." The southwest forests where they camp and the wet jungle of northern Kakadu offer no hookups for tape players — and none are needed, for the Latvian melody sings out now through their open throats. Under ancient Karri trees, the tallest and most beautiful of the eucalypts, I have seen the dance encircle a bulldozer and bring it to a halt. I have seen it stop the noonday traffic in downtown Sydney. At a demonstration against their government's support for the bombing of Iraq, I listened to the earnest, strident speakers at the mike and added my own words, too; but when my friends put down their placards and joined hands in the Elm Dance, I saw what happened to the whole event. In the surrounding crowd, as in myself, I felt a deepening and quieting of attention. The television cameramen, who had begun drifting away, hurried back, even crawled between us — forty of us by now — to film from below the patterns we made as we circled about and raised our linked hands. So the day's newscasts, between bulletins on the war, announced and showed how "people are dancing for peace."

Aboriginal Australians had something more memorable to say about the Elm Dance when our friends from Perth made a pilgrimage to their ancestral lands to protest a proposed uranium mine. As traditional owners of the sites to be excavated, the native elders have been mightily wooed by the mining industry and its proponents in government. The offers of jobs and money, with promises of more to come, have confused them as to what is best for their people; even the warnings from anti-nuclear activists have seemed like so many words. But when the pilgrims from Perth arrived and the old ones saw them circle up and move into the Elm Dance, they grinned. "You White fellas must know something real if you dancing."

25

Bodh Gaya

SOON AFTER SUNRISE, the marble is already warm under our bare feet. It is fresh — washed and wet, when we enter through the eastern gate and pause to take in the scene that opens out below us. It is a many-acred mandala of shrines and memorials, trees, flowering shrubs, with the towering temple in its center, almost yellow in the early sun. But we don't pause for long; like the other pilgrims, we have our circumambulations to make, and in another two hours the walkways not in shadow will be hot as a griddle. We won't descend the stairways yet, to walk the lower paths; we like to start out on the highest level. Opening our striped umbrella, whose shade can cover us both, we smile to each other and begin.

I have been to Bodh Gaya before, and treasure each visit to this hub of the Buddhist world, this spot of Gautama, the Buddha's enlightenment. But I never came with Fran. I never thought he wanted to come. Now here we are, in the fifth decade of our marriage, on either side of seventy, giving ten whole days to the enjoyment of this place.

At the tail end of the monsoon, it is sweltering — the off-season for tourists. Our fellow pilgrims are so few, their faces grow distinct and familiar. With a smile and a bow, we greet the regulars — the slender, bespectacled Japanese girl; the orange-robed Sinhalese bhikkhu, so sternly concentrated and so resonant in his solo chanting; the radiant, round-faced Burmese woman; the tall, fast-walking Tibetan monk, easily as old as we are. Like them, we come mostly in the mornings and again after sunset, to sit in our favorite contemplative spots and walk round and round the encircling pathways.

It is the bodhi tree, not the grand nine-story temple above it, that holds the center. In the course of the morning, Fran and I move ever closer to it, until its rustling heart-shaped leaves are overhead and we can touch the mammoth gold-flecked trunk. Here, two and a half millennia ago, under an ancestor tree to this one, Siddhartha Gautama sat in vigil, became the

Buddha. Here the pilgrims cluster today, as they have through the ages, offering flowers, intoning prayers, sitting in closed-eyed silence. The reverence of centuries bathes us.

Tree worship, I am telling Fran, was India's primordial religious practice. Yakshas and Yakshis, male and female tree spirits, were honored and their blessings sought because they represent the fertility of life. When Buddhism emerged, it did not set itself in opposition to this adoration of nature. It did not say "Cut down the groves" as Jahweh commanded when the Hebrews moved into Canaan or as Rome ordered when its missionaries spread out to convert Britain. The Buddha's followers simply, comfortably, used the much-cherished tree to represent the central event of the Buddha's life and the source of the truth he taught.

Fran moves off to sit on the petal-strewn pavement, knee to knee with a family of Thais, and closes his eyes. Leaning back against the stone railing, I stare up into the thick green canopy. It is fuller and darker than the maple in which I sat as a child on Ouie' farm, but the inner quiet I feel seems the same as the spacious stillness I knew then. I remember, too, the visions of roots and branches that cascaded through me after the blessing by His Holiness the Karmapa. And I recall how, when I was led then into the study of systems theory, tree imagery abounded, conveying the way open systems take form and grow out of each other.

On our first morning, I tell Fran about the Buddhist practice of "transferring the merit." On a three-month vipassana retreat, I had adopted that practice to dedicate each day to someone who mattered to me. When the long hours on the meditation cushion became hard, even scary, I discovered that the one to whose benefit I had offered the day buoyed me. Or at least my love for them did.

Fran likes the idea; it gives added purpose to our earnest pleasures. So here in Bodh Gaya we dedicate each day to those we hold in our hearts: friends with a teenage child in trouble, a couple struggling with their marriage, a neighbor in surgery, colleagues in Moscow caught in the collapse of the Russian economy. As we start out, clockwise from the eastern gate, we decide who it will be this day, then settle into the silence of mindful walking. It is such a luxury to be able to reflect at length on those who have graced our lives. Soon our concerns and intentions for them give way to thanksgiving for their existence; to see their qualities afresh is like opening a present on

Christmas morning. Already on the first circuit, by the time we reach the sun-baked northern side, we are telling each other about the wonderfulness of our person of the day.

We give a day, of course, to each of our children — Peggy, Jack, Chris. And the same magic happens. We start out picturing their lives back in Berkeley, focusing on the particular challenges they face. Soon they seem to be walking beside us in the bright, green morning. I pretend they can see through my eyes the emerald parakeets swooping by the red hibiscus blossoms and feel through my soles how the marble cools in the shade.

I have grown accustomed, once again, to our children's company. There were years when we lived far apart — Peggy in Ecuador with the Peace Corps, then in Paris with her lover Grégoire; Jack in Boston, settled into his circle of friends from college and his environmental work for Massachusetts; Chris wandering around Oregon, in and out of touch with us. Our family seemed permanently scattered when Fran and I finally sold the Lowell Street house in Washington D.C. and moved to California, where work and colleagues beckoned us. We never dreamed that we would all live close together again. But then, over the last ten years, like those parakeets dropping into the tamarind tree, our children settled around us.

The innermost walkway around the bodhi tree and its temple is enclosed by a stone rail fence. It was built, they say, by King Ashoka, twenty-two hundred years ago. Each pillar is carved with medallions, and on this day dedicated to Peggy and her family, I see that most of the medallions are lotuses, that many of the lotuses enclose sculpted faces, and that all of the faces are smiling. I see Peggy's smile, and Mama's too, for whom she was named. They are a lot alike in their loveliness and laughter. Mama never lost that buoyancy, even in the hardest times with Papa, and Peggy never seems to lose it either, though many of her children, in the pediatric AIDS service of Children's Hospital, die.

My fingers caress the lightly eroded face in the stone lotus. I see her sitting in the backyard of the two-flat house that Fran and I bought with her and Grégoire. She is making a quilt for the thirty children she lost, a differently colored and patterned square for each one. It is an act of completion, and also an act of hope, because the quilt is for the child she hopes to conceive. After two years of struggling with infertility, she now seeks, in this ritual of her own design, the blessings of those who best know the kind of mother she can be.

Now the smile in the lotus becomes *her* smile as she holds her baby boy, and Grégoire's as he roars home on his motorcycle to greet his "petit poussin." And it is Julien's as he climbs the stairs to our flat and heads to the toy basket, as if he owns the place.

After sunset, when the heat is spent, we return to the mandala rising around the bodhi tree, walk through pools of darkness and lamplight. On the evening of the day that is Jack's, a tide of chanting Sri Lankan pilgrims sweeps around us, sets the banks of oil cups ablaze. He loves South Asia, too, that earnest, blue-eyed son. I stop before a smoke-blackened deity in the temple wall, glinting in the glimmer of the candles below it. Who is this man, whose birth in Munich hung me on a turning wheel? Who forgave my maternal angers and outgrew his boyhood timidities, who has accompanied me into danger and discovery? As I stare into the stone's greasy glisten, I can almost see his face, grime-streaked at the encampment by the Seabrook reactor. And I'm crying a little, knowing, as I always have, how he impelled me to learn what I needed to learn about the state of our threatened world.

I move on to find Fran. He is on the temple's western side, watching the lines of Sri Lankan devotees; he is easy to discern, being so tall, with silver hair glistening in the light of their lamps. We take each other's arm for the one last go-round. We don't need to speak, for we know each other's gratitude: for Jack, for his decision to come west to direct San Francisco's recycling program and to settle in Berkeley close to our house; for beloved Charlotte who followed him from Boston; and for their child, year-old Eliza.

Huan Tsang came to Bodh Gaya in the seventh century. He is the Chinese pilgrim-scholar in whose guise I appeared at Huston and Kendra Smith's incarnation party. The place, as he described it, was a vast institution, anchored in wealth and prestige — monasteries and monuments jammed together for a mile and a half around the sacred tree. Then history intervened. Assaults by the Hindu priesthood and invasions by the Moghuls drove Buddhism from the land of its birth. It is hard, in the pious fervor of this place, to imagine the long centuries when it lay neglected, desolate, piled with refuse. Or to think it was only in the last sixty years, shorter than my lifetime, that it was restored as a pilgrimage site. I think of these reversals of history on the day we walk for Christopher.

As Fran and I head out on our rounds on Christopher's day, we step into our old patterns of worry on his behalf. How deeply we want stability for Chris — a relationship he can commit to, a job that can last, even a steady place to live. But once again, as happens so repeatedly here, concerns give way to gratitude. Chris is no longer lost, drifted out of sight. When he came down from Oregon to paint the rooms of the house we bought with Peggy and Grégoire, he stayed on. We see him continually, hear his stories of the life of a handyman around Berkeley. The instant he opens the door, I know it's him because gorgeous wolf-dog Esther is already up the stairs and in the kitchen. Then, after finishing off our meal, we may go out with them for a walk in the hills or a ramble through the Ashby flea market or an evening of jazz.

Today Fran and I branch off the south side of the perimeter and walk around Muchilinda pond, where a carved Buddha sits amidst the water lilies. He is protected by the serpent king, whose hood spreads above him like a parasol. The scene fades into images of Christopher in Nigeria, with his royal pythons around his neck and shoulders; and then of him scuba-diving with me in Tunisia as we spiral and somersault down through schools of colored fish.

When I turn back toward the Mahabodhi temple, I can almost see on its high, intricate facade a boy-form climbing — as ten-year-old Chris climbed the sculpted temples of Khajuraho when we lived in India. It scared me then, just as it did when he disappeared into the inner scaffoldings of the National Cathedral. He always treated the monuments of our civilization as if they were his playground. Or as if the proud achievements of our culture already lay in rubble, to be turned to new, ingenious uses. In any city, he still heads into the alleyways, the flea markets, the encampments of the homeless — as if what is broken and discarded has some meaning for the future. Chris, the paradox, who stockpiles old clothes and cars with rusted transmissions yet lives on nearly nothing. Chris, the survivor, who may help us pick our way some day through the ruins of our civilization. Chris, who follows, in every local speech and interview I give, the work I have chosen to do, and whose brown eyes both support and forgive my ambitions.

In the Mahabodhi morning, I follow Fran down the steps toward the great tree and let go, once again, of my worries for Chris. As the once-great Bodh Gaya establishment crumbled and then revived in simpler, truer form, so have my hopes for our first-born son.

To the north side of the temple, halfway up toward the perimeter, stands a venerable cousin to the bodhi tree. Carved figures, black from lamp smoke, cluster in the folds of its huge, gnarly trunk, and its far-reaching branches shade living figures as well — meditating, reading, doing prostrations. Fran and I have adopted this great being as our "ancestor tree."

Here we take time every day to place a flower by its roots and sit a while on its broad stone terrace, offering thanks for those who gave us life. Silently we remember our parents, and their parents too; then, finding a spot to talk, we speak of them together.

I sense Fran's gratitude that I loved his mother and father so deeply, sharing more of myself with them than I could with my own family. They saw me — saw who I was — as no one in my own family ever seemed able to do. And they loved me as the daughter they never had.

I had always delighted in watching my mother with Fran, chatting about people and plays over their ritual bourbon. He relished her warmth and wit. Having loved Mama so, he shares the loss I feel at her going, and also my relief with the end of the long vigil — kept most closely by my brother Harty — as that elegant woman faded and shrank into Parkinsonism.

For my father I do a number of circumambulations around the ancestor tree and light a candle stub in the recesses of its trunk. Making my peace with that man has been a lifelong undertaking. Gazing up into the leaves, I recall the long-ago morning when I awoke in Fran's arms and realized that my terror of Papa had relinquished its grip on my heart. After that I let myself begin to appreciate the strengths he possessed, and summoned in me. Years after his death, I can acknowledge that I owe to him much of my stubborn intellect, my love of languages and poetry, my eloquence. Perhaps his most valuable gift to me was the most painful to acquire: in countless confrontations he was the noble adversary who forced me to find my own integrity — and the power to defend it.

Our last night in Bodh Gaya, and out of a clear sky there's a light rain. Fran is sitting right under the bodhi tree with a passel of pilgrims; he sits as quiet as they do, though he's not used to the posture and his knees stick up. I'm glad that Herb King, at that Greenwich Village supper forty-six years ago, told me to keep seeing him as a stranger. Mostly I have done that. And so do I now as I walk by and let my eyes fall on him. His hands hold the prayer beads that Choegyal Rinpoche blessed for him two weeks ago; his eyes are closed. I imagine him hearing the rain on the leaves as we used to hear it on the walls of our tent when we camped in the Adirondacks. As I walk on round the temple, I seem to be dedicating these last rounds to him — to us. I let myself be thankful, once again, that we never turned our marriage into a prison, from which I would need to escape. It never became that bride-suffocating trunk I had feared as a child.

Tired, I sit on a low ledge in view of the tree. All the ones in many places, for whom we have walked, come again to my mind, and others around the world as well. They hover so close I can almost see their faces, hear their voices in the patter of rain on leaves. Rilke's poem murmurs in my mind, "I live my life in widening circles."

The young poet went on to say, "I circle around God." Whatever that meant to Rainer Maria Rilke, the widening circles of my life have not had as their center the Big Papa God of my preacher forebears. I walked out on that belief when I was twenty. What authority now holds me in orbit?

The soft rain has ceased. Above the bodhi tree, the moon appears, lopsided, almost full, and I am thinking: no, it is not Fran around whom I circle, nor my children, or even Julien and Eliza. It is not Khamtrul Rinpoche or Choegyal Rinpoche or Mummy, my honored Sister Karma Khechog Palmo, who brought me into Dharma practice. Nor is it Adekimba or Ocean of Wisdom, showing me, as they did, my heart's capacity; nor my dear colleagues in Germany, Australia, Japan, Chernobyl, showing me, as they do, the promise of our work together.

Is it my love for them all that holds me in orbit? Or is it the fate awaiting my planet's people in this harsh, momentous time?

The tall Tibetan monk strides by me, his lined face catching the lamplight. And there sits the young Japanese woman, eyes closed, still as a stone, and the Sri Lankan bhikkhu rearranging his robe, his sheaf of texts. For ten days their devotions have enriched my own. I want to say good-bye to them, to tell them that tomorrow I will be gone. But I don't. I only thank them, silently, for their company.

Appendix A

Glossary of Buddhist Terms

Note: Terms in use among Theravadin Buddhists, as in Sri Lanka, are in the Pali language; their Sanskrit form (Skt) is used by Mahayana and Vajrayana Buddhists, including Tibetans. Since I have lived in different Buddhist cultures, I've adopted a mixture of Pali, Sanskrit, and Tibetan terms.

anicca (Pali; anitya in Skt): impermanence, another of the three marks of existence.

arhat (Pali, Skt): one who has attained the highest level in Theravada practice, having extinguished all defilements.

Avalokiteshvara (Skt): celestial bodhisattva of compassion, known as Chenrezi in Tibetan.

bhante (Pali): form of address to a Theravadin monk.

bhavasota (Skt): stream of being; a term used by the Buddha to denote the self.

bhikkhu (Pali; bhikkshu in Skt): monk.

bodhi (Pali, Skt): enlightenment.

bodhicitta (Pali; bodhichitta in Skt): aspiration or resolve to attain enlightenment for the sake of helping others.

bodhisattva (Skt; bosat in Pali): "enlightenment being;" embodiment of compassion and insight; one who renounces entry into nirvana until all beings are enlightened.

bodhi tree: the *ficus religiosis* made sacred by having sheltered the Buddha during his enlightenment vigil; similar trees planted and honored at Buddhist temples.

Buddha Dharma (Skt): Buddhism.

Chenrezi (Tibetan): celestial bodhisattva of compassion, Avalokiteshvara.

dagoba (Pali): reliquary mound, a term for stupa in Sri Lanka.

dakini (Skt): a semi-wrathful female deity signifying compassion and emptiness.

dana (Pali, Skt): gift or alms; generosity.

dependent co-arising: the Buddha's central doctrine of causality (paticca samuppada), holding that all phenomena are interdependent and mutually conditioned.

Dharma (Skt; Dhamma in Pali): the teachings of the Buddha; the law of dependent co-arising. Also, distinguished here with a small *d*, as in **dharma**, the smallest unit of psycho-physical existence.

Dharma Chakra (Skt; Dhamma Cakka in Pali): Wheel of the Dharma representing both the teachings of the Buddha and the law of dependent co-arising.

dorje (Tibetan; vajra in Skt): thunderbolt; the ritual implement representing compassion in action.

Drukpa (Tibetan): dragon; subsect of the Kargyu lineage to which Khamtrul Rimpoche and the Tashi Jong community belong.

dukkha (Pali; duhkha in Skt): suffering or unsatisfactoriness, one of the three marks of existence along with impermanence and nonself.

Kargyu (Tibetan): one of the four major lineages of Tibetan Buddhism, which is headed by His Holiness Karmapa and includes the Tashi Jong community.

karma (Skt; kamma in Pali): action; the results of previous actions.

karuna (Skt): compassion.

kundun (Tibetan): presence, a name for the Dalai Lama, implying the presence of Tibet.

lama (Tibetan): religious teacher.

maha karuna (Skt): the great compassion.

Mahayana (Skt): Great Vehicle, the "northern" branch of Buddhism arising in 1st century BCE and spreading to such lands as Tibet, Mongolia, China, Korea, and Japan.

Manjushi (Skt): celestial bodhisattva of wisdom.

mantra (skt): a power-laden series of syllables repeated for protection and for centering the mind.

metta (Pali): loving kindness.

nirvana (Skt; nibbana in Pali): the ultimate release from suffering.

nundrel (Tibetan): extensive foundational practices in Tibetan Buddhism.

Pali: language of the earliest Buddhist writings.

paramita (Skt): "that which has reached the other shore;" perfection.

pindapatha (Pali): alms rounds, going out with begging bowl.

puja (Pali; Skt): worship, ritual prayers.

prajna (Skt; pañña in Pali): wisdom.

rinpoche (Tibetan): "precious jewel," honorific title for a spiritual master or tulku.

samadhi (Pali, Skt): state of nondual consciousness.

Sangha (Pali, Skt): the monastic order founded by the Buddha.

sarvasattva (Skt): all beings.

Sarvodaya (Pali, Skt): "awakening of all;" a people's self-help movement in Sri Lanka.

satipaathana (Pali): rigorous mindfulness meditation taught by the Buddha.

satori (Japanese): an experience of awakening or enlightened mind.

satyagrahi (Skt): practitioner of Gandhian nonviolent direct action, i.e. satygraha, or truth force.

Shambhala: a mythical kingdom described in the Tibetan Kalachakra Tantra as a source of learning and center of enlightened culture.

shramadana (Pali, Skt): the gift of labor.

stupa (Skt): reliquary mound, a dome-shaped sacred structure.

sutra (Skt; sutta in Pali): a discourse of the Buddha, or any Buddhist canonical scripture.

tangka (Tibetan): sacred scroll painted for meditative and devotional purposes.

tanha (Pali): craving, greed; one of the three fetters or causes of suffering (along with hatred and delusion) and emblematic of all three in the Second Nobel Truth.

Theravada (Pali): Way of the Elders, the "southern" school of Buddhism, based on the early scriptures or Pali Canon and primarily represented in Sri Lanka, Burma, Thailand, and Cambodia.

Togden (Tibetan): a Tibetan yogi.

Triple Gem: Buddha, Dharma, and Sangha.

tulku (Tibetan): one recognized as the reincarnation of a high lama.

Vajrayana: Tibetan Buddhism.

vihara (Pali): residence hall of monks.

vipassana (Pali): insight into the nature of things; a Theravadin meditation practice based on satipatthana.

yogi: a practitioner of yoga, one who is adept at spiritual exercises of a psycho-physical nature.

APPENDIX B

An Ethic of Nuclear Guardianship: Values to Guide Decision-Making on the Management of Radioactive Materials

1. Each generation shall endeavor to preserve the foundations of life and well-being for those who come after. To produce and abandon substances that damage following generations is morally unacceptable.

2. Given the extreme toxicity and longevity of radioactive materials, their production must cease. The development of safe, renewable energy sources and non-violent means of conflict resolution is essential to the health and survival of life on Earth. Radioactive materials are not to be regarded as an economic or military resource.

3. We accept responsibility for the nuclear materials produced in our lifetimes and those left in our safekeeping.

4. Future generations have the right to know about the nuclear legacy bequeathed to them and to protect themselves from it.

5. Future generations have the right to monitor and repair containers, and to apply such technologies as may be developed to protect the biosphere more effectively. Deep burial of radioactive materials precludes these possibilities and risks uncontrollable contamination to life support systems.

6. Transport of radioactive materials, with its inevitable risks of accidents and spills, should be undertaken only when conditions at the current site pose a greater ecological hazard than transportation.

7. Research and development of technologies for the least hazardous long-term treatment and placement of nuclear materials should receive high priority in funding and public attention.

8. Education of the public about the character, source, and containment of radioactive materials is essential for the health of present and future generations. This education should promote understanding of our relationship to the Earth and to time.

9. The formation of policies governing the management of radioactive materials requires full participation of the public. Free circulation of information and open communication are indispensable for the self-protection of present and future generations.

10. The vigilance necessary for ongoing containment of radioactive materials requires a moral commitment. This commitment is within our capacity, and can be developed and sustained by drawing on the cultural and spiritual resources of our human heritage.

Other Books by Joanna Macy

Coming Back to Life: Practices to Reconnect Our Lives, Our World, with Molly Young Brown. Gabriola Island, BC: New Society Publishers, 1998.

Rilke's Book of Hours, with Anita Barrows. New York: Putnam Riverhead, 1996.

Mutual Causality in Buddhism & General Systems Theory: The Dharma of Natural Systems. Buffalo, NY: SUNY Press, 1991.

World as Lover, World as Self. Berkeley, CA: Parallax Press, 1991.

Thinking Like a Mountain: Towards a Council of All Beings, with John Seed, Arne Naess, & Pat Fleming. Gabriola Island, BC: New Society Publishers, 1988.

Dharma and Development: Religion as Resource in the Sarvodaya Movement in Sri Lanka. West Hartford, CT: Kumarian Press, 1983.

Despair and Personal Power in the Nuclear Age, Gabriola Island, BC: New Society Publishers, 1983.

About the Author

Eco-philosopher Joanna Macy, Ph.D., is a scholar of Buddhism, general systems theory, and deep ecology. She is also a leading voice in movements for peace, justice, and a safe environment. Interweaving her scholarship and four decades of activism, she has created both a ground-breaking theoretical framework for a new paradigm of personal and social change, and a powerful workshop methodology for its application. Her wide-ranging work addresses psychological and spiritual issues of the nuclear age, the cultivation of ecological awareness, and the fruitful resonance between Buddhist thought and contemporary science.

Catherine Allport

Over the past twenty years many thousands of people around the world have participated in Joanna's workshops and trainings, while her methods have been adopted and adapted yet more widely in classrooms, churches, and grassroots organizing. In the face of overwhelming social and ecological crises, her work helps people transform despair and apathy, into constructive, collaborative action. It teaches a new way of seeing the world—as matrix of our own bodies and minds—reversing assumptions and attitudes that now threaten the continuity of life on Earth.

Joanna travels widely, giving lectures, workshops, and trainings in North America, Europe and Asia. She lives in Berkeley, California, with her husband Francis Macy, and close to her children and grandchildren. She serves as adjunct professor to three graduate schools in the San Francisco Bay Area: the California Institute of Integral Studies, the Starr King School for the Ministry, and the University of Creation Spirituality.

BOOKS TO BUILD A NEW SOCIETY

New Society Publishers' mission is to publish books that
contribute in fundamental ways to building an ecologically sustainable
and just society, and to do so with the least possible impact on the
environment, in a manner that models this vision.

Our books provide positive solutions for people
who want to make a difference.
We specialize in:

Sustainable Living
Ecological Design and Planning
Environment and Justice
New Forestry
Conscientious Commerce
Resistance and Community
Nonviolence
The Feminist Transformation
Progressive Leadership
Educational and Parenting Resources

For a full list of NSP's titles, please call 1-800-567-6772
or check out our web site at:
www.newsociety.com

NEW SOCIETY PUBLISHERS